Robert Gossip

History of Russia

From the Earliest Times to 1880

Robert Gossip

History of Russia
From the Earliest Times to 1880

ISBN/EAN: 9783337298760

Printed in Europe, USA, Canada, Australia, Japan

Cover: Foto ©ninafisch / pixelio.de

More available books at **www.hansebooks.com**

YOUNG FOLKS' HISTORIES.

HISTORY OF RUSSIA.

FROM THE

EARLIEST TIMES TO 1880

BY

R GOSSIP.

Author of "Turkey and Russia—Their Races, History, and Wars"

NEW YORK

JOHN W. LOVELL COMPANY

150 Worth Street, corner Mission Place

CONTENTS.

CHAPTER I.

Introduction—Government, Manners, and Distribution of the Slavonian Race, ... 9

CHAPTER II.

Legendary Russia and the Appanage Period (862-1223), .. 17

CHAPTER III.

The Period of Tartar Domination (1223-1533), . . . 39

CHAPTER IV.

Ivan "The Terrible" (1533-1584). 57

CHAPTER V.

A Troubled Interregnum—Serfdom Instituted—Accession of the Romanoff Dynasty (1584-1613), ... 73

CHAPTER VI.

The Romanoff Dynasty—Michael I. to Peter the Great (1613-1725), ... 94

CHAPTER VII.

The Period of Female Sovereignty—Catherine I. to Catherine the Great (1725-1726), ... 138

CHAPTER VIII.

The First Half of the Nineteenth Century, ... 182

CHAPTER IX.

The Reign of Alexander II., ... 219

CHAPTER X.

Extent of the Empire—Religion—Education—Manners and Customs, ... 244

PREFACE

THE history of Russia is little known. Yet the tale of her life, through long ages of obscurity, has a peculiar interest; while that of her recent advance, with a rapidity which has no example among modern States, to a pitch of territorial aggrandizement equally unparalleled, possesses an obvious importance. In the present little volume it has been sought to illustrate her condition during those early periods in which are hidden away a great deal of vigour and romance; to sketch the manner in which the institutions wherewith she started were decomposed and reconstructed; and to trace her course through various trials and transformations onwards to her present width of dominion, and the beginnings of that new social order which she is labouring to found. In doing this, while rigid compression has been studied, it has also been sought to combine scrupulous fidelity with something of picturesqueness and animation; and the hope is indulged that thus the attention of young students may be attracted and rewarded.

R. G.

HISTORY OF RUSSIA.

CHAPTER I.

INTRODUCTION.

Primitive Population.—The first inhabitants of Russia proper about whom anything is known were Slavonians. They belonged to the European branch of the great Scythian family. When they first settled in the country cannot be determined. At one time the territories of the race were very wide. The ancient Thracians are now thought to have belonged to it, probably with an intermixture of Pelasgic blood. So did the Dacians, the Mœsians, and other populations to the north of Thrace, as also the Venti of the Adriatic whom Cæsar conquered. The names of many places in the Morea are the same with those of places in Pomerania and round Moscow, while its popular songs are more deeply tinged with Slavonian than with Grecian superstitions. After the fall of Rome, peoples of the Slavonic stock occupied the whole of Hungary, Poland, and Bohemia, as well as the lands betwixt the Danube and the Balkans. Their chief seats, however, were further north, between the Dnieper and the upper reaches of the Volga, coming west to the Baltic, and sending their offshoots on to the icy seas. Their neighbours gave them various names. The Scandinavians called them the Vanar. To the Germans they were the Wenden. The Latins styled them the Venetæ. The appellation they took themselves was that of Sirbi

The name Slavonian is of comparatively recent origin, though its derivation is obscure. Some trace it to the native word "slava," which means glory; while others find its root in "slova," which signifies speech.

Government and Manners of the Slavonians.—Though great horse-breeders and cattle-rearers the Slavonians early settled in village communities, and addicted themselves to tillage. Gibbon quotes a manuscript referring to the close of the Roman period which states that there were 4600 villages dotted over the area of what was to become Russia and Poland. If the statement be correct, it is clear the villages must have been small; and it is curious to find, that to this day, among the Wends of Lusatia, the hamlets in which the inhabitants congregate are notably less in size than those of the neighbouring Germans. As to the social organization of the Slavonians, recent research has brought out discrepant views. The old chronicle, known as that of the monk Nestor, says "every man lived in his own *rod* separately," and every man ruled his own "*rod*." This word *rod* is now interpreted as meaning an association of relatives; hence some writers have concluded that the Slavonians were originally divided into clans. Others maintain that the term had an older use, which restricted it to a family, and so that all the statement implies is, that every Slavonian was master in his own household. In any case, it is plain that more general arrangements soon came to be adopted in respect of government and authority. Superior bravery and success in war led to the acquisition of superior influence; military chiefs became civil judges; and when the son of a hero inherited the qualities of his father, as well as his possessions, the parental dignity and power were continued to him. For a long while, however, any formal acknowledgment of hereditary title was most jealously excluded. The people reserved not only the privilege of choosing their chiefs, but likewise that of dismissing them. This was done whenever they were convicted of malpractices, and sometimes when there was nothing but suspicion to go upon.

The variety of names given to these chiefs was even greater than the distinctions in their ranks and duties, though that was considerable. We read of boyards, and voywods, and kniaz, of pans, and jupans, with many others, all of which names survive among different portions of the race. The two first, from *voyë*, a combat, were obviously applied in the outset to famous warriors, though ere long they came to designate great rulers and magistrates in general. The word kniaz is supposed to have meant the owner of thirty horses, whence it grew to the signification of noble captain or prince. For ages the most honourable functionary was the jupan. A cluster of villages was united in a jupa, which formed a district or hundred. At the head of each was the jupan. His chief duty was the administration of justice. Under him were several suddafs, sheriffs or inferior judges, who assisted him in his work. Above him, at least among certain tribes, was the pan, who had the superintendence of several districts, and who presided over the diets which the people of those districts held for common council. To this day there are tracts of country where the peasants call their judges by no other name than jupan; while in Polish pan is the name for a lord.

The Slavonians, as became an agricultural people, were peaceably disposed, simple, and hospitable. Yet they could fight well, and cherished several customs marked by great ferocity and barbarism. When attacked they drew a rampart of linked cars about their camp, and placed their women and children in the centre. If they succeeded, they showed themselves cruel and greedy of plunder. In time of peace, however, it was accounted disgraceful to turn a stranger from the door. Rather than deny entertainment, a poor man was reckoned to be justified in stealing from a rich neighbour the means of giving it creditably, the virtue being held far to outweigh the vice. Music was cultivated with enthusiastic ardour. Many Slavonic songs which are still popular seem to be very old. So are numerous Russian couplets in praise of the Danube and the gods of paganism, which are frequently quoted by the common people. The national instrument was the *gusla*, a species of guitar, played with a bow, to the accompaniment of the voice, though some sort of harps and lutes appear to have been in use also. Even on warlike expeditions these were not left behind, though the well-known story, told by Procopius, of a tribe of Slavi who were attacked at night by a Greek emperor, A.D. 592, being found with no arms, but only harps, in their camp, must be treated with scepticism— unless, indeed, the explanation be that he had come upon a number of minstrels like the Celtic bards, or the Scandinavian scalds, a class of men who, in all probability, composed those metrical romances about Kief and its glories which yet find recital even on the confines of Siberia. Polygamy was permissible, and widows were burned on the funeral piles of their husband. Male children were reared for war, being mounted on horseback, and having their hair cut, when they were eight years old; but superfluous daughters were destroyed at birth. Moreover, when people became aged and helpless, they were left to die of want.

Every jupa had its chief town, where all religious rites were celebrated. No separate class of priests existed. The religion was polytheistic. The principal figures in the Slavonian Pantheon were the Biel Bog, or white god, and the Cherni Bog, or black god, representing respectively the principles of good and evil. Among the lesser deities, who, however, received greater adoration, were Perune, the god of thunder, an image with golden whiskers; Radegast, the god of hospitality, a naked man with the head of a lion, crowned by a bird; Porenut, the god of seasons; Volos, the god of flocks; and Kupala, the god of fruits—whose fete-day, the 23d of June, is still observed in Russia, the name of the pagan deity being linked with that of a Christian saint, and the day being styled the festival of St. John Kupala. The god of war was named Rugevit, and was represented with seven faces. He had a colleague, Swiantovid, a figure with two bodies and four heads, whose worship took a form that ensured its observance. To him was consecrated a white horse, which only the keeper of the shrines erected in his honour was permitted to feed or mount, and beside him lay continually a saddle, bridle, and sword, that when it pleased him he might ride forth for conquest. This was only half of what he symbolised. In one hand he held a large horn, which, on his festival day, was filled with mead. According to the quantity which remained at the next anniversary, it was prognosticated whether the ensuing harvest would be plenteous or scanty. When the horn was emptied the people were invited to refresh themselves with the same kind of liquor as it had contained; and this they did so liberally that the day became one of unrestrained merriment and license—the feast of Swiantovid thus resembling that of Saturn.

Russian Subdivisions—Novgorod the Great.—Extending over an area so vast and so diversified, it was inevitable that the mass of Slavonic settlers should split into fragments, gathering peculiarities of feature, dialect, and custom. This befell naturally enough, the separation taking three great divisions—the south Slavonians or Czekhs; the central Slavonians, the ancestors of the Poles and Lithuanians; and the north Slavonians, now the Russians of Muscovy. None of the divisions was left to develop itself freely and naturally. Each was assailed, broken in upon, and disrupted, by foreign agencies. Goths, Huns, Tartars, and Mongols swept over the lands of the two first in successive waves of resistless inundation. For a long while the third remained exempt from such disturbance. The immunity is no doubt justly attributable to the bleak and barren character of the region they inhabited. They had fallen into four well-marked subdivisions. One group of colonists had settled in the richest parts of that great tract of country which is drained by the Dnieper and its affluents. To the north-west, another group peopled the basin of the Dwina. To the north-east, a third group were to be found among the forests that overspread the upper part of the Volgo basin. Round Lake Ilmen a fourth had established themselves. The development of regular institutions on a greater scale than the primitive "jupa," and the growth of towns much larger than the primitive "grad," were helped by the rise of trading employments. From time immemorial the products of the East have found transmission to Russia by the Caspian Sea, whence they were wont to be conveyed in boats up the Volga. A further journey, partly overland, brought them to the country about Lake Ilmen, on the shores of which, tradition says, centuries before the date at which authentic history opens, there sprang up the city of Novgorod. It grew till it became the capital of an independent community, governed by an elected president, and then of a confederation of such communities. Wider and wider spread its influence, till the inquiry, " Who can resist God and Novgorod the great?" passed into a proverb. Its prosperity, however, was marred by internal disorders, feuds, and revolutions, which it has been the fashion of historians to charge upon the democratic spirit of the people. "Unfortunately," says the Frenchman Levesque, before whose book nothing worthy the name of a Russian history had appeared, "it is rare that men are willing to be peaceable unless they are bound with chains." The time soon came when the northern Slavonians were to be thus bound. The foreign influences which had interfered with, overborne, and to some extent transformed, alike politically and socially, their kinsfolk in the south, were now to be directed upon them.

Arrival of Rurik the Varangian.—How the opportunity arose, or was taken avail of, is matter of great dispute. Some say that a soft-hearted president, feeling his death near, and vexed by a strife he had failed to quell, gave the counsel that some wise and strong man from the outside should be invited to take the office of governor. Others allege that a band of the Scandinavian pirates whom Harold Harfrager had driven from Norway, some of whom visited Iceland, while others descended upon Britain, and others voyaged to France, found their way to Lake Ilmen, and made themselves masters of Novgorod. Certain it is that, whether by force or by invitation, in A.D. 862 one Rurik acquired the sovereignty. He brought with him two brothers, Sineus and Trevor, one of whom obtained the government of a district called Bielo-Orzero, the other that of a district called Izborsk. But the brothers soon died, and thus Rurik became the master of northern Russia.

A modern school of Slavonic antiquaries and enthusiasts have set up the untenable theory that these incomers were not strangers, but kinsfolk who had located themselves nearer the Baltic. Despite the earnestness and erudition with which this conceit has been maintained, it must be put aside: it is scouted by every authority of note outside Russia. The very name given to the strangers, alike by old Nestor and by the Byzantine historians, "Varangians," goes to disprove it. The word in the northern tongues signifies sword-men or war-men; and it is a striking fact that, a hundred years later, when a Swedish king visited Constantinople, the Varangian guard, who were employed specially to protect the emperor, acknowledged him as their chief. Whether Rurik, instead of being a wanton aggressor, may not have been asked to compose the distracted condition of the state that yielded to his government, and then have been chosen to that office by the voluntary suffrages of its people, is more of a moot question. The case is probably similar to that of the Saxons and the Picts, or the people of Normandy and Duke Rollo—in both instances the invited allies became the ultimate masters.

Whence the name Russia? Three explanations are current. One derives it from Rurik. It is said he belonged to the Varangian tribe or family of Rus, and hence the land to which he came was called *Russkaya:* Russish or Russian. Another, with much more plausibility and weight of evidence, traces it to a Slavonian tribe or confederation, who seem to have made their power felt with extraordinary effect during the first centuries of the Christian era—the Rhoxolani or Rhoxani. Seeing that in the Doric and Eolic dialects of Greece the x was expressed by s, the transition to Russian was easy alike as regards sound and sense. Moreover, it is shown alike by Roman and Byzantine historians, as well as by ancient chronicles and traditions, that these people occupied in the three first centuries those parts of Poland, Red Russia, and Kiova, which the Russians occupied in the ninth. The third suggested explanation connects itself with the myth, growing out of the Slavonian disparting, which tells how, in vastly remote ages, three brothers left their home in the Illyrian Mountains, each to found a great state; that their names were Tchekh, Lekh, and Russ; and that, having succeeded in their object, they left their names to the people who sprang from them. This is obviously too romantic and air-drawn a fancy to be accepted by the most credulous in the present day. The second theory, which Malte Brun has the merit of having stated and recommended long ago, has been received even by enthusiastic Pan-slavists; and the word Russ has come to be applied with strictness only to the Kief and the mid-Dnieper district.

CHAPTER II.

LEGENDARY RUSSIA AND THE "APPANAGE" PERIOD.

The Reign of Rurik (862-879).—The advent of Rurik marks the period when the light of authentic history begins to dawn upon the fortunes of Russia. For a long while, however, the illumination it sheds is scant, feeble, and confused by the thick mists of tradition. The founder of the monarchy reigned for seventeen years. He ruled with a firm and vigorous hand. Yet, more than once, the continuance of his power was menaced by revolt. The last and most formidable of these attempts at rebellion was headed by a popular leader named Vadim. To subdue it was a task that gave Rurik much trouble, but he succeeded. Vadim was slain in fight; his followers were either exterminated or reduced to quietness; and henceforward the sovereignty of Rurik was acquiesced in.

Seizure of Kief—Reign of Oleg.—Two of his companions, Ascold and Dir, imitated his example on their own account. They left Novgorod professing an intention to seek a more brilliant fortune in the service of the Greek emperor. As they journeyed south they came to Kief, which was even then a considerable town. The Slavonian inhabitants of the district which had it for capital—those Rhoxani, who of old time had often harassed the Roman confines near the Danube and the Carpathians, who in 166 carried on war against the Marcomanni, and who in 270 were numbered among the enemies whom Aurelian conquered—had now sunk into tributaries of the Khazars, a half-nomad people of the Tartar race, the predecessors of their brethren the Turks. Ascold and Dir thought they could do no better than abide there, so, calling upon a number of their fellow-Varangians, they easily made themselves masters and rulers of the place. They soon became so strong that they were able to wage war against the Greek emperor, whom it had been their design to serve. Legends tell of how they were foiled in a manner they deemed supernatural, were so moved by the occurrence that they sent for a Christian bishop to instruct them in his faith, gladly receiving his words, and then built a church dedicated to Elijah the prophet upon the heights of Kief, where it was said St. Andrew the apostle, on his westward journey nine centuries before, had proclaimed the doctrines of the cross. The tale of this Greek invasion, it must be added, gets no countenance from the Byzantine annals.

A terrible reverse soon ensued. When Rurik died, the reins of government at Novgorod passed to his kinsman Oleg, either as being the eldest male of his family, or as the guardian of his infant son Igor. Oleg was ambitious, unscrupulous, and successful. The passion for an advance southwards was strong upon him. He followed Ascold and Dir to Kief. His party dropped down the Dnieper in a few galleys which it was given out were merchant craft. The two chiefs were tempted on board, were then seized by hidden warriors, and were forthwith put to death. Oleg and Igor were readily recognised as fit successors in the government, and thus the course of Russian annexation and conquest was begun. With the aspect and situation of Kief, Oleg was greatly charmed. He named it a "fit mother of cities," and transferred thither from Novgorod the seat of government.

He made his power felt all around. No doubt many of his wars were merely ravaging forays. He is credited, however, with having, like his predecessors, organised an expedition against Constantinople, which, unlike theirs, was attended by a measure of success. In this instance, too, the story is dubious, being probably invented to adumbrate what was to come after, under the strong influence which it has exerted. His death is said to have taken place in a manner which repeats a fable contained in a very old Icelandic saga. He had a favourite horse which he had ceased to ride, because the diviners had predicted it would cause his death. The animal itself died. Going to look at it, Oleg placed his foot on the skull, whence issued a serpent that stung him. The wound proved fatal.

Reign of Igor (912-945).—Igor succeeded him. His reign was long, but it was one of chequered prosperity. Twice over he certainly did make war against the Greeks. On the first occasion he was unsuccessful. His galleys were burned by Greek fire, and his land forces had great difficulty in making their way back. On the second occasion the tables were turned. Igor made way so far that the emperor was scared; the stoppage and return of the invaders were bought with gold; and a treaty was concluded between the powers, in which for the first time the term " Russian land" was used. At Kief, the confirmation of this bargain was made the subject of a religious ceremonial. The Christian Varangians, who had changed creeds with Ascold and Dir, repaired to the church, and took oath upon the gospel to its observance; Igor and his fellow-pagans laid their swords and shields at the feet of Perune, the thunder-god, and then swore to the compact.

He was killed in a contest with the Drevilians, an outlying Slavonian tribe, who held land among the forests and hills to the westward of the Pripet, and who were of a sterner and fiercer breed than the men of the plains. An attempt was made to exact from them a heavy tribute. They paid the first slight demand which was made upon them, but this renewed and increased imposition they resisted with great energy. In striving to make his levy Igor was worsted, was taken prisoner, and slain. His assassination was avenged in a perfidious and wholesale manner by his widow, Olga, a woman of great beauty and commanding talent, who bore rule during the minority of her son Sviatoslaf. She professed to desire peace with the Drevilians, invited their chief men to her court, and had them killed while enjoying a great feast she had prepared for them. Then she started with an army who pillaged and destroyed wherever they went, encountering little resistance except at the town of Korosten, the place where Igor met his death. It was taken by artifice. The queen promised she would raise the siege if she were presented with all the pigeons in the place. Having got them she had rags steeped in oil tied to each. After night-fall the rags were lighted, the birds were let loose, and they, flying wildly back to their homes, very soon set the thatched huts of the town in a blaze. In the confusion the inhabitants were cut off.

The Regency of Olga—Her Conversion to Christianity.—For the ensuing twelve years Olga guided the affairs of the principality Her conduct in that office was such as to render her a memorable personage in Russian annals. In them she is distinguished by the appellation of "the wise." Undoubtedly she was a woman of remarkable energy, and still more remarkable foresight. In various respects she was much before the ideas of her time and people, though in others she exaggerated their worst qualities, particularly those of deceit and cruelty. To the task of internal improvement she gave herself with unwearying diligence and sagacious knowledge. She founded many new villages in well-chosen sites. She developed means of communication by laying out suitable roads. She cared for the administration of justice with a jealous care. She endowed sundry institutions of a sort intended to mould and benefit the future. There is reason in the eulogy which pronounces her the mother of Russian civilization.

She tried to introduce Christianity as well. Her attention was turned to its claims when she had surrendered the throne to her son. The motives for inquiry may have been as questionable as the sincerity of her conversion; but, at any rate, she was led to abjure paganism. To inquire was the ostensible reason for a visit paid to Constantinople almost immediately after her abdication. The emperor at that time was Constantine Porphyrogenitus, the historian. From the description he gives it is plain she was received with much respect, which soon changed to admiration. She was impressed alike by the grandeur of the churches and of the services conducted within them. When she intimated her wish to be baptized, Constantine himself proffered to stand sponsor. The ceremony was performed by the patriarch, who pronounced over her the benediction: "Blessed art thou among Russian women, in that thou hast turned from darkness unto light. From generation to generation shall the Russian people call thee blessed." The prediction has been abundantly fulfilled. Before her death her fame as a ruler was an object of popular reverence; long after it the church added the honour of canonization; and to this day the wise and sainted Olga holds a pre-eminent place in the catalogue of Russia's worthies. Not that it can be averred her conduct, even after her change of creed, was above reproach. When she left Constantinople, the emperor loaded her retinue with valuable gifts. She promised in return to send presents of fur and wax, which were in much request, as also some recruits for the Varangian guard. These promises she found it convenient to forget. When the emperor, who had pressing reasons for urgency, reminded her about the recruits, she replied by evasions which were barely civil and largely false.

The Reign of Sviotaslaf (957-972)—Division of the Empire.—Sviotaslaf, much as he revered his mother, had no disposition to imitate her example in turning Christian. He regarded with aversion and weariness both her religious observances and the attention she bestowed on civil affairs. His tastes were all of another sort. He was a man of reckless, boisterous, jovial temper, fond of turmoil and adventure, who cared for nothing so much as war and the chase. Dismissing his train of menials, he placed himself at the head of a hardy band of soldiers whom he led from place to place, camping in the open air, broiling his food (which was often horse-flesh) on the naked fire, and cutting it up with his dagger. While

Olga lived he was content to leave the business of administration to her, so that no harm came of the style in which he indulged his likings, and her repute was exalted. During this period his constant wars led to a considerable extension of his dominions. After Olga died reverses came, and more than once the permanence of his possession was put in jeopardy. On one occasion, in his absence, Kief was besieged by the Petchenegans—a nomad and warlike race who had supplanted the Khazars, and roamed the wide steppes that lie between the Dnieper and the Don—who well-nigh conquered it. For years he was at feud with the Bulgarians, who had begun their long series of conflicts with the authorities of Constantinople, pushing them so hard that they were fain to pay for his help. When success shone upon his arms he formed the idea of abandoning Kief, and fixing his seat upon the Danube. His design was suspected, and he was put under a solemn engagement to evacuate the country. The pledge was given, but he so refused or delayed to fulfil it that the Greeks and Bulgarians came down in league upon him. He fought against them with extraordinary valour, but was overpowered and shut up within the walls of what is now Silistria. Here, at an interview with the Emperor John Zimisces, a fresh convention was agreed upon, and he took his departure. On his way he could not resist the temptation of dealing a by-stroke at the Petchenegans. They had been warned of his approach, and were ready for him. In the fight that ensued he was signally defeated. Only a few of his followers made their escape. He was among the slain. His head was cut off, and the skull was formed into a goblet, ornamented with gold, on which was carved an inscription to this effect:—" In trying to seize what belonged to others thou didst lose what was thine own."

Reunion of the Provinces.—For some time Sviotaslaf had exerted but a nominal sovereignty. The cares of state which he had gladly left to his mother he was fain to make over, soon after her death, to his three sons. The eldest, Yaropolk, was the ruler of Kief; Oleg, the next, had charge of the Drevilian land; while Vladimir, the youngest, was established at Novgorod. The arrangement was continued after their father's fall, each of the princes asserting a large measure of independence. This set the example of a style of partition which was often repeated in subsequent times. It always wrought ill, and never worse than in this first instance. The brethren were speedily at variance. Oleg was as devoted to the chase as his father. He caused a trespasser in his preserves to be slain. The youth was the son of Sviotaslaf's bravest and most influential captain, who was mightily incensed. In his rage he prompted Yaropolk to avenge the deed by making war, and in the strife Oleg was killed. Vladimir had an astute foreboding that his brother might desire to restore the unity of power, and be moved for that purpose to sacrifice him. He consulted safety, therefore, by hiding himself among his Varangian kinsmen beyond the Novgorod frontier. Tired of obscurity, however, he came back in a couple of years, recovered his position, and then successfully put in practice the policy he had dreaded as against himself. He robbed his brother of his betrothed bride, killed her father with her two brethren, and then forced her into a marriage. Next he declared war upon Yaropolk, besieging him in the town of Rodnia, the population of which were reduced to such straits that their sufferings became proverbial. At length Yaropolk was inveigled into a parley. As he entered the room where it was given out Vladimir would be found, two assassins, posted behind the door, plunged their swords into him, and thus freed their employer from all rivalry.

Vladimir I. (980-1015)—Christian Martyrs.—The throne thus foully won was filled with great distinction and ability during a long, eventful, and splendid reign. At first, Vladimir professed an ardent zeal for the old pagan faith. In token of his gratitude to the gods he erected new shrines in their honour, and reared new statues of themselves. The golden-whiskered Perune, in particular, was provided with a set of ornaments more

ample and costly than he had previously been decorated
with. Not satisfied with such homage it was decreed
that a human victim should be sacrificed. A young
Varangian, who was a Christian, was chosen for the
purpose. His father furiously denounced the project,
railing against the idols in language which his passion
rendered as eloquent as it was severe. His words so
excited the people that they set upon his dwelling, and
both he and his son were put to death in the tumult.
They were the first Christian martyrs in Kief. They
were also the last; for in a few years the greater part of
Russia was to embrace the faith for which they suffered.

Choice of a Religion.—They were years of immense
activity on the part of Vladimir. He displayed vast
powers of organization and government. He vigorously
promoted internal reforms. He annexed fresh territories.
He married many wives. Why or when his mind became
unsettled on the subject of religion is not precisely known,
but anyhow he determined to cast off the faith of his
fathers. Thus to resolve was an easy thing, however, by
comparison with the choice of a substitute. He gave
himself to this task in the most deliberate and philosophic
style. All round his territories he came in contact with
the professors of alien creeds—Mohammedans and Jews
in the east; Greeks in the south; the adherents of Latin
Christianity in the west. He sent for representatives of
each that he might learn from them the peculiar excellences of their diverse systems. The request was readily
complied with, theological zeal being quickened by the
prospect of acquiring a proselyte so renowned, who professed such a candid impartiality. The Mohammedan delegates were first heard. Vladimir's voluptuous disposition
was so much attracted by their permission of polygamy,
and by the account given of the Mohammedan paradise,
that he came near an acknowledgment of the prophet;
but then he disliked circumcision, and thought it foolish
to prohibit eating pork or drinking wine. " Wine," he
exclaimed, " is the delight of the Russians; we cannot do
without it." The deputies from Germany harangued him

on the greatness of God, and the vanity of idols, in a manner that won his assent; but what was told him as to the authority of the Pope awakened the suspicion that his kingly authority would be interfered with; and the shrewd surmise was fatal to the Romish claims. The Jews were next heard. They were posed by the inquiry, "Where is your country?" When the answer came that God in His anger had dispersed them, Vladimir broke into a fury, exclaiming, "What, do you, who are cursed of God, pretend to teach others? Away, we have no wish to lose our lands like you." Finally, there came a Greek sage who spoke of sin, of redemption, and of the final judgment, exhibiting a pictured scroll whereon was shown the spirits of the just, angel-led, winging their way to heaven, and the spirits of the damned descending, demon-driven, to hell. Vladimir trembled. He was powerfully affected. Yet he made up his mind that he would do nothing rashly. He sent ambassadors abroad to examine the character and effects of the various religions in the countries where they prevailed. They reported contemptuously of the Mohammedan worship, and with little favour of the Romish; but at Constantinople they were introduced to the church of St. Sophia when the patriarch was celebrating with the utmost splendour the divine offices, and so struck were they that they said, "the temple was verily the residence of the Most High, and the place where His glory was manifested to mortals." This report, sustained by the consideration that his grandmother, "Olga the wise," would not have chosen a bad religion, determined Vladimir. He resolved upon being baptized.

Like Olga, however, he disdained the thought of stooping to receive the rite at the hands of the Christian teachers in Kief; and he took even a stranger mode than hers for having his ambition gratified. He made war upon the Greek emperors (Basil and Constantine then reigned conjointly), while he demanded from them the hand of their sister, the Princess Anna. For a time it seemed he would have to endure disappointment. He had invaded the Crimea, and besieged Kaffa. The town was defended so stoutly that, after a six months' investment, he was about to abandon it in despair, and possibly his new faith as well, when an arrow was shot into his camp, having a letter attached which told where the springs were whence water was conveyed by pipes into the city. He tore up the channels, cut the connection, and so forced the inhabitants through the pangs of thirst to surrender. Then the emperors began to negotiate. They told him their sister could not wed a heathen. He replied that he was to become a Christian. The bride-elect had no taste for being joined to a barbarian she had never seen. At length, however, her scruples yielded or were overborne, and she sailed for Cherson. By the archbishop of that place baptism and marriage were celebrated with great pomp. Vladimir returned in triumph to Kief with his royal spouse, as well as with priests, books, vases, and relics innumerable.

A Nation Converted.—The new convert speedily showed himself even more zealous for the religion he had espoused than he had ever been for the religion he had abandoned. Needless must it be to say that his efforts on its behalf were more efficacious, in a sense, than the labours of a thousand missionaries would have been. First, his family and household were baptized. Then he proceeded to cast down the images he had set up. Some of them were burnt. Some were hewn in pieces. Perune, with the whiskers, was more ignominiously treated than any other. Tied to a horse's tail the deified log was dragged to the top of a hill on the banks of the Dnieper, was mercilessly thumped by a dozen lusty soldiers, and then rolled down into the stream. The method was a good one for banishing from the popular mind any idea of sacredness or of power. When the visible signs of paganism had thus been overthrown, the royal devotee issued a mandate that his people should conform to his adopted faith. The persuasions of a monarch are generally successful. On a set day all the inhabitants of Kief, men, women, and children, who had not been baptized, assembled on the banks of the Dnieper, into which they plunged at a given signal, some to the waist, others to the neck, while the priests and prelates who had come from Constantinople chanted psalms, offered prayers, and gave their benediction. Thus was the religion of a whole city revolutionised in a day.

Like scenes were repeated over all the land, till the old faith was everywhere displaced, save in some sequestered districts where it retained a hold for centuries. Of course, little can be said for the inward motive and effects of the change. Yet it was pregnant with great consequences. Had Vladimir become a Mohammedan, his subjects would no doubt have become Mohammedans too; and who can figure what would then have been the conditions and bearings of that Eastern question which has been the perplexity and despair of politicians for ages? In accepting the doctrines and ritual of the Greek church he took a step which has been mainly influential in leading up to that question in the shape we now have it, and at the same time has had a powerful effect in separating Russia from the civilization of western Europe. Throughout Europe the rise of Christianity found a civilization enriched more or less by the teachings of classical antiquity, and the new faith made its way through centuries of conflict. Thus the marks of what was old and what was new were impressed upon every sphere of life. In Russia there was almost no pre-Christian history, or pre-Christian culture, while the acceptance of the Byzantine ritual, ready-made and wholesale, was a proceeding that did not touch or raise the religious consciousness of the people. The effects of that easy compliance are traceable all through the centuries.

Civil Progress and Reform.—Though the style of his apostolate casts ridicule upon the spirituality of his faith, a decisive change was wrought upon Vladimir. It is traceable perhaps to the influence of his consort, whom he loved with all the deep and true attachment of his strong nature. She had left Constantinople with the sad remark, "I go into captivity; better were it for me to die here." But her forebodings were falsified, and she found no cause to wish an opportunity for return. Her husband was softened and humanised. He gave up his licentious habits. His delight in bloodshed passed away. Even the bishops he had installed remonstrated with him about his slackness and scrupulosity in ordering the punishment of hardened criminals and brigands. Some modern historians have suggested that very possibly these offenders were obstinate "heretics." The conjecture may be correct, but, apart from this, it is certain that Vladimir exhibited in manifold ways a clement and magnanimous disposition.

He continued to be successful in war, when occasion came; but his energies were devoted to the attainment of peaceful triumphs. He adopted the policy of Olga, bringing to its accomplishments greater authority and larger resources. Like her he made roads, built bridges, amended laws, and conferred permanent endowments upon what he deemed useful institutions. Greek architects planned his churches, one of which he reared on the hill whereon had stood the shrine of Perune, another on the site of the house wherein Feodor and Ivan were martyred. Greek teachers were brought to the seminaries with which he overspread the land—though in sundry places they found little employment, because many of his subjects thought of letters as a dangerous invention by the devil. He encouraged a system of colonising waste lands, more, no doubt, for the purpose of linking together the separate parts of his dominion than for benefiting the colonisers, though both ends may have been served. He approved himself a man of wide views and commanding forecast—doing so much for his country that it is no marvel his countrymen, through many centuries, should have joined with one consent in lauding his name. The old chroniclers describe him as the Solomon of his age. In his early days he had a good title to the appellation if it be true that, along with four wives, he had more than a hundred concubines. In his later years he established a more meritorious claim to the title by his wisdom, by his temperance, by the enlargement and profundity of his views, by the glories that gave splendour to his reign.

Yet his declining years had their share of sorrow. The pleasant vices of his youth became the whips by which he was scourged in his old days. He had extended his power so that his dominion reached from the Black Sea to the Baltic, and from the Volga to the ridges of the Carpathians, onwards by Lithuania and Poland, parts of which he had subdued; but he was tormented at home. Latterly his numerous family had been over-indulged, and they learned to take advantage of his weakness. Plying him with solicitations addressed both to his conscience and his affections, they moved him as they listed. Against his better judgment he consented to parcel out among his sons the kingdom he had consolidated, granting to each a hereditary fief. The evil consequences that followed such a partition in his father's time were repeated now in an aggravated form. The brothers set up as independent, and quarrelled among themselves. Even in his lifetime the strifes they waged gave premonition of the disasters that were to ensue. He was so incensed by the rebellious conduct of Yaroslaf, whom he had placed over Novgorod, that he started at the head of an army to inflict punishment. He had not proceeded far when a fatal illness suddenly seized him. He died in the summer of 1015. His death was kept secret till his body had been conveyed to his cathedral at Kief. There it was buried, amid the lamentations of his people, in a splendid marble tomb, which soon received the remains of his Greek wife. For his prowess as a warrior, and his eminence as a statesman, Vladimir was honoured with the designation of the Great, while the Russian Church enrolled him among her saints, giving him rank as an apostle.

Division and Strife.—Well might his subjects mourn. A brief period of great confusion ensued. The principality of Kief retained the first place among the twelve appanages into which the country had been divided. It was held by Sviatopolk, the eldest son, or, as some say, the stepson, of Vladimir, a sanguinary personage, who

conceived tne idea of killing off his rivals in order that
he might reunite the kingdom. He proceeded with
ruthless resolution to execute this design. The first
victims were Boris and Gleb, princes notable for their
strong attachment to each other, and both great favourites
with the people and with the army. The circumstances
of the deed aggravated its horrors, for Boris still survived
when Sviatopolk came to look upon his corpse, and spake
to him words which ever after sounded in his ears.
When a third brother had been slain, Yaroslaf declared
war against the usurping fratricide. At first he had an
easy success. The tyrant fled for refuge to the court of
his Polish father-in-law, who was induced to undertake
the task of his restoration. At the head of a large army
he crossed the frontier, ravaged the whole country up to
Kief, sacked that place, and left Sviatoslaf as its master.
Yaroslaf was so chagrined, perhaps so terrified, that he
contemplated leaving Novgorod, for the home of his
ancestor Rurik. His people, however, withstood this
design, rallying round him with an extraordinary enthusiasm, and volunteering great efforts for a renewal of the
campaign. Thus encouraged, he again challenged the
fortune of war in most propitious circumstances. Many
of Sviatoslaf's subjects deserted his army, forcing him to
call in the help of Petchenagans as well as Poles. This
proceeding inflamed still further the resentment felt
against him. Then, the field on which the encounter
took place happened to be in the vicinity of the place
where Boris was killed. Yaroslaf addressed his troops
in a speech of great eloquence, pleading the righteousness
of his cause, picturing his brother as a second Cain, and
praying God to avenge his foul deeds. A signal victory
was achieved. Sviatoslaf hied from the field terror-
stricken. His constant cry to his attendants was, "Onwards, onwards, we are pursued." This haunting dread
followed him all the days of his wretched life. After
many Cain-like wanderings he died miserably, leaving as
his designation Sviatoslaf the Accursed.

Yaroslaf the Law-giver (1019-1054).—For five and

thirty years thereafter Yaroslaf ruled at Kief, gradually gathering into his own hand well-nigh all the power his father had possessed. He ruled well. In his wars he generally succeeded; his most notable repulse being sustained in an expedition led by his son against the Greeks, which was sent forth on a most inadequate excuse, and conducted in a most inadequate manner. He founded cities, he reclaimed waste places, he extended his territories, he cultivated friendly relations with most of the powers around him. His own wife was the daughter of the Swedish king. His eldest son married a daughter of the Saxon Harold; his second a sister of Casimir, king of Poland; the third a daughter of the Prince-archbishop of Treves; and the fourth a daughter of Constantine Monomachus, the emperor at Constantinople. His eldest daughter, after a long and romantic courtship, became the wife of Harold Hardrada of Norway, who, after fighting the infidel in many far-off lands, was killed at Stamford in battle against the English Harold; his second, wedded Andrew of Hungary; his third, Henry I. of France, carrying thither, it is supposed, that famous copy of the *Evangelie* upon which the kings of France were sworn, though all knowledge of its language had died out, till it was shown at Rheims to Peter the Great, who at once read it off—its characters being those invented by the Greek monk Cyril (873), which were long used in the sacred books of the Slavonian Church.

Yaroslaf's fame chiefly rests upon the work which gained for him the designation of "The Law-giver." The first code of written laws which the country possessed was promulgated by him. In fact it was a compilation, but it contained divers new enactments. No one will pronounce it the work of a Justinian, yet it embodies many salutary provisions, as well as many that are abundantly curious. It legalised private vengeance for murder, and decreed that if the murdered person had no relations who cared to avenge him, then the assassin should get off by paying a fine to the public treasury. The amount of this fine was regulated according to the rank of the person killed.

What was called the double fine of eighty grivnas (*i.e.,* about thirty shillings of sterling money), was exigible for the slaughter of a boyard; for a free Russian, forty; for an artisan, schoolmaster, or nurse, twelve. The murder of a woman entailed only half the usual mulct, while that of a serf or slave was reckoned no public offence, the penalty being made payable to the owner. The whole district was made amenable to some extent in respect of the crime. Thus, "if in the heat of anger, or of intoxication, one man kill another and conceal himself, the district in which the murder is committed shall be responsible for the fine; but if the assassin keep his ground, he shall pay one half and the district the other." In pointed contrast with this cheap account of life was the stringency of the provisions as to personal insult, which was made severely punishable. So were all offences against property. If a servant through negligence suffered his employer's goods to be lost or damaged, the value was to be made good. Yaroslaf could not have liked money-lenders, for he provided that if a person borrowed money and then denied the debt, his oath was to suffice for his exoneration, without any appeal to evidence or question of prescription. Among the stipulations of a public nature was one which made the monarch the heir to every freeman who did not leave male issue. Apart from this there was no cupidity in the arrangements for maintaining the crown, while a maximum rent was fixed for land, corporal punishment was prohibited, and it was enacted that every one arraigned as an offender should be equal before the law. Besides his fame as a legislator, Yaroslaf achieved a grateful memory as a patron of literature and the arts.

A Period of Anarchy. — With all his wisdom he repeated the blunder of which his predecessors had been guilty, in dividing his territory among his five sons. The inveteracy with which this habit was adhered to and practised, despite its manifold and oft-illustrated evils, was due to a theory that every descendant of Rurik ought to have an appanage.

Yaroslaf made a well-meant effort to guard against the mischief he had so much cause to dread. On his death-bed he called his family together, and after having intimated his arrangements, made the younger sons vow subordination to the elder, whom he authorised to call for the aid of all the rest against any one who dared to break the peace. This precaution had little effect. Isiaslaf the eldest was a weak man, the others were greedy and ambitious. Instead of banding together for Isiaslaf's defence, they were more inclined to form a league for despoiling him. When sore bestead, he applied to his cousin Boleslas of Poland, surnamed the Bold, for assistance. Nothing loath, Boleslas raised a powerful army, invaded Russia, drove the disturbers out of Kief, and far away from it, set up the Grand Duke, and then entered upon the dissipations of the capital with so much zest, that it seemed likely he would never go away. At last he was called off by a summons to fighting in Hungary, which he obeyed with an eager gladness. Eight miserable years passed, during which the whole land, as well as Kief, became a prey to dissension, tumult, and virtual anarchy. In 1075, Isiaslaf was again in such straits, that, after appealing in vain elsewhere, he anew besought the help of Boleslas.

It was given with precisely the same results as before. The service sought was performed in the completest manner, and when the work was done, Boleslas and his companions found their reward in plunging with a reckless enormity into all manner of debaucheries. Their presence became almost as alarming to the feeble king as that of those from whom they had rescued him; and he bribed them into taking their leave. Money might not have quickened their departure, had not Boleslas been asked to take part in a campaign then raging in Bohemia. He went thither, taking with him one of Yaroslaf's grandsons, Vladimir Monomachus, a youth whose names were derived from his two grand-parents.

A year later Isiaslaf died. He was succeeded at Kief by his brother Vsevolod. This was in accordance with all arrangement which came to prevail for some time, by which the right of inheritance passed, not in the direct line, but to the eldest male of the family. Thus when a vacancy arose at Kief in the office of grand prince, there ensued a shifting of rulers throughout all the other principalities, such as mightily enhanced the confusion and discord which were so rife. During his father's lifetime, Vladimir really conducted the government. He ruled with firmness and with wisdom, though now and again in asserting the supremacy of Kief he was guilty of ferocious excesses.

Vladimir II. (1113-1125).—On the death of Vsevolod his eldest nephew came to the throne, and Vladimir fell for a time into obscurity. He soon found means, however, to preserve his reputation, or even to exalt it, by a series of contests with the Polovtsi, a barbarous race from Central Asia, who had squatted on the southern flank of the empire, and harassed the population most direfully. They made their appearance in Yaroslaf's time, and gave him a good deal of trouble. More than one great battle with them was fought during his reign. It will furnish an idea of the formidable character of these fights, as well as of the apprehensions which the strangers created, to quote a passage from a twelfth century poem, called "The Expedition of Igor." He was a son of Yaroslaf's, and Prince of Novgorod. He assembled his warriors to take vengeance upon the hated Polovtsi, vowing to "break his lance in distant deserts, where his ashes would remain if he could not dip his helmet in the Don, and quench his thirst in its waters." The poet describes the meeting of the host—how the neighing of horses is heard beyond Sula, the voice of glory resounds in Kief, the blast of the trumpet rouses Novgorod, and at Pontivle the standards float in the wind. There, Igor awaits his brother Vsevolod, who comes with his troops "like wolves eager for the carnage." Of course the barbarians are routed, though the carnage is dreadful, and the victory far from decisive. Says the poet: "The banks of the Niemen are covered with heads as numerous as the sheaves in autumn; and like descending flails, the swords separate warriors' souls from their mortal covering. Oh! mournful times! Why could not the great Vladimir remain on the mountains of Kief?" (that is, why was he not immortal?). Against these stubborn foes, who were afterwards absorbed by immigrants from the same region, the second Vladimir had no more lasting success than his uncle and father. In his old age he mentioned that he had concluded nineteen treaties with them, that he had taken more than a hundred of their greatest chieftians, whom he afterwards set free, and that he had punished or drowned in the river upwards of two hundred more. The earlier of these exploits kept his name in public view, as did his conduct upon an occasion when, having undertaken to punish the perfidy and cruelty of his cousin who reigned in Kief, he was induced, like a second Coriolanus, and by the like means, to spare the town. His forbearance had its reward. When his cousin died, the inhabitants, whose prayer he had heard, besought him to become their ruler. After some coy denials he consented. In 1113, being then sixty years of age, he mounted the throne, where he sat for thirteen years.

They were years of great prosperity. Vladimir was a man fully equal to the greatest of his predecessors. He had gained fame as a warrior; but when he came to the throne he illustrated the brightest qualities of a ruler. His aims were high and noble; in carrying them out he evinced great comprehension and energy; and the prosperity which crowned his efforts was very signal and encouraging. In his time Russia took higher rank among the nations than she had ever done. His most remarkable work was a rescension of the legal code which his grandfather had composed. The spirit in which this was done, was akin to that which inspired his last testament to his family—one of great benevolence and wisdom. "O my children," he therein wrote, "love God; love also mankind. It is neither fast, nor seclusion, nor monastic life which can save you; but good works. Do not forget the poor; feed them, and think that all goods belong to God, and are entrusted to you only for a time. Do not hide treasures in the bowels of the earth, for this is contrary to the Christian religion. Be fathers to the orphans; judge the widows yourselves, and do not permit the stronger to oppress the weaker. . . . In your households look to everything yourselves, without relying on your stewards and servants; and the guests will not find fault either with your house or with your dinner. In time of war be active, and be an example to your officers. Repose only after having established the nightly watch. Men may suddenly perish; therefore do not lay aside your armour when danger may happen, and mount your horses early. Above all, respect a stranger, be he a great or a common man, an ambassador, or a merchant; and if you cannot give him presents, satisfy him with meat and drink, because strangers spread in foreign countries good and bad reports of us. Love your wives, but give them no power over yourselves. Remember every good thing you have learned, and learn what you do not know." The precepts which he thus inculcated, Vladimir enforced by an appeal to his own example. "I have myself," he says, "done all that I could order a servant to do. In hunting and war, by day and night, during the heat of summer and the cold of winter, I have known no repose. I have never relied on magistrates and officers. I never allowed the poor and widows to be oppressed by the strong. I myself superintended the church, the divine service, the household, the stakes, the hunt, the hawks, the falcons. . . . Between morning and evening I have travelled a hundred miles. Amid thick forests I have, with my own hands, bound several wild horses at once, and I have had many remarkable escapes from the attacks of savage animals."

A Century of Confusion.—The death of this great monarch opened a long period of confusion and disaster. For a century onwards, the history of the country resolves itself into a sickening record of civil broils and wasted strength. The authority of Vladimir's successors in the

Grand Dukedom was set at nought. The commotions that agitated the provinces sometimes shook down the occupants of the principal throne. In more than one instance they were compelled to share the fate they had themselves dealt out to refractory and vanquished princes —having their eyes put out, and being forced to a lifelong retirement in a monastery. In these circumstances, the supremacy that Kief had so long possessed gradually waned and fell. It was finally overthrown by Andrew, the Prince of Souzdal, a large territory in the centre of the kingdom. A clear-sighted man, he perceived the terrible evils that connected themselves with the prevalent anarchy. An ambitious man, he conceived the idea of consolidating the various principalities, and raising himself to the first place. This design he pursued for many years with mingled adroitness and vigour. At length he was strong enough to assail the capital, in which, a short time before, his father had reigned. At the head of a confederacy, which included other ten princes, in 1169, he laid siege to Kief, which he took and sacked. Setting up his younger brother to bear rule in the desolated province, he transferred the seat of power to his own chief city, Vladimir, a town which had been founded by Vladimir Monomachus. For over a hundred years it retained the pre-eminence thus conferred, while the city of Ascold and Dir, " the mother of cities," as Oleg had named it, never recovered from this first shock of what was destined to prove a long succession of calamities.

Andrew did not fare so well in his attempt upon the independence of the prior capital. The corporate life and democratic spirit of Novgorod asserted themselves very determinedly. The inhabitants discarded the hereditary form of rule, constituted themselves a veritable republic, and insisted upon their right to choose and to dismiss at will their chief magistrate. No doubt they abused this power very grievously, for in a period of less than a hundred years thirty-four men filled that office. Despite this fickleness, the city grew in wealth and size; nor did their devotion to trade impair the prowess of its people. After the destruction of Kief, Andrew marched northward to subdue them. The citizens offered a stout resistance. Religion came in aid of patriotism to nerve their arms and sustain their courage. The archbishop with his clergy marched in solemn procession round the ramparts, carrying with them a picture of the Virgin. Report says that it was hit by a random arrow from the ranks of the besiegers. Straightway a fury of indignation was roused among the defenders. They rushed forth upon their adversaries with an impetuosity as irresistible as it was unexpected, routing them with a tremendous slaughter, and taking so many prisoners, that they were sold by the score for two pieces of silver. At a later date, a descendant of Andrew's did manage to bring Novgorod under his yoke; but the thraldom was short-lived, and except for the brief period of its duration, the place continued on till 1553 to be a free and thriving city, and a leading member of the Hanseatic League formed for the promotion of commerce and the repression of piracy.

Meanwhile, in the country at large, the confusion, degradation, and misery that prevailed, grew worse and worse. The bold attempt to restore internal unity made by Andrew of Souzdal, after having proceeded so far, was cut short by his assassination. His descendants gave themselves now and again, with a species of fitful energy, to a revival of the project; but their efforts went no farther than to enhance the widespread disturbances and embitter the civil strife. The internal history of the country became a dreary record of ceaseless wars and changes, through which the most patient of the Russian annalists can scarce thread their way, while all round the exterior, Hungarians, Poles, Lithuanians, Livonians, and Fins, began to press on the borders of the empire. But a more formidable enemy still was at hand, advancing from the east.

CHAPTER III.

THE PERIOD OF TARTAR DOMINATION.

EIGHT hundred years had passed since that Calmuck Napoleon, Attila the Hun, announcing himself as "the scourge of God," swept over Europe like a desolating pestilence, when a successor of the same type appeared in the person of Temudgin, a Mongolian chief, who, having formed the design of conquering the world, took the designation of Zingis Khan, or "most great ruler." The Mongols, or Moguls, over whom he ruled, had been for ages roaming about Asia, to the north and north-east of the Chinese wall. Under the spell of his ascendancy they were united in one great horde, who became the masters of all northern Asia, from China to the Caspian Sea. First they subdued their kinsmen to the east, the Calmucks, and other branches of the same race. Then they came westward, bending to their will the Turkish or Tartar populations, spreading terror wherever they appeared, killing innumerable multitudes or reducing them to slavery, sacking or razing cities, and doing it so thoroughly that Zingis boasted his horse could, without stumbling, gallop over the ruins of every place he had devoted to destruction. Following the southern shores of the Caspian they thus turned the flank of the Caucasus, and suddenly appeared in 1223 to the west of that mountain bulwark. The ancient foes of Russia, the Polovtsi, were the first to encounter these ferocious savages, by whom they were scattered like chaff before the wind. Fleeing in dismay to Kief, they carried thither the tidings of the terrible enemy who was at hand. The dread of a common peril overcame the feuds and jealousies of long years. The Russian princes entered into a league by which they bound themselves to stand true to each other in opposition to the hazard by which they were menaced; and the alliance was extended so as to include the fugitive Polovtsi. Marching eastwards, the combined forces met the invaders on the banks of the Kalka. A great battle ensued, in which some portions of the allies behaved ill. Whether from cowardice or treachery, the Prince of Kief hung back, and the Polovtsi gave little help to the common cause. The Tartars, as they were named, gained an easy victory, which they followed up in the ruthless fashion habitual with them. They ravaged the country on to the banks of the Dneiper, and had they chosen to persevere, might have overrun it at their pleasure. When they reached that stream they were overtaken by an order from their imperial master, directing their return. It was at once obeyed.ABheeling round their squadrons they rode back, disappearing as suddenly as they had come.

Baty's Invasion—Moscow Burned—Novgorod Threatened.—It might have been supposed that the relief thus experienced would have been turned to good account. The imminence of the peril, which had been so unexpectedly stayed, ought to have illustrated the folly of those internal divisions, which had reduced the country to a condition of impotence, and laid it at the mercy of this powerful assailant. Nothing of the kind took place. Civil discords soon became as rife and violent as before. Blood was copiously shed in quarrels the motives of which are as obscure as their results were lamentable. For the next dozen years the country seethed with meaningless contentions, which only exhausted its strength.

Then an event befell, the exceeding probability of which all wise men might have descried. The Tartars returned. They were led by Batu or Baty, the grandson of Zingis. They found the task of conquest even easier than before. Having subdued the Bulgarians on the Volga, they entered the principality of Raizan. The Russian authorities of that province sent north to implore assistance, but a deaf ear was turned to their petition. This callous indifference was speedily visited with a meet reward. The invader pushed steadily onward, burning and ravaging as he went. The city of Moscow, which had begun to rise into importance, was destroyed. That of Vladimir shared the same fate, after a courageous but ineffectual attempt to raise the siege upon the part of Yury, the prince of that province. He was killed in the height of the contest, and his followers were cut off to the last man. His wife, and the ladies who were her attendants, were burned in the principal church, to the altar of which they had fled for refuge. For a while Baty encamped near the blackened ruins of the capital. Then, resuming his march, he pressed on towards Novgorod. The energetic inhabitants of that place made every preparation for a stout defence, but there seemed little hope that they could beat back the conqueror, or escape that doom of torch and sword which he had inflicted elsewhere. When within sixty miles of the city, however, he halted, faced about, and left it unmolested, returning to the steppes of the Don, though overthrowing Kozalk on his way.

The alarm which the visit of these marauders created was intense and widespread. It extended to the furthest extremities of northern Europe. On account of it the inhabitants of Sweden and Friesland abstained from sending vessels to take away their usual supplies of herrings caught upon the British coasts. This failure, in what even then was a large and regular demand, caused a glut in the home markets, and the harvest of the sea was sold at lower figures than had ever been known. Gibbon has some very characteristic observations upon the astounding fact that the action of a Mongolian khan, whose seat was on the borders of China, should have reduced the incomes of fishermen at Yarmouth.

Kief Destroyed—A Cool Commander.—In 1239 Baty resumed his career of devastation. He now advanced across Southern Russia. His progress was even more destructive, had that been possible, than on the occasion of his former marches. "It seemed," says Karamsin, the famous Russian historian, "as if a deluge of fire had passed over the land from east to west; as if pestilence, earthquake, and all the scourges of nature had united to ensure its destruction." Tchernigof was the first city that fell. Then Kief was attacked. It was strongly garrisoned, and a very stubborn resistance was maintained. The stiffness of the contest only increased the fury of its assailants, and aggravated the horrors of its fate. The bastions of its fortifications having been broken down, the place was put at the mercy of the besiegers. Then, by means of huge battering-rams, breaches were made in its walls. Entrance having been gained the city was fired, and its inhabitants were slaughtered without regard to age, sex, or condition. Many of them found shelter in the church of St. Sophia, where they resolved to continue the defence, selling their lives as dearly as they could. An unfortunate occurrence prevented them from holding out for any length of time. They had stuffed the church with their treasures. Under the weight some of its chambers fell. Many of the refugees were bruised by the falling ruins, and in the confusion which ensued the others fell an easy prey to the Tartar swords. An incredible ferocity and ruthlessness marked the procedure by which ancient Kief was turned into a ruinous heap. Yet one incident stands out as exceptional, and proves that the leader of this barbarous horde was not incapable of magnanimity. The commander of the place was taken alive, and by Baty's orders, was conducted to his presence. In the interview which took place, the intrepid bearing and free speech of his prisoner powerfully impressed the victor, who suffered himself to be advised in a manner that brought important consequences. The miserable condition of the country was pointed out. It was told not only how it had been weakened by dissensions, but wasted by misgovernment. The conclusion was enforced that little would be won by subjecting it to conquest, by comparison with what might be gained by turning attention to Poland and Hungary.

This diversion was made. Baty held on his course westward, subduing provinces in Poland, Hungary, Croatia, Servia, Bulgaria, Wallachia, and Moravia. He burst over these lands like a thunder-storm. Fortunately for Europe, his advance received such a check as induced him to pause. Then hastily retracing his course to the Volga, he established his head-quarters upon one of its arms, and founded there the magnificent city of Sarai, the home of " the Golden Horde," as it was called, from which, for a time, the whole of eastern Europe was ruled, as being but a segment of the prodigious empire which stretched from sea to sea, comprehending both Russia and China.

"The Golden Horde."—In 1294, after the reign of Kubla Khan, the grandson of Zingis and a cousin of Baty, this empire fell to pieces. Yet the Khanate of Kiptchak, as the possessions won by Baty were named, continued to exist for two centuries. Of that khanate the whole of Russia formed a part. Ample pasturage was found in the valley of the Volga, and there the dominant caste had scope enough for that nomadic life which they preferred. The genuine Tartar lived most of his time on horseback, deeming a house less desirable than a tent, and the person who was content to spend his days in it unworthy of his manhood. His favourite meat was horse-flesh. His favourite drink was mare's milk, from which he distilled a species of intoxicating liquor, called *koumiss*. His family dwelt in waggons or tents. At first their religion was a mixture of Buddhism and other forms of idolatry, with ideas derived from the fire-worship of Persia. They were, however, very tolerant. Christianity was treated with respect and impartiality. Some of the early khans were suspected of secretly favouring it. One of them has a place upon the calendar of saints in the Russian Church. Even when, some sixty years later, the race accepted Mohammedanism, no change took place in the way they viewed the religion of those whom they held in thraldom. The scorn and hate which the adherents of the False Prophet came to cherish against the believers in Christ was not then fully matured. It was of later origin and accidental cause. But whatever of courtesy and moderation prevailed in that regard, it had no effect in mitigating the rigour of the tyranny under which the Russians were held fast. It was arrogant, oppressive, exacting, and capricious. A vast tract of fertile soil had been turned into a desert. The inhabitants of the regions beyond were kept in a state of abject and constant terror. Did they refuse to pay the exorbitant taxes which were arbitrarily assessed and insolently enforced, they were menaced by a visit of their spoilers, with intent to make the levy at their own hand; and this threat was always efficacious, for the idea prevailed that in such a case resistance or resentment would be alike foolish.

The Tartars did not interfere much with the framework of administration. So long as the machinery wrought in a manner that served their purpose, they were content to let it alone. Thus they preserved all the old divisions of separate provinces, and kept up the distinction of *Veliki Kneiz*, or Grand Prince. With consummate art, however, they contrived to foster emulation and variance among the different chiefs. They were especially careful to make it uncertain who should be exalted to the supreme dignity. This was an object of ambition to all. By dangling it before the eyes of each as an attainable prize, the perpetuation of mutual ill-will among them was ensured, while they were excited to a race of rivalship in the depth of servility to which they could stoop, and the amount of gifts they could offer. The humiliations to which the princes were subjected, when they were summoned to the camp of their suzerain, and when the khan or a representative visited them, were to the last degree mortifying and debasing. When a Tartar ambassador appeared at a native court, the prince had to spread a piece of sable fur under the hoofs of the envoy's steed, to receive on his knees the message which was brought, to present the messenger with a cup of mare's milk, and to lick from his horse's neck any drops that might have fallen thereon. Even the Grand Prince was expected to lead the horse through the streets, and to feed the beast with oats out of his royal cap. Reluctance or evasion was punished with remorseless severity. Several princes were put to death, and others had trial of cruel mockings and tortures. That such an extraordinary despotism should have been endured with patience for so long a time counts among the marvels of history.

Alexander Nevsky.—The condition of slavish dependence to which they had been reduced did, indeed, sorely gall both princes and people; and from time to time there arose men who addressed themselves to the task of emancipation. The measure of success which attended their exertions was small, and what was achieved by one was always speedily undone. The first person who meets the eye, as standing erect amid the general debasement, is Prince Alexander Nevsky. In 1236, the year before the second Tartar invasion, when he was only seventeen years of age, he had been elected Prince of Novgorod. That free community were then much harassed by Danes, Swedes, and Finns. The Finns had been recently converted to Christianity, and now, with the zeal of proselytes, they joined the Swedes in an effort to bring over the Russians of the north from the Greek ritual to that of the Western church. Force was used to induce compliance. A Swedish fleet entered the Neva with intent to sail into Lake Ladoga, and to disembark an invading army in the heart of the Novgorod territory. They loitered by the way, left their ships in the river, and encamped upon its banks. Mustering a number of hastily-equipped troops, Alexander swept down upon them and put them utterly to the rout, a very small proportion of Swedes regaining their vessels. In commemoration of this great triumph, in gaining which he displayed much personal valour, the name of Nevsky was bestowed upon him. It was the first of many signal services to the principality. Soon afterwards the Livonian Knights —an order of chivalry otherwise known as the Sword-bearers, whose habit was a white cloak with a red cross on the shoulder—essayed to do what the Swedes had been foiled in attempting. Under their guidance a strong force assailed the sister city of Novgorod, Pskof, built on the shores of Lake Pepius, and having taken it, advanced across the country to the capital. Trusting to its inhabitants being able to hold the foe in check, Alexander obtained reinforcements from Vladimir, retook Pskof, and attacked the rear of the invaders. They were thrown into confusion, and fell back in disorder. Re-collecting their forces, they were brought to bay at Lake Pepius, where, in the beginning of 1242, a great battle was fought upon the ice. For a time the superior discipline of the Germans enabled them to make way; but Alexander again circumvented them. While they were pressing right forward, their troops being massed in the form of a wedge, by a swift and skilful movement he planted a number of men on their flanks, whose onset carried all before them. The Livonians sustained an enormous loss, and for centuries the "Slaughter on the Ice" was coupled in popular fame with the "Battle of the Neva." A third time did Alexander draw the sword in defence of Novgorod, and again he wielded it successfully. The assailants were the Lithuanians, who, having slipped from under Russian control, were anxious to turn the tables upon their former masters. The attempt was often renewed, but never was it more decisively defeated than on this first occasion.

Tartar Supremacy—Heavy Taxes.—By such achievements Alexander inspired the hope that he might redeem the fortunes of his country. Brave and successful as he had shown himself, however, he shrank from a trial of strength with the Tartars. Some modern historians have blamed his acquiescence in their domination; and a controversy has arisen as to whether he was actuated by a wise prudence, or a venal selfishness. Baty, hearing of his prowess, sent for him to Sarai, where he was received with respect and kindness. From Sarai he was sent on to the interior of Asia, where he became the guest of the Great Khan himself. There also he was treated with favour. What he saw may have impressed him with a consciousness of the invincible strength that belonged to the power with whom he had to deal. At any rate, ever afterwards he counselled submission to its authority. He set the example himself, though it cannot be said that he went without his reward. He was first made Prince of Kief, and then Grand Prince of Vladimir. At various times he had much ado to maintain quietness. His freedom-loving friends at Novgorod gave him most trouble. They had never come under Tartar occupation, and were disposed to spurn every claim upon their homage. Baty's successor issued a decree, that, like the other Russians, they should be made amenable to a poll-tax. The angry resistance which this mandate roused, was such as Alexander could not appease. For one year its execution was delayed. In the interval Alexander persuaded the leading citizens to submission; but when he went back with the collectors the common people rose in tumult, vowing that they would not be numbered and taxed by accursed feeders on raw flesh. Not till he had left the city, warning the inhabitants of the fate they had provoked, did fear come upon them and a change of mind ensue.

This subject of taxation, however, continued to be a cause of great anxiety. Very soon the Tartars found it too troublesome a business to levy the taxes directly, and so they were farmed out to merchants from distant Khiva, who employed a class of men called Baskaks to aid them in the work. The Hebrew publicans of old time were not loathed with a deeper loathing than these men. Of course they made the exactions heavier than before, till at last the inhabitants began to refuse them as intolerable. In a number of towns all over the country payment was withheld, and the collectors were maltreated, killed, or sent empty away. Again, the anxious fears of Alexander were aroused. He hastened to Sarai with intent to appease the Khan, and to persuade him to overlook the offence. He succeeded in his mission; but it was his last public service. On his return journey he was seized with sudden illness, which was very generally attributed to the effects of poison. Convinced that he was dying, he had himself conveyed to the nearest monastery, was admitted into its order, received the tonsure, and expired soon after he had been clad in the monastic habit. His death caused a great outburst of superstitious veneration. It was said to have been notified by a voice from heaven to the Metropolitan of Vladimir as he was serving at the altar. When announced to the populace, they set up an universal wail of "We are lost." His burial was attended by thousands. It was believed that when the prayer of absolution was read, his corpse opened and raised its hands as it lay in the coffin. More than four hundred years afterwards, his dust was shifted to St. Petersburg, where it was laid by the banks of the river whence he derived his name, and where a great monastery was raised in his honour by Peter the Great.

Moscow becomes the Capital—"John of the Purse." —From Alexander's time the fortunes of Vladimir began to wane, and those of Moscow to rise. It was founded by Vladimir Monomachus, but for a long while it remained an obscure place. The youngest son of Alexander Nevsky, Prince Daniel, chose it for the capital of the small principality to which he was appointed, and in his time it made a considerable start in importance. Its progress was continued under his son Prince George, who greatly augmented the size of his dominion. He followed his grandfather's example in the maintenance of friendly relations with the Tartars. For several years he lived among them, so ingratiating himself with the Khan Usback, as to win his consent to a marriage with his sister, and to receive the dignity of Grand Prince, in which office Prince Michael of Tver was superseded. This change gave rise to a feud which cost the lives of both the principals, and was continued with fatal results to several of their descendants. Still, the influence of Moscow continued to increase. It did so especially during the long reign of Prince George's brother and successor Ivan, surnamed Kalita, that is, Ivan of the Purse. Tradition says he got the name, because, whenever he went abroad, he carried a money-bag, whence he gave alms to the poor with great liberality. The historian Bestujef Riamin thinks the designation arose from his reform of the coinage. The probability is that it came from the thrifty care with which he managed to keep a full treasury, conjoined with the free manner in which he spent his means when he saw an object worth a large outlay. Ivan was, indeed, a very astute person. From the first he adopted a policy of territorial aggrandisement, and very cunningly did he advance it on to large results. He used force against his rival the Prince of Tver, and thus annexed that territory to his own. He flattered the Metropolitan into becoming his tool, and induced him to leave Vladimir for Moscow, as his predecessors had left Kief for Vladimir. He acquired the right of levying the Tartar taxes, as a Tartar agent, and while he thus enhanced his importance he also replenished his exchequer. All through he played off Russ against Tartar, and Tartar against Russ with consummate dexterity, extending his power over his countrymen by dint of Mongol authority, and preserving his influence at Sarai by aid of Russian gold. He died in 1340.

Dimitry Donskoi (1362-1389). — He was succeeded first by his son Simeon, surnamed the Proud, whose arrogance and stiffness did something to endanger his father's acquisitions, and then by another son, Ivan II., whose soft and yielding disposition would have done still more, had it not been for the powerful influence of the Metropolitan Alexis. He entered thoroughly into the policy of exalting Moscow to the headship of the other principalities, and did much to further it. When Dimitry, the son of the second Ivan, came to the throne, he had a long struggle to wage with certain of the other princes who chafed under his supremacy; but his relations with the Golden Horde were not of the abject kind to which his predecessors had stooped. He still paid tribute, it is true, but the payment was made upon condition that the Russians should be exempt from all acts of violent interference. When summoned to appear as a vassal at Sarai, he refused obedience; and it indicates how much the power or spirit of the Tartars had declined that his refusal was winked at. The immunity did not long continue, however. In 1374, some disturbances in a provincial town, accompanied by insults to the Tartar representatives, stirred up the Khan of the day, Mamai, to send north a force charged with the infliction of punishment. It was opposed, and some desultory fighting ensued, ending in the Tartars being defeated. The Khan was so incensed that he vowed he would wreak a revenge which would bring to Russian recollection what had been suffered at the hands of Baty. An enormous force was raised for the fulfilment of this sanguinary design. Dimitry on his side did not flinch. He had been accustomed to warfare, and hitherto he had been uniformly successful. All the princes who had opposed him at the beginning of his reign he had overcome, and the growing power of the Lithuanians, who had made common cause with his hereditary antagonist, the Prince of Tver, he had three times met and checked in great battles. Therefore he was in nowise disconcerted by the peril which threatened him. His father's friend, the Metropolitan, entered with all the energy of a younger man into the arrangements for defence. He appealed, in the name alike of religion and of patriotism, to the other princes for aid against the foe of all. So influential were his exhortations and appeals, that a near approach to complete unity was established, only one prince, Oleg of Riazan, casting in his lot with the "Horde."

The host at the head of which Dimitry marched southward, was the largest that had ever been collected on Russian soil. It is said to have numbered 150,000 men, well equipped and fairly organised. Even this was inferior to the bands of Tartars, with whom there was a strong contingent of Lithuanians, who marched from Kief to effect a junction south of the Don. The two armies came in sight of each other across the stream.

The Russians were impatient for the attack. At first Dimitry was inclined to adopt the advice of the more cautious among his counsellors, who recommended the stoppage of his march. Moved, however, by the earnestness of his following, and by a message from the venerable superior of the Troitsa monastery at Moscow, which was regarded as oracular, he gave the order to advance. When the passage was made the boats used in it were destroyed, that there might remain no choice between victory and death. The Tartars were drawn up on the great plain of Kulikovo. In the early morning a thick fog obscured the dispositions of the combatants, but ere noon it had cleared off, and the sun shone forth brightly. The battle was then joined, and for a long time the contest was waged with great obstinacy. At last the Tartars began to gain the advantage. They pressed the Russians closer and closer, forcing them to give way. The retreat was likely to take on the character of a rout, when a sudden change was effected. The Russian reserve had been posted in a wood, out of sight, under the command of Dimitry's cousin, Vladimir the Brave. Holding his men in hand till he had the pursuing Tartars fairly before him, he then burst upon them with resistless impetuosity. They staggered and gave way under this unexpected blow. The Russians then halted, rallied, and turned upon their adversaries. For a brief space they held their ground with much gallantry, but the ascendant had gone from them; in their turn they were forced upon flight; and as they ran thousands of them were slaughtered. The victory was complete. From that day the name of Dimitry Donskoi was ranked with that of Alexander Nevsky in the Russian annals, as those of two men who alone during all the dreary period of Tartar domination signalised themselves by their martial prowess.

Overwhelming though the victory was, it did not produce any great result. With the joy of a prodigious deliverance there came a dissolution of the strength by which the deliverance had been wrought. The victors did not pursue their triumph. They soon began to quarrel with each other. The country was thus laid open to a fresh attack. In a short while that attack was made. Recovering themselves, the Tartars, in 1382, came on again with a tremendous force. Their invasion, which rolled on with an irresistible impetus, swept all before it, advancing as far as Moscow, whence Dimitry deemed it prudent to retire. His withdrawal has been very harshly judged of in late days, the idea being propounded that he played a cowardly part, and the conception of his character derived from his conduct two years before being thus greatly modified in the way of disparagement. Moscow was desolated by fire and sword; and when Dimitry came back his first work was to bury some 24,000 corpses that were found in the ruins of his capital.

The Tartar Decline.—This was the last of the Tartar inroads. Immediately afterwards the invaders became distracted by internecine disputes. Mamai, who was defeated by Dimitry at the Don, was succeeded by Tockhtamish, who ravaged Moscow. But Tockhtamish had the misfortune to incur the ill-will of the redoubted Tamerlane, who now took up the part of the great Zingis; and, although not dispossessed, he twice over was severely weakened and punished. Though weakened, however, his successors managed to retain their influence over Russia, and in the conflicts which took place alike between them and the great Khan, to whom they owed fealty, and between them and the Lithuanians, with whom they were frequently at war, the Russians suffered greatly. Their sufferings were intensified, no doubt, through the lack of headship which now prevailed. Moscow had come to be recognised as, in a sense, the chief of all the principalities, but its grand dukes were for years weak men, who addicted themselves to very cruel and violent proceedings. Especially was this the case with Vassily I., the son of Dimitry. His claim to the throne was contested by his uncle, and a civil war ensued. Capturing that uncle's son, Vassily had his eyes put out. Soon after, a brother of the blinded man made a successful insurrection, captured Vassily himself, and did to him as he had done to his cousin. The victor, another Dimitry, who gets the surname of Shemyaka, ruled for a little while; but ruled so badly that he was speedily displaced. From the monastery to which Vassily the Blind had been sent, he was brought forth to refill the throne. He did so with a wisdom, moderation, and sagacity such as he never displayed in his earlier years. No doubt many of his doings were savage. He had the man who dispossessed him poisoned. He got rid of other relatives in a summary fashion. Yet he added largely to the extent of his exclusive dominion, conquering some adjacent principalities, serving himself heir to others in default of what he held to be a legitimate succession, and keeping them all in peace. In a word, he prepared the way for his grandson Ivan III., to whom belongs the title of Consolidator of the Russian empire.

Ivan III. (1462-1505).—Ivan reigned for forty and three years. The time was one of the most prosperous Russia has ever known. His character as a great ruler stands out in a light that defies all controversy. Yet he was in no respect a great man. Personally he was a poor creature — small, ill-favoured, almost repulsive, sadly nerveless and timid when confronted with any hazard that threatened himself. Morally he was even worse— mean, tricky, false, a consummate hypocrite, an outrageous liar. Withal, he was a man who formed vast conceptions, which he pursued with rare sagacity, with marvellous patience, and with indomitable resolution, meekly accepting the buffets of adverse fortune, but never turning aside from his aims. In his time autocracy became almost supreme throughout Russia, while the country slipped from under the suzerainty of the Tartar horde. He took advantage of the dissensions which raged among them to form an alliance with one set, headed by the Khan of the Crimea; to declare war against another set, headed by the Khan of Kazan; and to postpone or evade for a series of years payment of the tribute which was due from him at Sarai. When his incensed overlord awoke to a discernment of all that was meant by his delays, excuses, and protestations, a huge army was at once set in motion for the purpose of bringing him to submission. Ivan behaved in a very craven fashion. He made numerous alliances. He collected a large opposing force. He vapoured about what he was to accomplish. Notwithstanding, he did not care to abide the onset of his foe. Retreating to a safe place he sued for peace, promising almost any terms the adversary cared to impose. That he was serious in his proposals can scarcely be doubted. Nevertheless when his ally, the Crimean Khan, fell upon the rear of the invader, subjecting him to utter discomfiture, he put forward the representation that all he had done was merely a device to gain time, and so that he was the true contriver of the happy issue. Such was the influence of the man that the story obtained credence, and he was forthwith hailed as the deliverer from Tartar bondage. That no more tribute was paid is true; but every student of history must be aware that Ivan would have had no qualms about paying any amount, provided he could not otherwise help himself. In commemoration of this achievement, he assumed the title of "Tsar" in his communications with foreign potentates, though at home he was content to be known by his old designation of Grand Duke. The word "Tsar," it may be explained, is not, as it is commonly supposed to be, a corruption of Cæsar. It is a Persian term indicative of supreme authority.

Ivan took for his second wife Sophia, the niece of the last Palæologus who reigned at Constantinople. When Byzantium fell into the hands of the Turks she fled for refuge to Rome. Her marriage to Ivan was suggested by a learned Greek, Cardinal Bessarion, and was ardently promoted by Pope Paul II., with the two-fold object of bringing about an union of the Russian church with that of Rome, and getting Muscovite aid for rescuing Constantinople from the possession of the infidel. The first object failed, for Sophia, instead of bringing her husband over to the Roman faith, herself underwent a re-conversion to his. But she did introduce western influences to a large extent, and powerfully helped in building up the fabric of empire. Embassies from Germany, Venice, the Papal States, and other distant parts of Europe were seen for the first time at Moscow; learned foreigners were induced to settle there; the Russian money was re-coined; gunpowder was manufactured, and cannon were cast; in short, a decided advance was made in all the arts of civilization, whether beneficent or destructive.

The Fall of "the Golden Horde."—At the same time the power of the Golden Horde was broken. Their dissensions prevented them from making any decisive effort to recover their lost supremacy. One ineffectual endeavour was put forth, and after its failure all relapsed into powerlessness and vanity. Split into fragments, each fragment gradually drew itself off, leaving only what had no close adhesion to the main mass. That the ties which induced many people to stop were numerous and strong can hardly be doubted; two centuries of occupation could not have passed without causing, all along the border-line, a great intermixture of races. That they were not so numerous or strong as to warrant the well-known assertion of Napoleon, "Scrape the Russian and you will find a Tartar," is also certain, for singularly few traces of the long domination can be discerned in the habits of the people, or ever were discernible. The whole period, indeed, seems to have suffered an effacement such as is almost unparalleled in history. Even the Tartar capital disappeared from the face of the earth. It was sacked, burned, and left desolate. So complete were the ruin and the desolation that its site was long unknown. In its day of pride, about the middle of the fourteenth century, it was described as a great, beautiful, and populous place, possessing broad streets, stately fanes for worship, and fine market buildings, wherein were to be found merchants from Syria, Egypt, Babylon, and many other places. For centuries not a vestige of it could be discovered. In 1840 an engineer, who was mapping the country whereon it was reputed to have stood, came upon certain "ground-swells," which struck him as being very peculiar. He ordered excavations to be made, and thus struck upon the ruins of the buried city. By and by its whole plan was disclosed. The khan's palace was uncovered — a very sumptuous building. The Russian quarter was found, recognisable not only by the meanness of its dwellings, but by the remains of what had plainly been a Christian church. And a great aqueduct was laid bare, which once brought for miles into the city the waters of a lake which had become a filthy marsh. The extinction of Sarai is strikingly typical of the fate which befell the power by whom it was built and peopled. Whatever remains of Tartar influence is matter of investigation by the ethnologist and the geographer. It has no place among things that are cognisable by ordinary men.

Vassily III. (1505-1534).—Of course the process of withdrawal and extinction took time for its accomplishment. It was hardly completed thirty years after Ivan's death, when his son, Vassily III., ceased to reign. Vassily was a strong and firm ruler. In his day Russia made great progress. He followed up with marked success the course of policy his father had pursued. No striking event illustrates the period of his administration, yet at its close the country was indisputably stronger, more compact, more prosperous, than at its commencement. The power of the rival princes was then completely overthrown. The last of those semi-independent appanages, the possessor of which had a reserved right to the grand dukedom, was annexed. At the same time the like fate befell the municipalities of Novgorod and Pskof; partly through intrigue and partly by force, the liberties of which they were so proud were destroyed. **Within an extensive circle autocracy** was now supreme.

CHAPTER IV.

TSARDOM—THE REIGN OF IVAN THE TERRIBLE.

Ivan IV. (1534-1581).—It must be admitted that, on the death of Vassily, the prospect that the system of rule he had established would have any continuance, was clouded by a great uncertainty. He had suffered domestic troubles. He got rid of his first wife, not without a resort to harsh and unjustifiable measures. His son by his second wife was, when he died, only an infant. The mother, who became regent, was a very unfit person to have charge of a lad upon whom, it seemed, that such a responsibility as awaited him would devolve. Happily, or unhappily, she also died when he was very young. The government then fell into the hands of a council of Boyards, whose self-seeking dissensions threw the country into great disorder. Every man was for himself, and outside enemies strove as they could to take avail of the opportunity. Prominent among them were the Lithuanians, now united with the Poles, whose demonstrations became more formidable, and also more successful, than they ever had been since the days of Alexander Nevsky. But the managing council cared for few of these things. So long as they could keep power in their own hands, and keep down alike the inquisitiveness of their ward and the discontent of the people, they were satisfied. In both instances it was a difficult task. It was especially difficult in the case of the young man they had to tutor, for Ivan IV.—Ivan the Terrible, as he came to be justly called—was endowed with faculties which made him dangerous to deal with.

The manner in which his guardians dealt with him

was most unwise. His natural disposition was cruel. It was his delight to torture domestic animals, to ride over old women, to indulge in all manner of wild freaks. This disposition was encouraged, as a method of diversion from more serious pursuits. The calculation was that so long as he was thus employed, and took delight in the employment, he would have no leisure or inclination for other concerns. In this the calculators reckoned wrongly. Ivan soon learned to see through the policy that was favoured. He detected that both he, and the nation over whom he was the nominal head, were really the slaves of a despotic oligarchy. He resolved to emancipate himself. Perhaps it is not wholly his fault that in working out this resolution he became the originator and instrument of a tyranny more remarkable than has ever been seen on European soil. Its cardinal idea was that of complete absolutism. He hated, even when he did not fear, every one who claimed any participation in the exercise of sovereign power. At the early age of fourteen he showed his temper unmistakeably. Prince Shovisky was the president of the council, and the man with whom the boy-prince was most familiar. But it was ascertained that Shovisky had quarrelled with some of his colleagues, that a cabal had been got up against him, and that he was left in a minority. The victors had the wit to know how Ivan could be moved to their side. He took up the cause gleefully. Without trial, without accusation, without warning of any sort, a lot of fierce dogs were let slip upon the unfortunate man at a signal given from the prince, and he was worried in the public streets in broad day.

His Good Years.—The people who thus gained the ascendancy abused it even more deplorably than their predecessors had done. The young prince was encouraged to the top of his bent in all his wild and violent courses. No sort of restraint was imposed upon him. He became almost as notable for his capriciousness as for his cruelty. It was impossible to guess what mood of mind he might indulge or affect for any length of time; but in all moods he was ungovernable, and his delights were uniformly treacherous and malevolent. The records of biography will be searched in vain for any example of a life like that he led during the period of his teens, though its counterpart exists in the still more revolting narrative of his old age. In 1546, before he had reached his twentieth year, he was crowned as Tsar of all the Russias, a title ever afterwards used at home, as well as in relations with foreign courts. Soon after he was married, his consort being Anastasia Romanoff, whose meek and gentle nature was in strongest contrast to his. For a brief space he continued his career of outrageous license, and then there came a sudden check and an entire change. Popular discontent had become irrepressible. Moscow had been repeatedly set on fire. One night Ivan was roused from sleep to find his palace in a blaze, and to hear himself made the object of most dreadful curses by the infuriated multitudes. He was stricken by fright and compunction. At this juncture a wandering monk named Sylvester made his way to the room where the monarch was, and addressed him in the language of sternest rebuke, denouncing upon him the vengeance of Heaven, here and hereafter, unless his evil doings were repented of and forsaken. In an access of awe, humility, and devotion he fell upon his knees and fervently promised obedience. For thirteen years the promise was kept. The fear that prompted it was reinforced by the love he cherished for his wife. While Sylvester and Anastasia lived he so acted as to win the confidence and attachment of his people to a remarkable degree. Indefatigable in discharging the duties of his office, he showed himself wise, clement, and generous. He drew around him as counsellors men who were prudent and upright. Taxation was revised and mitigated, the payment of the army being put on a better footing, while judges and governors were no longer permitted to remunerate themselves as they chose, but received salaries which were the product of a general assessment. Commerce was promoted, the town of **Archangel** being founded, and the northern parts of the empire being laid open to mercantile intercourse. The liberal arts were encouraged, letterpress printing being introduced, while, by permission of Charles V., architects, painters, and various persons of learning and skill were brought to the capital. At the same time a company of Russian merchants was formed in London, and numerous English factories were established on the shores of the White Sea. Withal, the boundaries of the empire were greatly extended. The territory of Kazan was conquered and annexed, the mosques being turned into Christian temples, and a large number of emigrants sent forward to take possession of that rich country. By the conquest of Astracan access was obtained to the trade of the Caspian, and another fertile province was added to the Russian dominions. Soon after Siberia, which had been discovered by an enterprising fur merchant and overrun by a Cossack adventurer, was settled in its habitable parts, garrisoned, and incorporated with the adjacent territory. All this middle period of the Czar's life was a time of contentment and prosperity.

His Later Life.—It ended in 1560. Anastasia died in that year. At once the slumbering demon which lodged in Ivan's breast was aroused. He plunged almost forthwith into the most appalling excesses of sensuality and carnage, alternating them with fits of what he named piety. That he became mad, in the medical sense, is the only rational conjecture that will apply to his conduct; but it is extraordinary that, all through, there was a method in his madness, that he always evinced a shrewd knack of venting his rage where it was most politic, and that in his wildest paroxysms of fury he could arrest himself in a moment, exchanging the whirlwind and tempest of passion for a calm that was even more alarming. He began by dismissing the counsellors to whom he had been indebted, replacing them by more congenial and pliant tools. Any remonstrance against the new departure he had taken was followed by immediate vengeance. Such remonstrances were offered, and those who did so were, along with their friends and partisans, put to death, imprisoned, or exiled. One prince, who had dared to disparage a worthless favourite, was stabbed by Ivan himself. Another, who refused to take part in some lascivious diversion, was poignarded in church. Death was the common penalty wherever an unquestioning obedience was not rendered to every whim. Many were killed on the mere suspicion that they intended to disobey; and the sanguinary tyrant complained that his victims were too few.

Revolt of Prince Kurbsky.—Disaffection spread rapidly among the nobles, who found a leader in Prince Andrew Kurbsky, a person who had rendered signal service to his country, alike in the cabinet and in the field. Ivan divined what was going forward, and took measures to have the prince seized. He was timeously warned, and made his escape to Lithuania, where he joined king Sigismund in an invasion of Russia. No sooner was he across the border than he sent back a confidential servant with a letter to Ivan, in which his iniquities were recounted with unsparing force and minuteness, and the question was put to him, what answer he could give when he met the spirits of those he had murdered before the throne of God? If the messenger who conveyed this epistle had any inkling of its contents, he must have been a bold man to fulfil his mission. When Ivan had read it he lifted an iron rod he was accustomed to carry wherever he went, and set upon him with such severity as to make blood flow. He then addressed himself to the task of penning a reply. He was very proud of his powers as a correspondent. The production he indited on this occasion is not a whit more extraordinary than others that have been preserved. He began in this strain : " In the name of the all-powerful God, the master of our being and actions, by whom kings reign and the mighty speak, the humble and Christian-like answer to the Russian exboyard, our counsellor and voyrod, Prince Andrew Kurbsky,—Why, thou wretch, dost thou destroy thy traitor-soul in saving by flight thy worthless body? If thou art truly just and virtuous, why not die by thy master's hand, and thereby obtain the martyr's crown? What is life? What are worldly riches and honours? Vanity! a shadow. Happy is he to whom death brings salvation!" He proceeds to controvert Kurbsky's charges, characterising some of them as "impudent lies," declaring that he was severe against traitors only, and asking "who ever spared them? Did not Constantine the Great sacrifice his own son?" The conclusion was as follows— "Thou threatenest me with the judgment of Christ in the other world. Dost thou then believe that the Divine power does not regulate things here below? Manichean heresy! According to you God reigns in heaven, Satan in hell, and men on earth. All error! falsehood! The power of God is everywhere, both in this life and the next. Thou tellest me I shall never again see thy Ethiop face. Heavens! what a misfortune! Thou surroundest the throne of the Highest with those whom I have put to death. A new heresy! No one, says the apostle, can see God. But I am silent, for Solomon forbids us to waste words with fools like thee."

Resignation of the Throne.—Kurbsky's revolt did not prove very formidable, but Ivan now became the prey of ceaseless alarms and suspicions. He was tormented by the apprehension that the nobles and the clergy were in league to compass his downfall. As against them he took a singular mode of appealing to the people. Among the lower orders he long had a sort of popularity. They liked him as the Romans liked Nero, as the Spaniards liked Ferdinand VII., as the English liked Henry VIII. They had suffered much at the hands of the nobility, and the curtailment of their power was not a thing to excite regret. The government of one tyrant, however oppressive, was more tolerable than the government of many. Conscious that such a feeling prevailed, Ivan resolved on putting it to the test and turning it to account. After attending divine service with unusual pomp and formality, he suddenly left Moscow, and for a month nothing was heard of him. Then two letters were received, one **addressed to the metropolitan,** the other to the inhabitants generally. In the first he represented that such disturbances as had afflicted and distracted the country in the early part of his reign were obviously being fostered anew; he complained that his desire to repress them had been thwarted by Athanasius, the metropolitan, and by the clergy; and he announced that therefore he had determined upon relinquishing the task of government. In the second he made the same announcement, coupling it, however, with an assurance that he had no reason to complain of the people, and that they possessed his affectionate good-will.

The consequence he had calculated upon was speedily realised. A vision of hapless anarchy rose before the thoughts of the multitude. Their superstitious veneration for the chief of the state was excited to unusual intensity. The remembrance of the prosperity they had enjoyed for many years came back upon them. It seemed a probability that Ivan might be in the right, for did not his knowledge far exceed theirs? Agitated by such feelings they cried out that, unless he returned, they were undone. "What are sheep without a shepherd?" they inquired. Then the resolution found a voice—"The state cannot remain without a head, and we will acknowledge none but him whom God has given us." "Let him punish all who deserve it," was added; "has he not the power of life and death?" The feeling grew till a deputation of nobles and prelates were forced into the acceptance of a mission to Alexandrovsky, whither Ivan had gone, beseeching him to return upon his own terms. At first he refused, thereby drawing forth such urgency of persuasion, on the score alike of religion and the interests of the commonwealth, that his reluctance was overcome. This consent proceeded upon an explicit pledge that the clergy were not to interfere with his treatment of persons who were plotting evil to the state, as well as the destruction of himself and his family.

A Restoration and a Reign of Terror.—He soon followed the deputies back to Moscow. The inhabitants scarcely knew him, so changed was his appearance. His frame had shrunk, his visage was dark, his eye had lost its lustre, and he had become both bald and beardless These outward changes were the concomitants of a more resolute sullenness and ferocity than he had before displayed. He addressed the people at great length. In his harangue he expatiated on the vanity of human greatness, and on the responsibilities of rulers. For himself he said ambition was dead within him, but he recognised the necessity of preserving peace by timely precautions against men who were factious and criminal. For this purpose he had to suggest the establishment of a new body-guard, to consist of a thousand well-born men, who should be embodied in a select legion. The suggestion was eagerly assented to, and thus originated the formidable corps that came to be known the as *Strelitzes*. Instead of one thousand men, six thousand were at once enrolled, while, far from being taken from the ranks of the well-born, they were largely recruited by the most infamous of the people. Ivan gave orders that each should carry at his saddle-bow a dog's head and a broom He intended thus to denote that they swept Russia and worried his enemies. This mission they discharged in a manner that merited his favour. They plundered and oppressed with impunity. Their word was evidence for any accusation they might allege; and when a rich man's goods were confiscated they shared in the spoil. They speedily became the objects of universal dread and execration.

From the day that Ivan reassumed the throne, a reign of terror, which continually grew more frightful, was set up. The butcheries he caused to be enacted were appalling, by reason alike of their number and of their atrocious character. Every species of torture that a malicious ingenuity could devise was brought into use. Princes and boyards were destroyed in crowds at a time, some by fire, some by the headsman, some by impalement, while such varieties of outrage as causing a victim to be drenched alternately by freezing and by boiling water, were common. Ladies were often stripped naked and exhibited to the populace before being slaughtered. At this odious form of cruelty the monster who ordered the sentence was generally present. Indeed, he made it a point to attend every great execution, his delight in giving the sentence being exceeled by his pleasure in seeing it carried through. How the indescribable horrors of which he was the author could have been patiently borne, surpasses all conception. People of every grade seem to have been terrorised into abject submission. "It is the will of God and the Tsar," was the exclamation which covered the acceptance of each new atrocity. Meanwhile not only did increase of appetite for blood grow upon the tyrant's part, but there came to him a reasonable conviction that it would be unsafe and impossible for him to stop in his career. He was haunted by a dread of treachery, which prompted from time to time the sacrifice of fresh victims in larger numbers. Then he would devote himself to a bout of riotous sensuality, in the course of which outrageous profligacy was substituted for the excitements of massacre and revenge. For weeks thereafter he might addict himself to a life of moroseness and austerity, rising early, praying much, fasting often, and doing menial offices with his own hand. Afraid to live in the magnificent palace at Moscow, he had a gloomy fortress built for his own occupation outside the walls of the Kremlin. Tormented by a sense of danger there, he then fixed his usual residence at Alexandrovsky, where he had the country for miles round carefully guarded. Here it was his humour often to play a religious life. The palace was made a monastery, three hundred of his most depraved legionaries were called monks, himself he dubbed abbot, and it need hardly be said his rule was very strict. Especially were the dungeons kept well filled; and it was his custom of an afternoon to relieve the tedium of existence by descending to them in order to witness their inmates put to the torture.

From his retirement this precious saint likewise sent forth some of his most terrific mandates. Whole cities were devoted to destruction on the most trifling pretexts.

So it was in the case of Torjek : some of the inhabitants having quarrelled with the Strelitzes, the population were declared rebels, and put to the sword. So it was at Kolomna : most of the people were dependants of an obnoxious noble, and all of them shared his fate. But the most ruthless and memorable deed of blood which can be laid even to Ivan's charge, is his visitation of Novgorod. The inhabitants of that famous city had evinced some symptoms of their old passion for independence. Ivan did not like their restiveness, and resolved that it must be curbed and punished. Whether by collusion or by accident, he soon found the occasion he wished. A vagabond from Volhynia, who was all his life a cunning scamp, had been punished for alleged crimes by the authorities of the city. He resolved upon revenge, and may have been instigated to the method he took in order to secure it by the influence of those above him. The plan he chose was to write a letter in the name of the archbishop, the governor, and the principal authorities, to the king of Poland, offering to put themselves under his protection, and asking him to come and relieve them from an intolerable bondage. A copy of this letter he hid behind an image of the Virgin in the church of St. Sophia. He then went to Moscow with a terrible tale of conspiracy and rebellion. When put to the question about it he hinted where the evidence was to be got. Those who hide are usually able to find; and the confidential servant who was sent with the informer was at once guided to the place where the treasonable document was concealed. Upon the evidence thus procured Ivan acted promptly. The condemnation of the whole city was pronounced, and in its fulfilment many other cities were desolated.

The Sack of Novgorod.—In December, 1569, the Tsar left Alexandrovsky, accompanied by his sons and his favourite legion, in order to execute the vengeance he had decreed. On his way he exterminated the population of Klin, in the province of Tver. Next, the chief city of that province, also named Tver, was destroyed.

There the man who had succeeded Athanasius as metropolitan was confined as a prisoner. He had been brought from the bishopric of an island in the White Sea to hold the first place in the Russian church. Ivan had imagined that he would prove an obsequious instrument. Instead, he turned out a stern reprover. The expostulations of Athanasius were mild in comparison with the severity of Philip's deprecations and remonstrances, and these the monarch could not brook. He was therefore taken from his see and thrown into a dungeon at Tver. No sooner had the troops entered the place than Skutarof, a confidant and favourite of the emperor, who held the office of sacristan at Alexandrovsky, repaired to the cell in which the good prelate was immured, and there strangled him. Even the awfulness of the crimes perpetrated throughout the city lost, in the popular estimation, something of its blackness when compared with this evil deed, which did not at once become known. That Ivan approved it is certain; that he regretted he was not a witness may be presumed; but he had prudence enough to insist upon secrecy for a while.

From Tver he proceeded onwards to Novgorod. On the 2nd of January he was at Ilmen. That city was sacked. There was a suspicion that the treasures of its monastery had not been got at. Therefore the monks were ordered to produce twenty roubles each, and those who could not were flogged. The same plan was followed at Godroditche, a town near the ill-fated capital. At length, upon the 8th of January, Novgorod was reached. Ivan was met on the bridge by a procession of clergy, headed by the archbishop, having with him certain miraculous images belonging to the place. The ecclesiastic gave the monarch welcome, and offered to pronounce over him the customary benediction. The offer was spurned, and the offerer was treated to a tedious harangue, abounding in malediction and anathema. Suddenly the rush of invective was stayed, and the orator proposed an adjournment to the cathedral of St. Sophia. There he heard mass; then he prayed for a long time in private with great apparent fervour; and when he had risen from his knees he announced that he would accept the archbishop's hospitality. With his chief following he went to the episcopal palace, where a great banquet had been prepared for them. They had not been seated long when Ivan uttered a wild shout, upon hearing which a host of his satellites rushed in, seized the entertainer, his officers, and servants, and proceeded to pillage the palace and cloisters.

This was the beginning of sorrows. For five weeks the city was made the scene of murder and pillage. Day by day from five hundred to a thousand of its inhabitants were brought forth to die. Their doom was inflicted in divers modes: some were shot; some were hacked and mangled by the sword; some were smeared over by inflammable materials and then set on fire; some were tied to sledges, were dragged through the streets to the bridge over the Volkhof, and were thence thrust into the stream, while soldiers, armed with lances or hatchets, were placed to prevent any of them from swimming to the side. To this day it is a belief among the common people that the reason why the river at that place does not freeze, even in the most severe winters, is because of the blood shed then and there. To this day a huge mound near one of the Novgorod churches is pointed out as the burial-place of Ivan's victims, the common idea being that it is a heap of bones. At last the progress of devastation and massacre was stayed. The place had been despoiled of everything that was valuable, and one-half its inhabitants had been slaughtered, when Ivan condescended to pardon those whom he had left alive. He commanded them to appear before him. They assembled, a pale and ghastly crew, worn out with fright and despair, wholly uncertain as to what was intended to befall. They were addressed in mild and unctuous phrase, were told all that had happened was for their good, were exhorted to pray that their benefactor might have a long and happy reign, and then were graciously bidden adieu. The solemn derision which was thus used to crown an awful tragedy was in some respects even more hideous than the tragedy itself. Nothing could have so shown the hardness and perversity of heart which distinguished its author. It is computed that sixty thousand persons perished in this massacre, which extinguished the glory and greatness of Novgorod.

From Novgorod Ivan went to Pskof. Its panic-stricken inhabitants naturally imagined that it would be desolated like its neighbour city. Their fears turned out erroneous. Accounts differ as to the causes which prompted the tyrant to hold his hand. The one most generally received imputes his mercy to no scruples of conscience, or compunctuous visitings of nature, but to a superstitious dread. Outside the place he was met by an impostor or magician, who is described by Sir Jerome Horsey, an Englishman then resident at the court, as "a fowll creature, who went naked both in winter and sommer; he indured both extreame frost and heat, and did many streinge things thorow the magicall illusions of the Divell." This uncouth being accosted the Tzar, offering him a bit of raw flesh to eat. The proffer was declined, with the remark, "I am a Christian, and eat no flesh during a fast." "But thou doest worse," was the response, "thou dost eat the flesh of men," and this observation was followed by a threat of dire calamities should he dare to injure the people of Pskof. The affrighted monarch withdrew, though not without plundering the richest houses in the city.

Murder of the Tsarovitch.—Time would fail to recapitulate with any minuteness a tithe of the terrible enormities perpetrated by this crowned miscreant. The climax of his wickedness was reached in the murder of his son. The lad was a high-spirited youth, bold and dignified, if also cruel and licentious. His wife had been abused by his father, and a remonstrance on his part led to a quarrel. Before a reconciliation was completed, he asked to be put in command of some troops that had been collected to repel one of the constant Polish invasions. The request awakened the old man's anger and suspicion. "Rebel!" he exclaimed, "thou wishest to dethrone me."

Then lifting the iron rod, he inflicted upon his unresisting victim blow after blow till he fell to the ground bleeding profusely. At once Ivan's fury was allayed. In a little while his paroxysm of rage was succeeded by one of remorse and despair. He fell upon the body of the lad, kissed him, fondled him, at one moment besought his pardon, with an abject humility, the next cursed the surgeons, who would not do as he wished, and anon frantically implored God for mercy. "I die an obedient son and a faithful subject," quoth the lad four days later to his father, who had never left him; and so saying he expired.

The Death of Ivan. — From this time onwards the monarch's fits of mental anguish became more frequent and severe. So touched was he even in his lifetime by the gnawings of the worm that never dies, so excited by the awful representations of an alarmed fancy, that he often rose in the middle of the night, knocked his head against the walls of his chamber, or threw himself on the floor, uttering the most frightful yells and imprecations. At length in the winter of 1580, his strength began visibly to decline. In the following March he became dangerously ill. His illness in nowise altered his character, save by rendering it more capricious. At one time he would give astute directions for the government of the realm after his decease, counselling a diminution of the taxes, and the maintenance of peace. At another he would gloat over the treasures he had amassed, feasting his eyes upon his diamonds and jewels. Even on his deathbed he attempted the chastity of his daughter-in-law who was waiting upon him. A few months before he had sought Queen Elizabeth of England for his eighth wife, and later his ambassador tried to induce Lady Mary Hastings, the Earl of Huntingdon's daughter, to accept that honour. At one time he would direct the liberation of all prisoners, save those confined for capital offences. At another he would order some unlucky wretch who had incurred his displeasure to be tortured. One of these was a physician, Eliseus Bomelius. Sir Jerome Horsey tells how he was racked: "His armes drawen back, disjointed, and his leggs streiched from his middle loynes, his backe and bodie cutt with wyer whipps," after which he was bound to a stake, and "rosted and scorched till they thought noe life in him." Then he was put on a sledge, and brought through the castle, where Horsey saw him. "He cast up his eyes naminge Christ," and was then thrown into a dungeon to die. Ivan's premonitions of his own approaching death were confirmed by some astrologers whom he consulted. Nevertheless he caused them to be warned, that if they breathed a syllable on the subject, he would have them roasted alive, and he ordered them to be kept in confinement till the day they had named. When it came he had a warm bath in the morning, and was much refreshed by it. "Go," said he to Prince Belsky, "and order those astrologers to be put to death; according to them this is my dying day, and yet I feel stronger and better." "Wait," replied the intended victims, "for the setting of the sun." In the afternoon he called for a chess-board, and sat up in bed to play with Belsky. He arranged his pieces, "all savinge the king," we are told, "which by no means he could make stand on the plain board." While thus employed he suddenly fainted, fell backward, and closed his eyes for ever, so ridding the world of a tyrant whose crimes against freedom and morals surpassed those of a Nero or a Caligula, while his cruelty, his cunning, and his contemptible meanness find but a faint parallel in Louis XI. of France.

The later years of his reign were unfortunate for his country. Twice was it invaded by the Crimean Tartars, who, in 1571, advanced to Moscow, which they laid in ashes — Ivan, instead of encountering them with the valour he displayed in his early years, retiring to a safe distance to await their withdrawal. The Poles made frequent incursions, in which they were generally successful, though the Tsar contrived to neutralise the effect of their victories. One method he adopted was to get Pope Gregory XIII. to mediate in his behalf. This he accom plished by professing a desire to be instructed in the Romish faith. A monk named Possevin was despatched to be his tutor. He fared badly. In the course of their many interviews, Ivan always started off into denunciations of papal arrogance and ostentation. To a statement that the honours paid to the Pope were his due as "the head of Christianity, the guide of all faithful monarchs, a sharer of the throne of the Apostle Peter, nay, of Christ himself," Ivan shrewdly made answer, "Christians have but one father who is in heaven. We, princes of the earth, are raised to our thrones by a worldly law. The disciples of the apostles should be humble and wise. To us, princes, belong Cæsarean honours; to popes and patriarchs the honours of episcopacy. . . . He who dares to call himself a sharer of Christ's throne, who has himself carried on a seat (as on a cloud of angels), who does not live according to the holy Christian doctrine—such a pope is a wolf and no shepherd." With unflinching pertinacity, the monk returned again and again to his task; but his zeal led to no results. Ivan's purpose had been served, and so Possevin was dismissed with the curt but emphatic declaration, "Roman Catholics are at liberty to live with us a godly and honourable life; that's enough." A request to expel "the venomous Lutherans" was point-blank refused. It is, indeed, one among the few redeeming features of this reign that religion was never made an excuse for persecution.

CHAPTER V.

A STORMY INTERREGNUM—SERFDOM INSTITUTED—THE ACCESSION OF THE ROMANOFFS.

Ivan's Successor (1581-1597).—Ivan left two sons, Feodor and Dimitry. Six weeks after his death, Feodor, the eldest, was proclaimed as his successor. He was a soft-witted youth, very amiable, timid, and superstitious. By some of his people he was despised as a simpleton. By others he was lauded as a saint. He saw visions, and dreamed dreams, and was so abstracted, benevolent, and pious, that it was given out he received special communications from heaven. His father, discerning his unfitness for rule, had placed him under the guardianship of three boyards, with whom he associated a board of thirty councillors. It seemed a provident arrangement, but it did not work well. From the outset the council addressed itself to a reversal of what had been Ivan's settled policy—to depress the influence of the nobles. Soon the councillors began to wrangle, intrigue, and conspire. In a short while Ivan's chief nominee secured an indisputable ascendancy. He gathered all power into his own hands. Throughout the thirteen years of Feodor's nominal reign he was the actual ruler, a veritable Mayor of the Palace; and at its close he possessed himself of the crown.

This man was Boris Godunoff. He was the great grandson of a Tartar noble who had embraced Christianity, and whose descendants had thriven greatly. In Ivan's lifetime, Feodor had taken Godunoff's sister to wife. The match had Ivan's approval, for Boris was himself a favourite, insomuch that he alone had dared to interpose when the old Tsar was murdering his son. A man of great comprehension and energy, daringly ambitious, yet able by his strong judgment to control his ambition, he turned to good account the advantages he enjoyed as the sovereign's brother-in-law and prime adviser. His administration was vigorous and far-sighted. Towards the Tsar he behaved with wisdom and fairness, shielding his weakness, and taking thought for him in every way. His conduct made him popular, and he cultivated the attachment of the masses by well-timed displays of liberality. Feodor was childless, his only daughter having died when an infant. The heir to the throne was thus his half-brother, the young Dimitry. This boy showed much of his father's disposition. There is a story, that one winter's day he formed a number of snow figures, which he named after Godunoff, and his friends. Then he amused himself by beating them, having their hands, feet, and heads struck off, and saying, when his mandates were obeyed, "That's what I'll do when I am in power." The tale, however, may only illustrate the nature of the apprehensions that were entertained, and be an invention of later date, contrived to suit the facts that came out afterwards.

Murder of the Young Dimitry. — Dimitry and his mother were sent to Uglitch, a town far from Moscow. They lived there for a time in a sort of honourable banishment. On the 15th of May 1591, according to the most circumstantial among the many versions of what happened, he felt unwell, but went to church as usual. On his return he was left by his nurse and governess to play in the court-yard of the palace. Soon afterwards he was found dead with a gash across his throat. He was found by his mother, whose outcries raised a great tumult. At once she denounced certain adherents of Godunoff as being the assassins. The accusation found ready credence on the part of the excited crowds who gathered at the sound of the church bell. They seized the alleged offenders, and put them to death on the spot.

To the last the Regent steadily denied that he had any hand in the deed. He imputed the occurrence to accident. An inquiry as regards all the circumstances was ordered. The issue of it consisted in a representation that the boy was subject to epilepsy, and that in a fit he might have fallen upon a knife he held in his hand. Whether that was the mode of death or not, it was determined at any rate that the wound was self-inflicted. So much having been fixed, Boris turned to consider the precipitate and unwise conduct of the people who had massacred his retainers. A terrible vengeance was inflicted upon them. The Tsarina was forced to take the veil. Her brothers were cast into prison. The ringleaders of the riot were slain. So many more of the inhabitants were banished that Uglitch was left desolate. Of course this excessive severity only tended to spread and strengthen the sinister rumours that provoked it; though there came a time when it was widely believed that the rumours themselves were fallacious—that Dimitry had never been killed. Meanwhile the injurious reports received colour, if not confirmation, from alleged facts that began to be whispered about. Other members of the royal house had died suddenly. Nephews and nieces of the Tsar had disappeared in a mysterious manner. The agency of poison was hinted at; and suspicion pointed to Godunoff as the man in whose interest, and probably by whose orders, they had been cut off.

He held on his course unmoved. The country prospered under his rule. His general policy was as enlightened as it was firm though cautious. He executed many great works. He founded Tobolsk. He strengthened Smolensko. He carried civilization into Siberia. From his own enormous fortune, which he husbanded with a prudent care, he contributed with a lavish generosity to all public objects. Moscow was half consumed by fire, and he took upon himself the chief burden of alleviating the distress thus caused. But nothing could overcome the dead weight of mistrust and dislike he had to face. Even his best deeds were suspected and misrepresented, insomuch that the common people believed the conflagration was of his own kindling, that he might divert attention from Dimitry's death and win a repute for generosity. In war he was both able and fortunate. When his kinsmen, the Crim Tartars, invaded the country, sweeping up to the heights that surround Moscow, Feodor contented himself with announcing his conviction, derived in answer to prayer, that they would be discomfited. Boris put himself at the head of the army, and in the course of a brief campaign, in which he displayed signal skill and courage, routed the foe with immense loss. On his return from this campaign he banished many of the nobles who were most hostile to him, while he bought the support of others by establishing the institution of serfdom.

Serfdom.—The change he made seemed at first sight of trivial moment. It was no nefarious scheme against human liberty, planned with deliberate adroitness and carried out with ruthless determination. On the contrary, it was introduced in an incidental manner, and was justified by reasons so plausible that its author may well have deemed that he was conferring a benefit upon all concerned. Certainly he had no forecast of whereunto the thing would grow, the number of persons it would affect, or the tremendous consequences it would involve. The history carries one back to the old Slavonic times, with their "*rods*" and "*jupas.*" A survival of the "*jupa,*" or village community, so well known in the infancy of most states, by whatever race they are peopled, exists in Russia under the name of the *mir*, or commune. It existed long before Godunoff's day. To such *mir* every Russian who is not of noble rank, or a citizen, behoved to belong. In it his rights as regards the state were gathered up. The state took no account of him individually, but dealt with the *mir* as an unit. The *mir*, according to the orginal idea, was the peasant's world. Indeed, it is the same word as that he uses when he would express his idea of the *kosmos*. Within that world he could move with a considerable degree of freedom. Each *mir* possessed a certain portion of land, which was divided anew among the families composing it every nine years, the right of ownership always remaining in the general community. But the whole land was not so allotted. The communes were isolated and often far apart. Great estates intervened betwixt them, though a portion of these estates had to be assigned to the *mir* that lay nearest them. In return the community were bound to furnish a certain amount of labour, and a peasant might hire himself out for a fixed period, or for life, as he chose. In cases where a tract of time was not specified in the bargain, then, on St. George's day of each year, the labourer was free to shift.

For some time previous to 1593 the shiftings had been very frequent. A strong migration towards the south had set in. It had come to be known that there more genial skies and a richer and more easily tilled soil were to be found. Some of the free communes were largely deserted. The nobles, to whom they were pledged for a certain amount of labour, complained of annoyance and deficiency. Very strong measures were resorted to, in many cases, to arrest the movement. In some communes it was enacted that no member should leave without providing a substitute. On many estates arbitrary and violent methods were taken to prevent desertion. The state of rural society in the northern parts was confused and embittered to an extraordinary degree, while there was some hazard that the land would be left uncultivated. It was in these circumstances that Godunoff legislated. His proceeding was simplicity itself. He decreed that, after St. George's day of 1593, the privilege of free movement should cease. By this law multitudes of men over a wide tract of country became *adscripti glebæ*—slaves to the soil, bound to work for their lords three days in the week, or to pay him a rent which was called *obrok*. The system hardened, extended, and became one of the most striking characteristics of Russian government.

Boris made Tsar.—Early in 1598 Feodor died. It illustrates the inveteracy of the mistrust with which Boris was regarded that evil surmises were circulated to his prejudice regarding the mode and cause of death. There is almost complete unanimity among historians in pronouncing them unwarrantable. Even writers who stand in doubt as to his conduct towards the young Dimitry agree that there is no reason for imputing to him any foul play in respect to Feodor. There is probably as little truth in the tale that, when Feodor felt himself dying, he offered his staff, the emblem of sovereignty, to several persons, who refused to take it; that then, in a fit of petulance, he cast it upon the floor; and that Boris at once lifted it up. When the Tsar's will was read it was found that he had named his widow, Godunoff's sister, as his successor, with the proviso that Godunoff should continue to act as regent. Feodor was the last male representative, in a direct line, of the dynasty which had ruled Russia by the space of seven hundred and thirty years. Collateral branches of the family founded by the Scandinavian Vikings did exist, and to one of them the present imperial house belongs.

If Boris had been anxious to win the crown, he was now in no hurry to take it. His sister was proclaimed as sovereign within a week after her husband's death, but a few days afterwards she resigned the office, retired to a convent, and took the veil. Then her brother was invited by the council of boyards to mount the throne. To their surprise, and very much to their bewilderment, he refused persistently. Weeks passed, and a general assembly of the states was convened to consider what should be done. It met at Moscow towards the end of February, a body containing 474 members, of whom 99 were ecclesiastics, 272 nobles, land proprietors, or government officials, 33 deputies from towns, 27 representatives of the mercantile class, and 16 of the common people. With virtual unanimity they declared Boris the most competent person to save the state from the anarchy which threatened it, and a large deputation was chosen to wait upon him with the prayer that he would assume this ministry. He had retired to the convent where his sister was, and it was given out that, tired with the cares and worry of public life, he intended to take monastic vows and end his days there. When the deputies arrived he was at his devotions, and declined to be disturbed. When the decision of the assembly was made known to him, and he was humbly entreated to comply with their request, he solemnly vowed, "Never will it enter into my thoughts that I should reign. How could I possibly think of aught so exalted! God is my witness such a thing never came into my mind." At length, in answer to the long-continued and increasingly-urgent expostulations and appeals by which he was assailed, he burst out with the utterance, "O Lord God, I am thy servant! Let thy will be done!" The scene is suggestive of many parallels, though the closest of them—closer than that of Cæsar or of Cromwell—is to be found in the case of Richard III., as narrated in the old English chroniclers and preserved in Shakespeare. The resemblance extends to the language used. The part played by Buckingham on the English stage was performed in the counterpart drama by the Patriarch. This man, named Job, was a mere creature of Godunoff's. He was the first who held that exalted office in the Russian Church, and he owed his appointment to the powerful Regent. Some years before Boris had obtained from Constantinople, from the Patriarch Jeremiah, the nomination of a colleague, who was endowed with the right of consecrating archbishops to all the Russian provinces, subject only to a *pro forma* recognition of supremacy in his Greek brother. That the reluctance to accept the throne which Boris showed was but a piece of coy dissimulation, is inferred not only from the fact that Job was his most active partisan, and the chief spokesman at the conference, but that his agents, by the coarsest means, including threats and blows, coerced the representatives of the common people among the deputies into a display of earnestness on his behalf.

The First False Dimitry.—His reign was brief, and despite his enlightenment and ability, it was far from prosperous. He sought to strengthen it by uniting his family with the reigning houses of Europe; but one after another these matrimonial projects failed. He sought to found universities for the diffusion of scientific knowledge and the study of foreign languages, but the opposition of the clergy defeated his plans. He proposed first to Austria, and then to Persia, the formation of a league against the Turks, but neither of them would listen to him. Though Poland and Lithuania had recoiled from the keen edge of his sword and the force with which it was wielded, he tried most anxiously to make friends with them, and events arose which embittered the chronic hostility. A succession of bad harvests rendered the years 1601-3 years of terrible dearth; but though he exerted himself with immense activity and munificence to mitigate its effects, the people murmured against him as if he had been somehow the cause of the disaster. Amid these unfortunate and disquieting conditions a strange rumour spread from lip to lip that Prince Dimitry was alive, that he had found favour in the eyes of the Polish king, and that, with Sigismund's help, he was preparing to claim his brother's and father's seat. At another time the tale might have been scouted as incredible. As things were, its unlikelihood was readily overlooked. The story was held true in relation to a youth who asserted that he was Dimitry. If an impostor, as is now generally supposed, though there always have been upholders of his claims, he managed his imposition with consummate skill and with exceeding good fortune.

The account he gave of himself was, that the intention of Boris to murder him had been discovered, that a priest's son was found who met death in his stead, and that he had been conveyed to a convent where he was educated in secrecy. He showed a seal bearing the arms and name of Dimitry, and a valuable diamond cross said to have belonged to him, as corroborative of his statements. Soon persons were found who spoke with great confidence as to his identity, specifying certain marks and peculiarities which were known to them as characteristic of Dimitry, all which were found in the pretender. Handsome, plausible, confident, well versed in all the circumstances it concerned him to know, he made a great impression, and gained over to his cause many of the Polish nobles. Among others he obtained the friendship of the Pala ine of Sandomir, who showed a thorough belief alike in his claims and his prospects by consenting that he should wed his daughter. The young man was introduced to the King of Poland, who at a solemn audience professed his conviction that the representation made was true, exclaiming, " God preserve thee, Prince of Muscovy. Thy birth is attested by satisfactory evidence. We assign thee a pension of forty thousand florins, and as our friend and guest permit thee to accept the counsels and services of our subjects!" Of this permission the pretender hastened to take avail. He ingratiated himself still farther with the Poles, by abjuring the Greek faith, and entering the Romish church. He was soon at the head of a small army, and at the close of 1604 he invaded Russia.

Boris acted with his customary promptitude. He collected evidence to show that the fellow was one Gregory Otrepief, the descendant of a noble though poverty-stricken family, who had been trained for a monk, and, not liking that life, had run away from it. He procured from the living mother of the murdered prince a testimony that her son was indeed slain. He made an exposure of the conspiracy to the Polish sovereign, appealing to his honour to desist from the course he had begun, and threatening him with vengeance should he persevere. When this appeal was disregarded, he forbade all intercourse between his subjects and the Poles; he got his friend the Patriarch to fulminate his anathema against all who should abet Otrepief's pretensions; and he collected an army wherewith to crush him. In vain were all this energy and precaution. The Cossacks of the Don declared for the pretender, giving earnest of their adherence by sending a contingent to the force he led, which more than doubled its strength. As he advanced he was joined by multitudes of disaffected people. He was successful in his first encounter with the troops of Boris; and the victory was of course interpreted as a sure presage of his final triumph. He behaved with courage and energy in the

F

field, and with still more remarkable discretion and humanity when the fight was done. Conduct and fortune thus combined to recommend his cause. It is true that Boris sent out large armies against him, by whom he was repeatedly subjected to defeat; but these victories did not tell. They appeared to have no effect in arresting the development of popular feeling on his behalf. The prejudiced and superstitious multitude were swayed to his side by an impulse which prompted them to construe all things in his favour. His defeats were as gainful as if he had been the conqueror. Every move made by his antagonist served a purpose directly the reverse of what was intended. A report that Boris had sent emissaries to his camp who tried to poison him was greedily believed, and inflamed popular passion greatly. Meteors in the heavens were regarded as omens of God's wrath against the usurper, and warnings of evil should the rightful prince not be reinstated. The progress of the defection shook the vigorous mind of Boris. He fancied that, instead of the impostor, the reanimated corpse of young Dimitry was at the head of the army that had given him so much trouble. That prince's mother was sent for, and questioned privately as to her son's death. When she now answered that she could not tell whether he was alive or dead, she was fearfully abused by word and deed, and ordered off to close confinement. It is a marvel she escaped alive. His terrors and suspicions led Boris for a brief space to imitate the cruelties of Ivan the Terrible. He trusted no one, not even the spies by whom he surrounded himself. The prisons were filled. Tortures and executions were frequent. No one could guess what was likely to happen; when, on the 13th of April, 1605, the Tsar who had that day shown unusually good spirits, who had eaten heartily, and who after dinner had ascended to a chamber which gave him a view of all Moscow, suddenly expired. It was said that, failing to poison his rival he had poisoned himself, but the circumstances of the death contradict that notion.

The Reign of Dimitry.—Next day his son Feodor, an

amiable youth, sixteen years old, was proclaimed as Tsar, under the guardianship of his mother. His reign was short and tragic. At first there seemed to be in Moscow something like a cordial acquiescence in his support. It may have been an enforced conformity, for there is evidence that the common people had largely turned away from his father, and were much incensed against him. In the meanwhile the news that Boris was removed, with the reports as to how the removal had taken place, strengthened by a new and powerful force the claims of the false Dimitry. It had been gathering support from many diverse quarters. It now broke forth in an overwhelming rush. On the 7th of May the army declared for the pretender. On the first of June a vast crowd assembled outside the Kremlin to hear a proclamation that he had issued as Tsar. The excitement was intense. A great tumult arose. The buzz of curiosity and speculation was heard all round. People were determined to be satisfied; and the means of satisfaction were easy. Before the surging and eager multitude, Prince Shouisky, one of the house of Rurik, a direct descendant of St. Vladimir, the man who conducted the inquest at Uglitch when the alleged murder or suicide was supposed to have taken place, was brought forward to make a declaration. He declared, " Boris ordered Dimitry to be killed, but the Tsarevitch was saved. The son of a priest was buried in his place." The statement was received as conclusive. Forthwith cries of " Hail, Dimitry Ivanovitch," rent the air. Then there came shouts of " Down with the Godunoffs!" Moved by the spirit that thus prompted them, the Kremlin was stormed. The mob rushed pell-mell into the palace, to find, when they reached the presence-chamber, the young monarch on his throne, with his mother and sister beside him, holding holy pictures. They were all three seized, were imprisoned in a private house, and a few days later were strangled by order of two boyards of the ascendant party. A story of self-poisoning was invented in their case also. Following upon its acceptance, their corpses were buried without funeral rites, while that of Boris was dug up from the place of royal sepulture, where it had been interred with much pomp, and was flung into the same hole.

On the 20th of June Dimitry entered the capital. His reception was a triumph. No apparent touch of scepticism affected the welcome by which he was greeted. Any latent feeling of the sort was overcome by the scene which was enacted a week or two later. The coronation of the new-found Tsar was postponed till his mother could attend it. She was brought with great pomp from the convent to which she had returned after her liberation from the confinement to which she was ordered before Godunoff's death. The Tsar went forth to meet her with an immense cavalcade. When her litter was stopped, and she drew back the curtain, he leapt from his horse, and amid sobs and tears, embraces and gratulations, they attested before all the people, in a most impressive manner, their instant mutual recognition and remembrance. On the 30th of July the so-called Dimitry was crowned in the Moscow cathedral with even more than the usual pomp and ceremony. For a time all went well. The qualities which made him popular in the camp made him popular also in the city; and he was assiduous in their cultivation. Very soon, however, it became clear that the height to which he had so unexpectedly climbed was too much for his head. He became indifferent, arrogant, imperious. These faults were intensified when he brought home his espoused wife. She was a Pole of the Poles, and flaunted in a most injudicious way, alike her religion and her nationality. It speedily became evident that her husband was either completely under her domination, or that if a Russian by birth he had ceased to be a Russian in feeling. He outraged the habits and sympathies of his people with a scornful glee it was hard to abide. Foreign customs were introduced at court. Foreign guards were placed in attendance at it. Foreign favourites were suspected of bearing sway. The Tsar had sense enough to make no parade of the Roman Catholicism to which he had been converted; but his wife insisted upon affronting the professors of the orthodox faith. All this brought about swift recompense of a direful sort.

Dimitry's Downfall.—A conspiracy was formed against the sovereign who had been so lately welcomed. Its chief was that Prince Shouisky whose testimony had extinguished any lingering doubt that the alleged Dimitry was no impostor. From that time Shouisky had chafed and sulked, the supposition being that his chagrin was due to disappointment at not receiving higher honours and a larger confidence than were awarded him. Though a weak and vacillating man he had a measure of adroitness, which he turned to account in fostering opposition to the new monarch. His plot was discovered; and, along with his younger brothers who were convicted of participation in it, he was condemned to die. He had actually been led out on the scaffold to suffer execution, when the Tsar ostentatiously intervened, and granted him a pardon. Gratitude for having his life spared proved less powerful than the annoyance and vexation he experienced over the frustration of his schemes, and the galling manner in which he had been humiliated. Moved by a desire for revenge, he fell to plotting anew in a style more deep, patient, and subtle than before. Among his own class his overtures were received with much favour. The leading members of the clergy fell in with his counsels, and they in turn zealously promoted his object among the populace. Upon the 28th of May, the signal for revolt was given by tolling the great bell of Moscow. It was answered from all the belfries in the city. Aroused from the festivities at which he was enjoying himself to ask the cause of the clangour, the Tsar was told "it is a fire;" and with that explanation he was content. He was speedily undeceived. The conspirators had secured every entrance to the Kremlin. As the populace came surging up, their fury was turned upon the Polish guards, whom they sought out and slew. Headed by Shouisky, a party of armed men burst into the palace, exploring room after room, in quest of the man to whom they had sworn allegiance. He behaved in rather a craven fashion. He rushed to his wife's chamber, telling her to save herself, which she did for a time by aid of a lady-in-waiting. After a vain attempt to hide, he jumped from a window thirty feet from the ground. He was taken up with his leg broken, by some of his guards who remained faithful. In reply to the denunciations of him as an impostor, they said they would surrender him were his reputed mother, who was in the palace, to repudiate him. Such a repudiation was given, or extorted, and at once proclaimed. The people were in the mood to believe it, and the belief excited a fierceness of rage which was uncontrollable. The ill-fated youth was thrust through with a spear; his naked corpse was stuck up in the Red Square of the Kremlin, where it remained for three days, a mark for every species of savage contumely; it was then flung into a hole in the "stranger's field," otherwise called "the House of the Poor;" and finally, owing to a superstitious belief that the sorceries of which he was now accused were still working mischief, it was dug up, and was burned to ashes, which, mixed with gunpowder, were fired from a gun pointed along the road by which he came to Moscow. His wife and father-in-law, who were caught in the palace, were kept in confinement for a while, but were not unkindly treated, and were afterwards sent home.

The Reign of Vassily Shouisky.—The false Dimitry having been removed, the ulterior aim of the leading conspirator was revealed. Prince Shouisky was raised to the vacant throne, taking the title of Vassily IV. It was a natural enough appointment. On the ground of hereditary right, Shouisky, who belonged to the family of Souzdal, and could trace his descent back to Alexander Nevsky and St. Vladimir, had as strong a claim as any competitor; while his recent services were of course accounted deserving of recognition. Unfortunately for him, he or his friends were much too precipitate. The form of an election was gone through on his behalf; but the proceedings were forced and irregular. He was the nominee of the boyards alone, who exacted as a prior condition a pledge that he would rule in accordance with their wishes. His name was never submitted to a properly-called and properly-constituted general assembly. This omission was pointed out and protested against when the people of Moscow were summoned to the grand square to hear him proclaimed. It was averred, in particular, that without the assent of deputies from the Muscovite towns the choice was invalid. These unwelcome representations were drowned amid the obstreperous shouts of Shouisky's partisans. His acceptance was carried; he was forthwith sworn in; allegiance was vowed to him in return; and a circular message was sent to all the towns with news of what had taken place.

The difficulties Vassily had to face were in their own nature sufficiently complex and formidable. They were much aggravated by the manner of his elevation. It soon appeared there was no disposition throughout the country to confirm the action of the boyards. The people felt they had been outwitted. The questionable conduct of Vassily towards the late pretender was canvassed much to his disadvantage. Sorrow for the miserable fate of that promising and attractive youth, mingled with doubts as to whether the evidence upon which he had been so hastily deposed and condemned was not weaker than the evidence upon which he had been so enthusiastically welcomed. The workings of the popular mind as thus influenced took a strange development. It is comprehensible that there should have been a reaction from the outburst of fury in which the pretender was slain; but one might have deemed it incredible that any scepticism as to the fact of his death should arise.

The Second False Dimitry.—Yet during all his brief reign, Vassily was plagued by the appearances of men who asserted themselves to be the late sovereign, maintaining that the corpse which had been exposed, buffeted, and spat upon was not his, but that of a substitute. More than one such pretender came forward ere Vassily could be aroused out of his amusement and indifference. At length a schoolmaster in Sokola obtained such a following, that it was deemed necessary to hang him. Other claimants to the throne sprang up in swarms. One said he was a son of Ivan the Terrible, others that they were grandsons, either through Ivan (whom his father killed), or through Feodor; but the most formidable of all was another spurious Dimitry. Who this daring adventurer really was is uncertain. His face and figure resembled those of his predecessor. Like him he was a man of address and tact. The Polish leaders espoused his cause with an enthusiasm equal to that they had previously displayed. A great point in his favour was made when Marina of Sandomir was induced to acknowledge him as her husband. No doubt she was animated by a desire for revenge, as the Poles were by motives of policy. For a while it seemed as if both would be gratified by a repetition of the success which had formerly been gained. Russia was invaded; the people declared for the pretender; the armies sent out to check his progress were defeated; and the tide of conquest rolled up to the walls of Moscow. In a little time the capital opened its gates, and the whole country round about submitted to the new authority, the only exception being the monastery of Troitsa, itself a fortified town, which was gallantly held by a handful of brave men for more than sixteen months. At the end of that period the siege was raised by the appearance of Prince Schopin-Shouisky—a man of far more nerve and ability than his imperial cousin—at the head of a strong body of Russian troops and Swedish auxiliaries. In a few weeks the pretender was forced to withdraw from Moscow; and good hopes came to be entertained that the tide of fortune had turned. The expectation was belied through the occurrence of two events which altered the whole condition of affairs. Prince Schopin died suddenly; and Sigismund of Poland declared war upon his own account. Success attended his arms everywhere; while the Russians were left without any adequate leadership. They were repeatedly defeated; Smolensko was taken by siege; and Vassily was reduced to such straits that he could not pay the

Swedes, who went over to the enemy. The road to
Moscow was now clear, and the alleged Dimitry, with
Marina, and her father, joined the victorious host that
marched upon it. The inhabitants seized Vassily, forcing him first to abdicate, and then to turn monk. The
assumption of the cowl did not save him. He was subsequently dragged from his monastery, sent on to Warsaw, and immured in a dungeon where he was confined
for life.

A Pole as Tsar.—Whether Sigismund would have
set up the second false Dimitry on the throne, now that
he had the power, is more than problematical. He was
relieved from the difficulty of deciding by the fact that
almost simultaneously with the enforced abdication of
Shouisky, his rival was accidentally killed by a Tartar
chief when out hunting. A few months of sad disorder
and embroilment ensued, during which the Polish king
cautiously and sedulously advanced a project he had long
cherished. This was nothing less than an union of
the crowns. With a little less of crooked policy in the
arts by which this design was pursued, with a little more
of conciliation in the terms it was sought to impose, and
of patience in waiting for the upshot, success might have
been achieved, Russia might have been annexed to
Poland, or partitioned with Sweden, and there would
have been a different Europe from that which now exists.

Sigismund had reinforced the influence acquired by his
victories through a lavish distribution of gold among the
boyards. Yet he did not dare to suggest that they should
choose himself as their sovereign. He was content to
recommend the council of nobles to elect his son Ladislas.
This they did with an unanimity and a readiness that
surprised him, provoking his regret that he had not
embraced the chance for having his purpose made an
immediate fact rather than a prospective contingency.
He knew that the so-called election was open to the same
charge of irregularity as that of the late monarch, the
consent of the nation having been neither asked nor
given; but he thought nothing of this neglect, and the

alacrity with which town after town accepted the proclamation of Ladislas might have seemed to excuse his indifference. He ought not, however, to have left the clergy out of his calculations. They had often exhibited much patriotic feeling, and their religious *esprit de corps* was now appealed to as well. They could not be blind to the hazards which their church would incur at the hands of a sovereign professing an alien faith. This consideration they pressed upon their people with an earnestness that produced a profound impression. Their warnings and exhortations led to a representation being forwarded to Warsaw, where Ladislas still was, that it would be indispensable he should conform to the Greek ritual. The king was staggered; but the condition was distasteful, he underrated the influence, sincerity, and zeal of those who preferred the demand; and he fell into the blunder of meeting it by a haughty refusal.

The Polish Invasion Repulsed.—This was the turning-point in the history of a well-contrived scheme, prosecuted with patient energy, and more than feasible. From that moment it encountered a determined resistance. Mistrust grew to aversion, and aversion to a pitch of animosity it was as impossible to subdue as to reason with. From one end of the country to the other, there arose a cry for the expulsion of the foreigners. The inhabitants of Novgorod, with a revival of their ancient spirit of independence, scouted any allegiance to Ladislas, and, under the leadership of a patriotic butcher named Kosma-Minin, rose in force to maintain their protest. Their example was followed by the people of other cities and towns. Moscow was held by a Polish garrison, who had been cordially received in September 1610, though six months later they were as heartily detested. They had themselves done much to cause the change. Made aware of what was taking place outside they began to swagger and oppress, subjecting the inhabitants to insulting usage and grinding oppression. Of course quarrels ensued, and the city became a scene of bloodshed and confusion. The garrison, however, kept the upper hand, and made its weight ever fall more heavily. Then a league was formed by the insurgents for the deliverance of the capital, and by the end of March it was well nigh completely invested. The Poles made preparations for defence, compelling Russian carters to drag their artillery to the ramparts. A dispute arising, the soldiers fell upon the unarmed throngs, and as the strife spread killed a great many persons. In that part of the city called the Bely-Gorod or White-town, the Muscovites threw up barricades behind which they defended themselves courageously. Irritated by this defiance, the Poles set the place on fire, and all that quarter was destroyed, as were the others where the natives principally dwelt. The inhabitants took flight, wandering about the adjacent country in quest of food and shelter, and suffering terrible privations consequent upon the severity of the weather.

The summer that succeeded was a dismal time. Never had the country been so distracted and abased. From Smolensko King Sigismund threatened to overrun and rule it as a conquered territory. In the north, the Swedes whom Vassily Shouisky had brought to fight against the Poles seized several towns, Novgorod among them, in the name of their own sovereign. The Cossacks of the Don, to one of whose chiefs Marina of Sandomir was now married, upheld the cause of her son. The Tartars of the Crimea overspread the whole country farther south. Brigandage was common; the land was left untilled; suffering, uncertainty, and dread were everywhere prevalent.

Nevertheless the spirit of the people was not broken. Some few grandees stood erect amid the general servility, animating the people by an example of probity, disinterestedness, and public virtue. The clergy remained staunch in their adherence to the national cause, and contributed powerfully to keep others true. Among the middle and lower orders the crisis called forth several great men, other than the heroic butcher of Novgorod, of the stamp qualified to meet a great occasion. In

October 1611, a general assembly was convened at Nijny Novgorod. After divine service a summons to action received from the monastery of Troitsa was read. Minin came forward with a proposal that it should be obeyed, even should they have to sell their homesteads, and give their wives and children to temporary serfdom. The earnestness that fired his rough oratory was catching. A great united effort to free the country was resolved upon. Prince Dimitry Pojorsky, whose name and character were alike fitted to evoke patriotic ardour, was placed in command of the army which was raised in a few weeks. Minin was entrusted with the appropriate task of seeing to the commissariat. Success was found to be easier than had been anticipated. The uprising was that of a whole people, and before it opposition was swept away. The only stubborn difficulty was presented at the capital. For two months, from August till October, the Polish garrison kept the place, against overwhelming numbers, suffering straits so dire that it is said they had to eat human flesh; but at length they capitulated, and Russia was freed.

Accession of Michael Romanoff.—At Christmas a general assembly met for the choice of a ruler. It was an anxious business. In preparation for it a three days' fast was observed throughout the country, and prayers for divine guidance were offered in all the churches. For a time it seemed as if these supplications were to be unanswered. The early meetings of the assembly were marked by long, stormy, and fruitless debates. The names of several boyards were mentioned as eligible for the throne; but Prince Pojorsky, who might have looked for the honour himself, wisely counselled, that after what had happened, the choice of a noble would breed fresh jealousies and dissensions. Then the claims of several among the clergy were canvassed; but the idea of raising a priest to the supreme power in the state was repugnant to many. Some thought was next entertained of inviting a Swedish prince; but a majority of the assembly protested against the inconsistency of driving out one foreign ruler in order to bring in another. At length a nomination was made which conciliated all diversities of opinion. It was that of a lad, sixteen years of age, son of Philaret, the Metropolitan of Rostoff. He was a scion of the house of Rurik—so that he had the claims of royal lineage and divine right. His father had been conspicuous among the clergy for his services and sufferings in the national cause—so that patriotic and class feelings were both gratified in honouring him. Withal his age, his nurture, his disposition suggested that he would be amenable to advice. These considerations sufficed to secure virtual unanimity. On the first Sunday of Lent, in 1613, it was proclaimed to the crowds who thronged the great square of the Kremlin, that the assembly had made choice of Michael **Feodorovitch Romanoff as Tsar**

CHAPTER VI.

THE ROMANOFF DYNASTY.

Origin of the Family.—An immense amount of most ingenious research has been expended in the endeavour to trace out the early history of the Romanoffs. According to Müller, a distinguished Russian antiquary, they are of German origin. They are said to have had the same ancestor with the Chérémétiefs, one Andrew Ivanovitch, s rnamed Kobyla, who came to Moscow in the reign of Ivan Kalita, or of his son, somewhere about the middle of the fourteenth century. Having regard to the circumstances of the country at that time, Müller says, "it is permissible to represent the ancestor of the Romanoffs and Chérémétiefs as a knight who went first to Livonia, and thence to Russia, to conquer the infidels." The representation may not be more fanciful than those which genealogists are accustomed to assume and retail, but it cannot pretend to any basis of certainty. The future course of the Romanoff branch of the Kobylin family has been traced out. Andrew became a boyard. So did his fifth son, Feodor, who grew a much richer man than his father. The younger sons of the house seem, indeed, to have had the knack of outstripping their seniors. Feodor's youngest grandson was the founder of the Zacharin family. One of Zachary's grandsons was named Roman. He had a daughter, Anastasia, the first wife and the good genius of Ivan the Terrible. He had also a son, Nikita Romanoff. The affectionate veneration with which the popular mind cherished the memory of Anastasia made her nephews the objects of mistrust and dislike to the usurper, Boris Godunoff. There were five of them. Two were exiled. Two were imprisoned, the heavy chains with which they were loaded in their dungeons being still preserved. The fifth, the youngest, the handsomest, the gayest, was torn from his home and forced to become a monk, receiving in religion the name of Philaret. On the downfall of Godunoff he was made Metropolitan of Rostoff. In that capacity, while other towns were welcoming the second false Dimitry, he kept it faithful to Vassily. In revenge a number of the pretender's partisans made a sudden onset, and carried Philaret off a prisoner. He soon contrived to make his escape; and on the abdication of Vassily he was one of a commission sent to treat with the Polish king. At first they were received with kindness and respect, but the consideration of their business was adjourned time after time to wait the development of events, and in the end they were thrown into prison. Philaret was a captive when his son was chosen Tsar.

Michael I. (1613-1645).—At first the lad declined the dignity. He was supported in his refusal by the advice of his mother and his female relatives. No doubt the fate of the last two monarchs prompted their disinclination. In the end, however, the appeals that were addressed alike to pride and patriotism, were efficacious. A reluctant consent was given, and conditions of acceptance were adjusted which were marked on either side by singular prudence and wisdom. They were embodied in a formal deed which set forth the legality of Michael's election, contained a promise of true allegiance, and guaranteed, under the most solemn sanctions, the hereditary succession to the throne in the order of primogeniture. On the other side, Michael was taken bound to protect and support the Greek religion; to enter upon no war, promulgate no new law, nor alter any old one, without the consent of the imperial council; to decide no dispute, except in conformity with existing laws, the intention and application of which were patent; and either to surrender his private estates to his family, or to incorporate them with the crown domain. The deed was in fact nothing less than a well-devised national constitution, the observance of which would have rendered impossible the establishment of that arbitrary and rigorous despotism which soon came to prevail.

Michael did observe it. During the thirty-two years of his reign he was careful never to overstep his prerogatives. His public conduct was uniformly honest, moderate, and wise. His reward came in the respect and prosperity he enjoyed. At first he was plagued by various attempts at revolt, but they were subdued without trouble; and though some of the ringleaders were punished, their followers were treated with great clemency. Old Philaret was made Patriarch, and was associated with his son in all the cares of the empire. The proceeding might have excited jealousy, but not a murmur was heard against it. Instead, it was praised as a becoming instance of filial devotedness, and Michael was the profiter, not only in respect of the public approbation accorded to his conduct, but of the salutary counsel he became entitled to invite, and the lessened responsibility he had to bear. A period of order, reformation, and advancement, succeeded the long term of confusion, imposture, and decline, which had proved so harassing and deplorable. Commercial enterprise took a start which carried it a long way farther than it had ever previously attained. Treaties to regulate mercantile intercourse were concluded with China and Persia on the one side, with England in 1623, and with France in 1629, upon the other. Everything throve to which Michael put his hand, except when he engaged in war. The relations of Russia towards Sweden and Poland led to repeated embroilments, the issues of which told heavily against him.

War with Sweden.—The Swedish difficulty was an inheritance from the days of Ladislas and Vassily Shouisky. It has been told how Vassily hired Swedes to help him against the Poles, and how, when Ladislas obtained the ascendancy, they proceeded to help themselves. Vassily was responsible not only for arrears of pay to the Swedish troops, but for money lent by the Swedish king.

When payment was asked Michael thought himself entitled to repudiate the obligation. Charles IX. was furiously incensed. He sent a strong army to exact both payment and revenge. Hardly had it set out when Charles died, and thus proceedings were delayed for a time. His son, Gustavus Adolphus, however, had no mind to relinquish the claim. Putting himself at the head of a second expedition, he soon acquired possession of the large district called Inghermanland, and reduced various strongly-fortified places. The Russian troops could make no stand against him, and Michael was fain to sue for peace. In the spring of 1617 the negotiations took shape in a treaty by which, in addition to handing over two hundred thousand roubles—the original cause of dispute—he ceded all the Russian territory up to the line of the Lava. This was a severe loss, and a terrible humiliation.

War with Poland.—Even worse was his fortune in the case of Poland. King Sigismund had acquiesced, with the best grace that was possible for him, in the settlement of affairs by which Michael was raised to the throne. Yet he felt very poignantly the discomfiture of his plans and the disgrace that had been inflicted upon his son. When the rupture with Sweden occurred he was ready to take avail of it for his own behoof. This he did in rather a treacherous mode, by declaring a separate war upon his weakened and preoccupied adversary. No great success attended his endeavours. He was baffled and beaten back; but the victories which Michael gained seemed to him not worth their cost. Therefore he assented to a treaty which was to last for fourteen and a half years, by which he surrendered a large slice of territory. He seems to have thought this advantage was gained trickily, and to have cherished a feeling of resentment and a purpose of retaliation. Unfortunately for himself, he condescended to tricky methods for carrying out his design. When King Sigismund died he conceited himself that he had found his chance. He then ostentatiously renounced the bargain to which he was pledged,

G

and delivered a bold stroke for the recovery of what had been taken from him. It failed, however, as it deserved to fail. His forces were superior in numbers, in equipment, and in handling, to those brought against them, yet they were utterly foiled. Instead of winning back what he had lost, he lost much more. Livonia, Esthonia, and Courland were taken from him. All that he was promised in exchange was the document announcing the election of Ladislas by the boyards in 1610. He evinced a lawyer-like anxiety to get possession of this deed, apparently from a fear that it might be used at some after time to give a semblance of validity to pretensions adverse to his own or those of his descendants. Either he betrayed an excessive solicitude, or those with whom he had to deal befooled him. Perhaps both elements entered into the case. At all events he never got the paper. The Poles said they did not value it, but that it had been either lost or burned.

An Interregnum.—It soon appeared that the concern about the succession which prompted his wish was by no means misplaced. Though he had a long reign yet he lived a short life. He died at the early age of forty-nine. Considering what he had done for his country—the peace and well-being it had enjoyed, the respect and confidence in which he was held—it might have been supposed that he had left a smooth path for his heir. It was not so. The heir was a lad only fifteen years of age. His father had chosen for him a tutor and guide in the person of one Boris Morosoff, a noble of ability and influence. This man was fired by the idea that he could re-enact the part of Boris Godunoff with a success more complete and enduring. He devoted himself to the task most assiduously and most unscrupulously. He filled the court with his minions. The chief posts in the army were assigned to his favourites. He amassed enormous wealth, which he used for purposes of corruption. He induced the young Tsar, Alexis, to wed his wife's sister. He got himself recognised as the one centre of influence, the true depository of power. But he allowed his ulterior aim to appear too quickly and plainly; and while over-precipitate he was also over-exacting. He sold monopolies. He imposed a grinding taxation. He encouraged the judges in the imposition of large fines, the produce of which he shared with them. His tyranny became monstrous, even as his ambition became evident. The inhabitants of Novgorod rose in revolt. The inhabitants of Moscow were also ripe for rebellion, when a fortunate incident averted the temptation, and perhaps saved the monarchy. Alexis was intercepted one day as he came from church, had a number of moving petitions addressed to him, was told how often and urgently relief from the alleged grievances had been asked, and was assured that he was not personally blamed for the infliction or continuance of the evils under which the petitioners smarted. The interview aroused the man to a new sense of responsibility and of power. Morosoff was exiled, clamorous requests for his execution being peremptorily refused, and from that time Alexis was his own prime minister.

Alexis I. (1645-1696).—He ruled wisely and happily. In domestic affairs he followed his father's example. In many respects he bettered it. The resources of Russia acquired a prodigious development in his time. He established a mounted postal service only a few years after England had become accustomed to it. He caused treatises on mathematics, geography, and military science to be translated and studied. He tried to introduce the manufacture of silk and of linens. He encouraged the working of iron and copper mines. He brought shipwrights from Amsterdam, with the intention of building a merchant fleet for the navigation of the Caspian Sea; and it was the sight of a pleasure-boat, constructed under his orders, that inspired his son, Peter the Great, with the enthusiasm he showed in the same direction. And he convoked a general assembly of the States, such as had not been convened since his father had been elected, in order to consult with them upon various reforms which he was anxious to carry through, notably upon a revision of the existing code of laws, which at his instance was simplified and amended in a very remarkable manner. No one can refuse to see in this proceeding the nascent possibilities of a representative system, the growth of which would have given Alexis a higher fame than belongs to him, while it would have mightily altered the complexion of Russian and of European history.

In his foreign policy he was largely fortunate. He disliked war, but he seldom fought without gaining his end. In this respect, and especially in his contests with Poland and Sweden, he was much more lucky than his father. He retrieved the major part of his losses at a very small expenditure of effort, and some of his conquests had very wide and far-reaching consequences. Hostilities with Poland broke out in 1654. They were undertaken in alliance with the Cossacks of the Dnieper and the Ukraine. For more than a century their kinsfolk, the Cossacks of the Don, had been feudatories of Russia, but they had placed themselves under Polish protection. By the Poles they were excessively ill-used. No sort of regard was paid to their traditions and peculiarities. They were subjected to heavy and galling exactions. Their lands were parcelled out into estates for the great nobles, who made it their sole concern to raise as large a revenue as possible. For this purpose they farmed out the collection of their rents to middlemen, among whom were many Jews, well skilled in acquiring a double profit. The marvel is, not that a revolt came, but that it should have been so long delayed. When it did come it was formidable and decisive. Its origin and progress were on this wise.

Alliance with the Southern Cossacks.—A veteran chief named Bogdan had been subjected to very oppressive treatment. He roused his people to sympathy with his wrongs and to a purpose of vengeance. A mission to the Khan of the Crimea was successful in procuring his co-operation. Very soon Bogdan was at the head of a powerful force, the Tartar contingent of which was forty thousand strong. He speedily overran the province of the Ukraine, twice over defeating the army sent to withstand him, acquiring numerous accessions to his forces as he advanced, and gaining a position whence he might have struck a blow at the capital. At this juncture King Ladislas died, and the diet was convened for the election of his successor. Bogdan encamped at Zamosk, pending the deliberations which led to the choice of John Casimir. At first it seemed as if his magnanimity was to receive a suitable reward. The new king frankly admitted the enormity of the wrongs he had endured, and tendered a promise of redress. At the same time, while he was thus lulled into security, the general in command of the Polish troops perfidiously invaded his camp, committing terrible havoc. Bogdan escaped with a considerable part of his following, which he soon recruited to more than its former strength, and led back to wreak a hatred more implacable and vindictive than ever. Again the diplomacy of the wily king proved too much for him. The Tartars were detached from his cause and induced to go home. Consequent on their defection he made suit to Alexis for help. The bribe held out in exchange was a tempting one—that the Cossacks would transfer their allegiance to him. Alexis was not insensible to the value of such an acquisition, nor to the chance of recovering from Poland the provinces his father had lost. Nevertheless he was very chary about moving. It required the strongest incitements from the clergy, and those in whom he trusted, to make him stir. When he did move it was to enter upon a conquering march. Kief, Tchernigoff, Smolensko, were soon in his possession. So rapid and wide were his conquests that Swedish jealousy was excited, and King Charles Gustavus thought it necessary to strike in against Poland also.

He entered Pomerania at the head of a small force, and found his advance as easy as that of the Russians had been. The Polish sovereign fled to Silesia, and everywhere between Courland and the Carpathians the Swedes were received with ready submission. Could the victors have agreed the events of history might have been antedated, and Poland been then divided betwixt them.

Alexis was greatly indisposed to meddle with the rival invader, so long as he was himself let alone; but the action of the Lithuanians, in casting off his authority for Swedish protection, led him to deliver a counter-stroke. He made an incursion to an undefended part of Sweden, laying waste the country, sacking the villages, and putting the inhabitants to the sword. He seems, however, to have been afraid of the chastisement this inroad was fitted to provoke; he shrunk from an encounter with the veteran troops of the "Thirty Years' War;" and he was fain to arrange a truce for three years. It formed the basis of an arrangement which was ratified at Kardis in 1661, by which time the Poles had recovered strength, and were engaged in a desperate grapple with Sweden. It endured for well-nigh half a dozen years, up to the treaty of Andrussoff, which was concluded in 1667. To that settlement Russia, though she had scrupulously held aloof from the later quarrel, was a party, and by it she became a great gainer. All that she had won back at the outset of the strife was confirmed in her possession, and her authority over the Cossacks of the Dneiper received formal acknowledgment. They were joined spontaneously by their brethren, the Zaporofskian Cossacks, and it is probable that the whole of these communities might then have come under Russian sway, had it not been for a difficulty that arose with the most loyal, gallant, and powerful among them, the Cossacks of the Don.

Quarrel with the Cossacks of the Don. — These people were then in the condition they were found by Dr. Clarke a century later, before the legislation of Alexander I. Bold, hardy, independent, severe in their morals, thrifty in their mode of life, good farmers, capital riders, famous marksmen, they were allowed to govern themselves after their own fashion, and were dangerous to meddle with. A Russian commander, Dalgoruki, had behaved to them in an overbearing manner, and caused a brother of their hetman, Stenko Radziin, to be executed. The maltreatment of Bogdan, which alienated the Cossacks of the Dneiper from Poland, did not create anything like the commotion and anger which this act excited. It led to an insurrection on a great scale. At the head of a large army Stenko devastated the valley of the Volga, overran Astrakhan, and is said to have entertained the idea of setting up as an independent monarch. While he dallied with this project Dalgoruki defeated his forces, and obtained an interview with himself. It was represented to him that the Tsar was anxious to confer with him personally. Accepting this assurance he went willingly to Moscow. There he was executed as a rebel. Those of his followers who accompanied him shared his fate. A feeble attempt of his countrymen to continue the struggle, and to avenge his death, was visited by a terrible retribution. The terror which the rising had caused was shown by the remorseless severity with which it was suppressed. It is said that twelve thousand Cossacks were gibbeted along the roadsides. This ruthless conduct was successful in its main object. The population were utterly cowed, although it was deemed wise, as soon as they submitted, to leave them alone. Their kinsfolk to the south, however, who meditated a revolt from the Polish yoke, were scared from coming under that of Russia. They preferred to make a proffer of their allegiance to the sultan, Mohammed IV. By him it was eagerly accepted, the acceptance leading up to that Polo-Turkish war in which the imbecile Michael, who succeeded John Casimir, bought off attack by ceding to Turkey the whole of Podolia and the Polish portion of the Ukraine.

Views as to Turkey.—The diet repudiated this bargain, entrusted John Sobieski with the task of reversing it, and called upon Russia, in compliance with the treaty of Andrussoff, to give her help to the enterprise. Alexis did not refuse, though he was in no hurry to fulfil his obligation. He interfered so far on his own account as to demand that the Turks should give back Azoff, which they had taken from his Cossacks in 1642; and then, while his army was being organised, he sent a representation to the chief

European powers of the peril that menaced Christendom, pointing out how much their interest in averting it exceeded that of Russia, and proposing the formation of a common league against the Ottoman power. It was a sagacious and statesmanlike proposition, even if there was in it some amount of selfishness. No response was vouchsafed, though a few years later its wisdom would have been generally acknowledged. Meanwhile Sobieski gained the great fight of Choczine, and was then recalled to assist in choosing a new king; while on the 10th of February, 1676, Alexis died.

The Reign of Feodor (1676-1682).—He left three sons, two of them, Feodor and Ivan, children by his first consort, the third, Peter, born to him by his second, Natalia Narishkin. She made a bold attempt to have her own boy, then an infant three years old, appointed to the succession, on the ground that his half-brothers were imbecile. Ivan was weak-minded, but Feodor's feebleness was only physical. The scheme for setting him aside was frustrated. At the age of nineteen, amid general good-will, he ascended the throne. His reign was short, but not unimportant. The war with the Turks was prosecuted rather more energetically than in his father's time. Considerable successes attended the Russian arms. Their adversaries suffered terribly from the climate. Besides, they were made desirous for an acoommodation in order that they might be free to strike for an object of much greater magnitude than anything then involved in their quarrel with Russia. The foolish policy of Leopold I., the German emperor, and the ceaseless machinations of Louis XIV. of France, had inspired the Sultan and his Vizier, Kara Mustapha, with the idea of annexing Hungary and South Germany. Preparations for that design were now on foot. In view of it an easy assent was given to terms that would otherwise have been scouted. By the peace of Radzin, concluded in 1680, Russia was enabled to advance her frontier southward on the condition that she would refrain from erecting fortifications between the Boug and the Dneister. At the same time the Cossacks, who had proffered their services to Turkey, feeling themselves despised and cast off, went over to her antagonist, whom they have ever since served with remarkable fidelity.

The Regency of Sophia (1682-1689).—Feodor applied his mind to the duties of government with an assiduity and vigour that sufficiently belied the reports of his incapacity. He carried through sundry notable innovations of a beneficial character against very determined resistance. But his mental activity was too much for his bodily strength, and he died childless after having filled the throne for six years. Before his death he acquiesced in the proposal that his half-brother, Peter, should be his successor. This arrangement was vehemently contested on Ivan's behalf by his sister Sophia. A woman of great personal beauty, she was also endowed with a masculine vigour of intellect and tenacity of purpose. She seems to have loved Ivan with an attachment that derived strength even from his silliness. The idea of passing him over she resented, not only as a wrong to him, but as a slight to herself, and to all her mother's family. Her enthusiasm, her eloquence, her earnestness gained many friends for the cause she championed. Still, the Narishkin influence was potent; and, in order to overcome it, she resorted to a hazardous expedient. She convened the chiefs of the select legion formed by Ivan the Terrible, now known as the Strelitzes, and put her case into their hands, supporting it by the fervid importunities of her tongue, by the more moving eloquence of her tears, by lavish gifts of money in hand, and by yet more lavish promises of future recompense. She gained her point for the time. The Strelitzes took possession of the capital, forced the Narishkins to flee, and pursued mother and son so closely that they barely saved their lives by finding refuge in the convent of the Holy Trinity. There is no proof that Sophia wished them murdered. Upon the contrary, even in the hour of her triumph, she consented to have Peter proclaimed as joint-sovereign. The regency fell to herself; and she recalled to power her brother's prime councillor, Prince

Galitzin, a man with a great repute for ability and energy, though his talent seems to have deserted him when a serious pinch came.

Presuming upon the services they had rendered, the Strelitzes waxed arrogant and domineering to an intolerable degree. They acted as if the regent was wholly at their mercy. Their cupidity prompted demands which her wealth could not satisfy, while their lust of power made them insist upon claims compliance with which would have made her their tool or their screen. She was not the woman to be thus ordered or superseded, but she kept down her wrath till their commandant impudently insisted upon getting her younger sister for his wife. Then it burst forth in a manner which goaded its victim to attempt his worst. She was prepared for his effort, and defeated it. The Strelitzes were overpowered, and every tenth man of them was ordered for execution. At the last moment, however, Sophia cancelled the sentence. A few of them were sent away to serve with regiments stationed on the distant frontiers, but a general pardon was accorded to the rest. It did not quiet their malicious and convulsive hostility. A second rising was soon organised. Again it was met and subdued with intelligent firmness. Again a free pardon was granted to the mutineers, though the ringleaders had to sue for it in the great square of the Kremlin, where they appeared for the purpose with ropes about their necks, ignorant whether they would be strung up or let go.

Apart from these disturbances Sophia's government was fairly prosperous. A religious controversy arose over certain innovations introduced by the Patriarch Nikon, which were vehemently resisted by the old orthodox party. It had a lasting effect upon the country; but left her unaffected. She was not so fortunate as regards a war into which she was forced. The Tartars of the Crimea, in 1688, made another of their expeditions against Poland. As aforetime, the Poles appealed to Russia for assistance under the treaty of Andrussoff, which still remained in force. Sophia was averse to interference, her disposition being, as her father's certainly would have been, to hold aloof, leaving the combatants to weaken and despoil each other; but Galitzin had imbibed strong ideas as to the need of intervention, and the advantages that would accrue from it. Like many a clever man he made a huge mistake. His ideas of policy seem to have been twisted by his personal predilections, for, although no soldier, he took the leadership of the army which he organised for the invasion of the Crimea. He never reached the peninsula. When he got to the Isthmus of Perekop in the late autumn, it was to find that the retreating Tartars had set fire to the rank dry grass of the steppes, and had turned the country into a desert over which advance was impossible. Next year he fared no better. At the same place he came upon a powerful Ottoman army, who not only barred his passage, but drove him back with tremendous loss. As lying bulletins had been distributed representing his progress as a continuous triumph, the revelation of the unwelcome truth, which was made worse by sundry attempts to gloss over the facts, had a very disastrous effect.

Education of Peter the Great.—The course of events had no more diligent and reflective student than the young joint-emperor Peter, now in his seventeenth year. By this time he had developed a remarkable degree of shrewd insight, stubborn self-will, and patient courage, mated with curious dashes of passionate temper and wild self-indulgence. He had been sent off to an obscure village with a set of boisterous companions, named his "amusers." They were left to do as they liked, and it can hardly be doubted that the hope was the boy would be so corrupted and engrossed that all regard for the cares and duties of his position would be deadened within him. It was not so, partly by reason of the strong though wayward genius which he possessed, partly because of the instruction he received from one of his companions, an adventurer named Lefort.

This man was more than double his pupil's age when

he forced his way into the circle of which Peter was the centre. The latter half of his life had been a constant whirl of vicissitude, comprising many marvellous adventures, many hairbreadth escapes. He was a veritable citizen of the world. Born at Geneva, he had been placed in a mercantile situation; but he neglected his work, spent his money, and ran away. He took service in the French army, where his behaviour did not improve, and finding the employment irksome, he took French leave of it. Hiding himself on board a ship, he was carried from Marseilles to Holland. There he suffered such straits that sheer necessity forced him to join a body of troops that were being raised for the Tsar Alexis. With them he went to Archangel, where, when Alexis died, they were left, utterly forgotten, or at least unheeded. He used his abundant leisure to add an acquaintance with Russ to his knowledge of the French, German, and Dutch languages. Then he made his way to Moscow, where he became a favourite in society, married a rich wife, and resolved upon attaching himself to Peter. He succeeded at once in his design. The two became fast friends and almost inseparable companions, save when the younger man broke away now and again to indulge in a period of profligate or riotous amusement. His bouts of dissipation soon grew less frequent and of shorter duration, while they were always succeeded by a severe spell of work. It was his humour for a time to convert his companionship into a mimic army *corps*, and to place it under camp rules, which were enforced with scrupulous exactness. He entered as a drummer, and wrought his way up through all ranks. Not only was regimental discipline maintained, but the military art was carefully studied, especially in regard to fortification. Everything was done with exemplary thoroughness. In the performance Peter put his hand to shovel and wheelbarrow, and attached himself now to the besieging forces, and now to the besieged. The bent thus given to his disposition never left it. His native force of will, steady resolution, and ascendancy of character, were unquestionably developed and strengthened by this training, as well as the physical energy for which he became distinguished. At the same time he received from Lefort other lessons that were not less important. His eyes were opened to the facts of life. He learned something of the outer world. He was made aware of his own position. This knowledge if it increased, as it certainly did, his tendency to wilfulness, also inspired him with purposes of high ambition and vast reach. His wilfulness was illustrated by the obstinacy with which he persisted in wedding Eudoxia, the daughter of a Colonel Lapuchin— a marriage which turned out unhappily. His ambition was shown in the manner he took to dispossess his sister, and assert his own authority.

Peter Seizes the Throne.—Sophia had regarded with a quiet scorn the employments to which he was addicted. She thought them boyish follies which had the good effect of keeping him from mischief. So long as he did not interfere with her she cared little what became of him. She was therefore puzzled and alarmed when he began to present himself at the council, to insist upon being informed of what was taking place, to gainsay her wishes, and to dispute her policy. With the swiftness of feminine comprehension she discerned how mistaken and heedless she had been, read off his purposes, and perceived how easy would be their accomplishment. At all hazards she resolved to forestall him. Her project was to shut him up in prison. In order to effect his capture, she stooped to entreat the aid of her old allies the Strelitzes. Six hundred legionaries were sent out to seize him; but they came back with their errand unfulfilled. A hint of the design had been communicated to his followers; a stout resistance was offered to the band; and, in the confusion, Peter made his escape to his early refuge, the convent of the Holy Trinity. From thence he issued a manifesto denouncing the usurpation of his proper authority, and appealing to the loyalty of his subjects to aid him in redressing their wrongs. Sophia proposed as a compromise, that, while he should be recognised as sovereign, she, as the representative of Ivan, should share his power. This suggestion was scouted, and the mediators, whom she sent as its advocates, remained as the partisans of Peter's exclusive claims. She then besought a personal interview; but some of his advisers knew what cause there was to dread her influence, and the request was refused. The mob now turned against her, instigated by reports that she had sought to take her brother's life. Nothing remained but submission or flight. She tried to make her escape to Poland; but was caught on the road, separated from her friends, forced into a convent, and stripped of all authority. Prince Galitzin was degraded, and banished to Archangel. The chief of the Strelitzes was beheaded. The knout and Siberia became the doom of others. From 1689 Peter reigned without a rival; for though Ivan lived, during the next seven years, and his name continued to be associated in the sovereignty, he exerted no sort of influence upon affairs.

Creation of an Army.—At once the new Tsar devoted himself to the creation of an army. Except a few regiments maintained at frontier posts, the Strelitzes were the only permanent soldiers in the empire. To Lefort, and to General Patrick Gordon, a Scot, were entrusted the task of procuring foreign levies who might become the nucleus of a native military force. Lefort obtained the services of some three hundred fugitive Huguenots. Gordon was successful in recruiting a still larger number of his own countrymen. Thus aided, the two were soon able to gratify the imperial desire. A standing army was brought together respectable in its numbers, its equipment, and its organization.

Formation of a Navy.—To form a navy was the Tsar's next resolution, though one of more gradual growth. The rotting remains of the pleasure-boat which his father had placed upon a lake in the gardens of Imaeloff struck his observant eye. A Dutch ship-carpenter was found in Moscow who undertook its reconstruction. Peter evinced what might have seemed a childish delight in the work, and in its result. He never tired of sailing in this tiny craft; had others of a larger size built; and got himself educated to seamanship in connection with his miniature fleet as he had formerly learned soldiering with his playmates. In 1693 he visited Archangel, and first saw the ocean. He spent that summer and the next cruising about in English and Dutch vessels, making himself familiar with the duties of every one on board, from the man at the mast upwards. His perseverance is the more remarkable because he had a nervous dread of water. He could not for a long while embark upon it without breaking forth into a cold sweat, which ended in violent spasms. His force of will was called upon to subdue this weakness. He accustomed himself to a daily use of the cold bath; he extended his voyages and kept longer afloat; and at last he acquired the delight of a genuine sailor in feeling the waves bound beneath him.

The White Sea is frozen for half the year. Archangel is thus precluded from becoming a great port. Peter understood this, and lamented it. He understood also that the Caspian, to which he had access, being no more than a land-locked lake, could not be so utilised as to remedy the complaint he expressed in a saying which was often on his lips, "Russia has too much land without water." Nevertheless, he determined to see what could be done on that behalf. This purpose first led him to visit the southern part of his dominions. It led, at the same time, to his first experience of war. He renewed the demand which his father had preferred for the restitution of Azoff, and as the Turks refused compliance, he resolved to enforce it. Gordon and Lefort were placed in command of his troops, he himself serving as a volunteer. After a protracted siege, an attempt, which was defeated with great loss, was made to storm the place. Next year another effort was put forth with more adequate means and preparation. By incredible exertions a flotilla, in the construction of which Dutch and Venetian shipwrights were employed, had been launched. However much the reverse of formidable it may have been, it sufficed to prevent the Turks from provisioning the place by sea. Half the land forces were detached for the frustration of any attempt to give succour otherwise. Upon them the hardest portion of the task fell, for they had repeatedly to fling back expeditions sent from the Crimea with that object. By the end of July the place was starved into capitulation. The victors were greeted with immense enthusiasm when they returned to Moscow. They made a triumphal entry, planned by Peter, though he assigned himself an obscure place.

Escape from Murder.—Soon afterwards his extraordinary presence of mind was illustrated in a narrow escape from murder. The bold innovations he had made, though the mere prelude to vastly more extensive changes, had been viewed with disrelish by many of his subjects. The Strelitzes, who had grievances of their own, arising out of their subjection to regular discipline, were particularly active in fostering discontent. At last they formed a scheme for assassinating Peter and restoring Sophia. The plot was divulged on the night fixed for its execution. Peter wrote an order to have the house where the conspirators were to meet surrounded by troops at eleven o'clock. Through mistake he inserted this hour instead of ten, as he had intended. Shortly after ten he repaired to the place, and found to his astonishment no soldiers there. Assuming that they must be inside, he entered to see what they had done. He thus walked into the midst of the conclave who were pledging themselves to his death. Though much taken aback, their confusion far exceeded his. He explained that he had seen the lights, and heard the sounds of merriment, and that it had occurred to him he would like with their permission to join them, adding a hope his presence would not disturb their enjoyment. So saying, he seated himself at the table, drank to their healths, and soon had them engaged in a course of carousal and compliment, which was kept up till the arrival of the soldiers enabled him to drop the mask of hypocritical complaisance he had worn so cleverly. Fortunate was it for the commander of the troops that the order he had received was distinct, and terrible was the punishment inflicted upon the duped revellers.

He Visits Western Countries.—In the summer of 1697 Peter started upon an European tour. He travelled as one of an extraordinary embassy headed by Lefort and another companion. Proceeding through Esthonia and Livonia, of which provinces they made a careful examination, they pushed through North Germany to Holland. At Amsterdam they made a considerable stay. Here, greatly to Peter's rage, the secret of his identity was discovered, and the freedom of his movements was hindered by crowds of curious people who flocked about him. He outwitted them, however, by donning a deeper disguise, calling himself Peter Timmerman, the name of his mathematical tutor, and hiring himself out to work as a common ship-carpenter at Saardam. He took a turn at everything that had to be done—rope-making, sail-making, blacksmith work, as well as carpentry. He associated freely with his fellow-labourers, lived like them, dressed like them, drank with them, did his work as well as the best of them, and accepted his wages with perhaps less of grumbling.

From Holland he crossed to Britain. He was hugely delighted with his reception, and especially with a beautiful yacht which William III. presented to him. He did not seek to conceal his rank here; yet he plied his craft of shipbuilder both at Rotherhithe and Deptford, where vessels were being constructed to his order. This enjoyment he alternated with other gratifications. A public-house near Towerhill was a favourite resort for a pot and a pipe; and the Marquis of Carmarthen he deemed a splendid fellow, because he was able to sit him out while they drank brandy mixed with pepper, their debauch lasting a whole night. Yet the amazing versatility and splendid purpose of the man were exemplified as strikingly as his disposition to wild excess. His interest in useful and refining studies was made manifest by an assiduous attendance upon certain systematic courses of instruction, as well as by the keen insight with which he canvassed the tuition he received, and the puzzling questions with which he tormented his instructors. His attention was specially turned to his old study of fortification, as to which he had his views expanded and corrected; astronomy, also, was a branch of science to which he gave himself with a peculiar zest; while chemistry and anatomy excited an interest in him which they never lost. Still, the ruling passion was strong; and he left Britain with the remark, "If I were not Emperor of Russia, I should desire to be a British Admiral." No doubt the perfect order observed on board a man-of-war, and the despotic authority which the captain exerts, were extremely to his taste.

A Frightful Punishment.—When he left London he returned to Amsterdam, whence he made the best of his way to Vienna. There he had to talk with the German Emperor about the treaty which was afterwards framed and ratified at Carlowitz, while he wished to acquaint himself with the constitution and rules of the imperial army. It was his intention to visit Italy, but his travels were cut short by an intimation that the Strelitzes were again in revolt. They had refused an order to take up quarters on the frontiers of Poland, which was then convulsed by a double election to the throne. At once he hurried home, after eighteen months absence, to find that Gordon, who had been left in charge of the army, had subdued the mutiny, had arrested the offenders, and was detaining them to await the punishment it might please the Tsar to adjudge. It was ferociously severe. Two thousand persons are said to have suffered death. Circumstantial accounts, put forth with the attestation of professed eye-witnesses, relate how Peter, in the case of the ringleaders, emulated the worst cruelties of Ivan the Terrible. He had them put to the torture in order to make them confess. Whether a confession was extorted or not, he found them guilty. Then, not content with having acted the part of judge, he took that of executioner likewise. The story is told in the Memoirs of the Comte de Segur, how, "drunk with wine and blood, the glass in one hand, the axe in the other, in one single hour twenty successive libations marked the fall of twenty heads, which the emperor struck off, piquing himself on his horrible dexterity." This tale is also narrated by Voltaire, upon the authority of Frederick the Great, who said he had it from M. Printz, the Prussian ambassador at Moscow. One shudders to imagine such a frightful atrocity. Yet it is not out of keeping with what Peter is proved to have done otherwise. There is no evidence that his sister had anything to do with the disturbance except passively, as an object of hope to the insurgents; but he had two hundred of them hung up in front of her windows, while a form of petition that she should resume the crown was placed in the stiffened fingers of a corpse, the arm being then cut off and thrust in at her chamber-door. His young wife was also suspected; and, mindless of his own marital infidelities, he had her divorced and imprisoned, while her alleged lover was impaled. Of course the Strelitzes were disbanded. Their numbers had been woefully thinned; the curtailment of their privileges had checked the desire to join them; and their dispersion to different services in far-apart regions, so that they could have no communication, made an effectual end of them.

Internal Reforms.—Rid of this trouble, the Tsar now turned the whole force of his mind upon the accomplishment of what he thought desirable reforms. His ideas were very comprehensive. They reached also to things that are very minute. Never was there such a combination of what is vast, difficult, and far-reaching, with what is trivial, arbitrary, and sure to pass away speedily. It was hard to know in regard to which class of subjects the autocrat was most peremptory, or to which ideas his attachment would longest abide. He altered the mechanism of administration, at least in all its highest departments. He did what was more difficult, for, by the institution of what is called the "tchinn," he changed the whole rules of society. Nothing was too great to withstand his revolutionary vigour, if it offered itself as an object of assault. Nothing was too small, did it chance to attract his regard, to escape his persistent hostility. He ordered every man to shave—an edict which so wounded the feelings of the people, that many of them preserved the hair which was cut off their faces, in order that it might be laid in their coffins. He insisted that tight-fitting clothes should be worn by all males —and the change from the wide-flowing garments of the east was to many as embarrassing as it was distasteful. Amusements were prescribed and regulated—aristocratic and rich families being forced to entertain their neighbours, who, in turn, contrary to old usage, were compelled to bring their wives and daughters with them. He established an uniform system of weights and measures, and he reformed the calendar, making the year begin with the first of January instead of at the beginning of harvest—though, unhappily, he adopted the old Julian reckoning, which is eleven days behind the Gregorian. Taxation was increased and re-distributed— all exemptions being abolished, even those of the clergy. They were further irritated by a prohibition of monastic vows, except under certain very hard conditions—insomuch that some ardent members of the priesthood were moved to denounce Peter as the veritable antichrist. With seeming carelessness he held on the even tenor of his way, speedily widening the sphere of his recognised authority, bending all things within it to the despotism of his arbitrary will, and imposing upon them what he deemed the semblance of western civilization.

St. Petersburg Founded.—One of his most characteristic works was the creation of a new capital, named after himself. St. Petersburg has a history such as can be matched by that of no other city. The site chosen for it was a mere swamp, at the edge of a recently-won conquest, and bordering a sea which the first breath of winter regularly congeals. The difficulties of construction were enormous, for the ground had to be piled, stone had to be brought from a distance, and the whole process was so toilsome that, time after time, Peter's advisers counselled its abandonment as an impossible task, though he would never hear of it, impossibility being to him a word without meaning. More men were crowded on to the work; money was expended without stint; lives were sacrificed every whit as heedlessly; and in nine years the marsh, which had been the home of the bittern and the sea-mew, was covered by a spacious city,

ST. PETERSBURG.

having wharves, canals, bridges, and long rectilineal streets, lined by imposing buildings, many of them such as would be beautiful if seen through a keen Attic atmosphere, though they are out of place where they stand. It is said that during these years 100,000 soldiers and work-people, who were virtually slaves, perished consequent upon the severity of their toil, the rigours of the weather, and the scarcity of provisions. In 1714 the seat of government was shifted to the new metropolis, which was at the same time peopled by a forced migration; but the advent of winter always sets some of its population flying southwards, and to this day, through all its splendours, every returning spring brings evidence that it is built on a morass.

Catherine and Menschikoff.—The superintendence of this great scheme did not engross the energies of the Tsar. His versatility found other employments of widely different sorts. For one thing, he re-married. His life with Eudoxia Lapuchin, his first consort, had been unhappy. Her friends resisted and condemned those departures from traditional etiquette in which Peter delighted; and other causes bred domestic dispeace. In 1696 the Tsarina was divorced and confined in a convent, a boyard named Gheloff, who was accused of being her lover, having been impaled. In a short while her place was filled by a Livonian peasant girl, who exerted a remarkable influence upon the fortunes of Russia. She was born in the small village of Ringhein. Her parents died while she was a child, leaving her poor and friendless. The parish clerk in the neighbouring town of Marienburgh took pity upon her, received her into his house, giving her food, clothing, and some little education, in recompense for the share she took in the domestic drudgeries of his small establishment. She grew up a pretty girl, *petite* in figure, animated and engaging in manner, sweet-tempered, but a little self-willed. Falling in love with a Swedish dragoon who was quartered in the town, she insisted upon marrying him, though the fellow was under orders to leave, which he did next day, and was never heard of more. When Marienburgh was captured by the Russians she attracted the notice of General Bauer, who took her to live with him. Thence she was transferred to the protection of Prince Menschikoff, a prime favourite with the Tsar, and a man whose rise had been as extraordinary as hers was to be. At fourteen years of age he came to Moscow in quest of work. He was taken as an apprentice into the shop of a pastry-cook. It was part of his duty to sell pies and patties in the streets. A handsome boy, with a fine voice, and a knack of making rhymes, he was accustomed to recommend his wares in songs of his own composition. While thus engaged he drew the attention of Lefort, who took him into his service. So he came under the notice of the Tsar, who formed a great attachment to him. It was well deserved and well repaid. Menschikoff grew up a shrewd, capable, brave, and loyal man. He never overcame the defects of his early education, for he never learned either to read or write, and he had sundry foibles at which Peter was wont to laugh—in particular, at his egregious vanity and his fondness for pomp, traits so much at variance with the simplicity of the Tsar's own habits. Yet the two understood each other; they remained fast and helpful friends; and in his later years no one except, indeed, Catherine had so much influence with Peter. She had been living with Menschikoff for about two years when she was transferred to the imperial palace. Entering it as a mistress, she soon ruled it as a wife. The Tsar's affection for her was genuine. In turn, she gave herself up to him with a complete devotion, amusing his leisure, soothing his fretfulness, allaying his most tempestuous gusts of passion, sharing in his councils with an intelligence he respected, and participating in his dangers with a heroism that filled him with admiration and delight.

Peter's Wars and Aggressions. — His wars were numerous, and in the main successful. He pursued a policy of aggression all round. He aimed at governing the Baltic and confining the Swedes to their peninsula; at fomenting the divisions of Poland in order to profit by the weakness they caused; at circumscribing the territory of the Ottoman empire, and subjecting to his own ascendancy the Christian populations that bore the yoke of Turks or Persians; at extending his commerce and his dominion to the far east; and at the same time acquiring weight and consideration in the affairs of the west. It was a comprehensive and difficult programme; but he laboured at every part of it with an amazing diligence and a remarkable success. By sheer pertinacity he obtained from the Turk much better terms than the diplomatists who drew up the treaty of Carlowitz in 1699 had formulated on his behalf, acquiring possession not only of Azoff, for which he had fought, but also seven leagues of territory in the direction of the river Kuban, while it was stipulated that the Tartars of the Crimea should be restrained from those harassing incursions to which they were prone. Even this did not content him; he accepted the bargain as binding only for a limited period, and no sooner had it been concluded than he began arrangements for throwing it aside at a convenient opportunity. The fortifications of Azoff were strengthened; those of Taganrog were built; certain old works at Kamienska, on the Dnieper, were restored—all in violation of the compact; while other menacing steps were taken that pointed clearly a purpose of further aggrandisement. Its execution was delayed consequent upon the outbreak of a Swedo-Polish war.

Poland and Denmark thought they saw in the youth of Charles XII. a chance for recovering the territories which Sweden had reft from them. Peter was willing enough to co-operate for this end, provided he got Ingria and Carelia to himself. Upon these terms he raised an army and took possession of the provinces. Sweden acted against the confederacy with admirable promptitude. Before the Danes knew what they were about, Charles was before their capital, and had extorted from them a confirmation of his title to the disputed provinces of Schleswig and Holstein, as well as an indemnity for the trouble to which he had been put. Turning next upon the Poles, he suddenly swept them out of Livonia. For the Russians he professed an utter contempt; and the ease with which at Narva 8000 of his soldiers routed a force six times their number, no doubt tended to justify and to enhance his scorn. Peter was in the Polish capital when the battle was fought. He received the news of it with great composure. "The Swedes will teach us how to beat them," he observed; and the prediction speedily came true.

All the winter of 1701-2 was spent in the most indefatigable preparations for a renewal of the campaign. Troops were enlisted and drilled; cannon were cast; the Tsar threw all the enthusiasm of his nature into the work; and he succeeded in kindling among his men something of his own ardour. Re-entering Ingria as soon as the weather would permit of movement, he marched upon various points of vantage, forcing the Swedes to retire, beating them time after time in trivial skirmishes, and at last obtaining a decided victory over their main force, who were encountered at Dorpt. Very soon the whole province was in his possession up to the confines of Livonia. Leaving Menschikoff in charge as governor, Peter himself advanced upon Courland. Here he was defeated in his first onset, but rallying his troops and bringing up reinforcements he obtained various successes, which were consummated by the capitulation, in the early autumn, of the capital.

Invasion of Russia by Charles XII. — Meantime Charles had pressed hard upon the Poles. The weak and fickle Augustus of Saxony he dethroned, setting up Stanislaus Lecinzky in his place. Peter, while sedulously guarding his own conquests, exerted all his powers of intrigue to rouse the Polish people, and especially the Polish grandees, against an acceptance of the new sovereign. His efforts had a measure of success sufficient to excite the wrath of the hot-tempered monarch of Sweden. The Swedish treasury was full; Charles had a seasoned army of 50,000 men who had never known defeat; and he vowed that he would punish the presumptuous interference of Peter by an invasion of his kingdom. The adoption of this resolve marks one of the most critical moments in Russian story. No one conceived that the Tsar would be able to withstand his assailant. The general impression was that his armies would be overthrown, and he himself deposed. He had no ally to whom he could look for succour. The resources of Poland were to be used against him. The Ottoman power was so hostile that he had reason to dread it would join his antagonists, as indeed it would, had not the pride and self-confidence of Charles prompted him to disdain such help. His temper was illustrated by a remark he addressed to the French ambassador at the court of Saxony, who inquired if an accommodation was impossible. "I will treat at Moscow," was the haughty response. When it was reported to Peter he quietly remarked, "My brother Charles wishes to play the part of an Alexander; he shall not find a Darius in me."

His preparations for defence were made with the utmost care and forethought. Yet the patient sagacity he bestowed upon them was not incompatible with the exercise of great dash and swift decision. The conduct of his antagonist was highly favourable to a display of his best skill. Charles vapoured and dawdled, thinking, no doubt, that he could strike whenever it suited him. Peter planned and toiled with an anxious zeal that put all his faculties on the stretch. After Charles was ready to advance he suddenly called a halt, in order that he might visit at Dresden the Polish king whom he had displaced. This ostentatious proceeding made it necessary that his army should winter in Lithuania. Peter immediately advanced his forces to Grodno, in order that he might be able to contest every inch of the ground over which his adversary was to advance. At Grodno he made a narrow escape from capture. Charles heard of his arrival, ordered a sudden dash upon the place, gained admission by a *ruse*, and came so very near the attainment of his object, that, while he was entering at one gate, in all the pride of pomp, Peter was shuffling out in disguise at another. The case was very soon, however, almost completely reversed; for Charles, who was attended by a very small guard, took up his quarters at a Jesuit college, where he enjoyed himself heartily at the expense of the fathers who hated him, who found means to communicate with Peter as to the weakness and negligence of his foe, and who thus brought on an attack which was as nearly successful as the previous surprise.

When the regular campaign opened, Peter's strategy

showed to great advantage. His force was twice as large as that of the invader. Yet he was very careful to avoid a pitched battle, knowing well that his raw recruits could no'. stand against the disciplined battalions they had to meet. His hordes of Cossacks did admirable service in this emergency. They assailed the foe on all sides, and when they drew notice scampered off at a rate which made it impossible to catch or suppress them. Moreover, they devastated the country all about, so that the Swedes, who had trusted for supplies to the territories they were to pass through, soon began to be pinched by straits. In these circumstances the advance was hindered; Charles was compelled to canton his army in order to procure supplies from the rear; and the delay so chafed his spirit that he was betrayed into an irredeemable act of folly. His true policy was to march upon Moscow and crush it. Instead, he suffered himself to be seduced upon a fool's errand away to the steppes of the Ukraine.

The tempter was that Mazeppa, part of whose story has been made universally familiar by Lord Byron's poem. Originally a page at the court of John Casimir, he had provoked the jealousy of the nobleman he served, who had him bound naked to a wild horse, and sent adrift. He was carried from the centre of Poland away to the deserts of the Ukraine. The barbarous people showed him great kindness, and he was fain to make his abode with them. In their frequent contests with the Tartars he acquired much distinction, and by-and-bye he was made their hetman. A fancied slight, of which he was the object at Moscow when on a visit to the Tsar, filled him with inextinguishable hatred. He tried many methods of revenge, and when the war broke out he lighted upon one that he conceived would be more efficacious than them all. He wrote to Charles offering to join him, should he come south, with all his people. The bait took; Charles struck away from his right path for a place of rendezvous in the province of Pultowa, near where the Drevna falls into the Dnieper. At first Peter could scarcely credit the news. When the movement, and its motive, became clear he acted with his customary decision. Mazeppa was superseded; his accomplices when caught were put to death; the strong places in which the insurgents might have found shelter were levelled; the loyalty of the population was appealed to with great effect; and when the leader of the revolt reached the appointed meeting-place, instead of arriving at the head of a formidable force, he appeared with only a few ill-equipped battalions. At the same time the Swedish force was terribly broken and distressed. General Lewenhauft, who brought up its rear, had much difficulty in making way at all. The Russians hung upon his track, clustered thick about him, interfered with his every movement, and forced him more than once to halt in order to strike back. At last they engaged him in a pitched battle which lasted two days. The Swedes fought with a desperate valour; but they were hopelessly outnumbered, and the number of their slain was very great. On the evening of the second day they rested behind their train of baggage waggons, which was drawn up as a defence. All night the gleam of their watch-fires was discernible from the Russian camp. In the morning it was found they had had made their escape, leaving their wounded, their artillery, and their stores behind. Not more than a third of them got away, so as to join their comrades. In the conflict the Tsar distinguished himself by his prowess and vigilance. It was the greatest contest his army had ever waged against regular troops; and he was much elated by the issue.

The Battle of Pultowa.—Charles, meanwhile, was in a sorry plight. He had too small a force to retrieve the fortunes of the war, while yet it was too large for the amount of provisions he could collect. His advisers joined in urging that he should endeavour to get back to Poland; but he would have none of their counsel. He insisted that he meant to conquer the Ukraine as a preliminary to the subjugation of Russia. All through the winter, which was unusually protracted and severe, he abode where he was. When spring came, making movement possible, he marched in a south-easterly direction till he came to the barren territory that borders the region inhabited by the Cossacks of the Don. There his obstinacy gave way; and he was obliged to admit that there remained nothing for it but to retrace the steps that had been taken so wearily, without any intelligible object. At the head of eighteen thousand jaded and dispirited troops he came back to the Ukraine, and sat down before the town of Pultowa, a fortified place on the banks of the Vorskla, from the line of which several mountain passes open on the road to Moscow. The garrison was small, and would speedily have been obliged to yield, but for the alacrity with which Peter advanced to its relief. He came at the head of fifty thousand men. By means of a dexterous feint, which called off the attention of the besiegers, he was enabled to throw into the town a reinforcement of troops, and store of provisions. Having accomplished this, he turned to prepare for the decisive contest that was to ensue.

His superiority in strength did not induce any relaxation of wariness. He knew well that the conditions of the contest were not so unequal as at first sight they appeared. The Swedish troops were veteran soldiers. They had confidence in their leader, who had never been personally discomfited. The magnitude of the danger which now threatened him exerted a special call upon his genius, and ensured that his followers, who were alive to the perils of their situation, would fight with a determination equal to their vigour. Before the battle began, Peter gained a great advantage by choice of ground. He threw his troops across the peninsula formed by the Dnieper and the Vorskla, confining his antagonist to the acute angle of it. He drew up his army in two lines, his cavalry being held in reserve, while his flanks were protected by redoubts carrying artillery. These arrangements he was suffered to carry through without molestation, for Charles was confined to his tent during some days by reason of a wound in the foot received in a skirmish under the walls of the town. As soon as he was allowed outside, he directed that the enemy should be at once assailed. His orders were given from a litter in which he was carried to the field. When it was knocked from under him by a cannon ball, he was hoisted on a platform, which was borne aloft on the pikes of four soldiers. After a time the Russian first line was broken in more than one place, and began to give way; but the second was immediately hurled upon the wearied victors. Its weight drove them back; and as they gave ground the pressure increased, till they were at last penned into the narrow corner formed by the junction of the two streams. Here they were fixed as in a trap. It was impossible to fight longer, and it was almost as impossible to flee. Many who tried to get away were drowned. Those who did escape managed to carry Charles with them. Guided by Mazeppa he made for Oczakoff, on Turkish territory, remaining for years a refugee, though an exceedingly troublesome one.

Peter had behaved with an intrepedity equal to that of his rival. He exposed himself in the most heroic fashion, and had two extraordinary escapes from death. His hat was pierced by one ball, and his saddle was struck by another. When the victory was won he exclaimed, "Now has the son of the morning fallen from heaven, and the foundations of St. Petersburg stand firm." He did not exaggerate the meaning of his triumph. With reason is the contest waged on that 8th of July, 1709, reckoned among "the decisive battles of the world." It abased the power of Sweden, which was then very great, in a manner from which she has never recovered. It brought upon the European stage, almost for the first time, a new rival, whom she had hitherto checked and kept at bay. It led up to the acquisition by Russia of the Baltic provinces she has ever since possessed. Amid the multifarious activities and vicissitudes of his career, this was an object Peter kept steadily in view, and followed up with most persistent resolution. Time after time, now with one ally, now with another, and then alone, at one time by land, at another time by sea (where he served as rear-admiral, being duly promoted to the rank of vice-admiral, after gaining a victory over a Swedish fleet off the island of Elend), he renewed his aggressions, carrying them farther and farther, till at last, by the peace of Nystadt, concluded in 1721, there was ceded to him the whole of Livonia and Esthonia, with great part of Finland. It shows his eagerness to grasp this enlargement of empire that he should have consented, for himself and his successors, to acknowledge the preponderance, throughout Livonia and Esthonia, of the Lutheran religion, of the German law and language, and of the subsisting hereditary constitution. Up till a very recent date this bargain was faithfully observed. The consequences have been very extraordinary. In each province the mass of the population belongs to one race—Lithuanians, Letts, and Fins. In each there is an ascendant minority of a different race, who have given a peculiar colour to the prevailing civilization—Poles, Germans, and Swedes. At the top there is a third power, foreign to all the rest in origin, speech, manners, and ideas. In 1868 an attempt was made to Russianise them, by introducing the Greek religion and making Russ the language of law and administration; but the design has had little success, German influences remaining supreme.

A New War with Turkey.—Immediately after Pultowa, the agents of Charles began to stir up Turkish enmity against Peter. An active and influential party in the Divan at Constantinople remained in favour of fighting him. Chief among them was the Sultan's mother, who perpetually asked her son, "when would he help her lion against the bear?" Sultan Achmet was desirous of maintaining peace; but such was the pressure urged upon him, such were the representations of Russian menace with which he was plied, that the task became one of exceeding difficulty. The Khan of the Crimea was incessant in his complaints of proceedings that threatened his territory. From the other side came allegations that the Slavonic and Græco-Christian inhabitants of Moldavia and Wallachia were being excited against the Porte. A spirit of warlike enthusiasm animated the people and carried away the Grand Vizier. At last, account being taken of Peter's engagement in north-western Europe, it was resolved to assail him.

However indisposed to hostilities, Peter lost no time in taking up the quarrel. He hurried from the scene of his operations against Sweden to Moscow, where he made fresh arrangements for the conduct of the government in his absence. He would have been content to delegate the superintendence of affairs to Catherine, his private marriage with whom, said to have been celebrated four years before, was now first avowed; but she insisted upon going with him, and he would not balk her of her wish. The counter declaration of war to that issued by Turkey was solemnly proclaimed in the principal churches. It described the contest as one in defence of religion. Every effort was made to arouse the feelings of the people upon that score. Red standards were distributed to the army, bearing on one side the motto, " In the name of God, and for the cause of Christianity," while on the other there was displayed a cross, with Constantine's well-known inscription underneath it, "By this we conquer." The enthusiasm excited was widespread and intense. It extended far beyond the bounds of the empire. It was fostered and sustained by a rumour, often revived since, that in the tomb of Constantine there had been discovered a prediction that the Russians would chase the Turks from the city he had founded. In a word, there was brought into play for the first time the subtle influences of religion, lineage, and destiny, which have been appealed to with large effect in the later history of the two countries. On this occasion, however, they were appealed to in vain.

The campaign was, from first to last, the most disastrous Peter ever knew. His plans were formed with all his accustomed comprehension and foresight, they were acted upon with his characteristic energy and decision, and yet they broke down hopelessly at every critical juncture. He started on his southward way at the head of eighty thousand men, but he expected to be joined ere he left his own dominions by forty thousand more, who never appeared. He had intrigued with the Hospodars of both Moldavia and Wallachia, receiving engagements of support from both, while playing off the one against the other; but he was thus made the victim of a double treachery, for the Hospodar of Wallachia, being suspected by the Turks, sold himself to them, and did his best to mislead their antagonist, while the Hospodar of Moldavia, who was equally in the confidence of both, though leaning decidedly to Peter's side, was unable or afraid to do anything upon his behalf. At Jassy, the Moldavian capital, where he expected to find store of provisions, he was met by an apology for their absence, and thus his army was reduced to severe straits. Learning that the Turks had formed great magazines near Galatz, he sent two divisions of his force along the western bank of the Pruth in order to seize them; but they had not proceeded far ere they were arrested by the alarming intelligence that the Turks were advancing up the other side. Before it could be determined what ought to be done the advance-guard ot the two armies confronted each other, with the stream between. Scherematoff, who was one of Peter's most trusted generals, held the command, and he immediately made the best dispositions possible in order to prevent the Turks from crossing. His efforts were wholly vain, for thousands of Crimean horsemen forded the river at divers places, and four bridges were speedily thrown across it. The best he could do was to draw off his troops, falling back upon the main army. Peter could not blame, for he had no choice save to fall back himself in quest of the most defensible position he could find. His selection was made with the clear and sagacious sense which seldom deserted him, even in his most vehement paroxysms of passion. The ground he fixed upon for making a final stand was guarded by the river on his left, and by an extensive marsh on his right, so that he calculated on the enemy being compelled to

I

deliver his attack right in front. It was a reasonable conjecture, yet it proved wholly erroneous.

The Battle of the Pruth.—The Turkish army was three or four times larger than what the Russian force had now become. The Turkish leaders had learned much of the disappointments the Tsar had met with, and the straits to which his men were reduced It was resolved to turn this knowledge to account by starving them into a surrender. For days on end the Tsar was left to use pick and spade in laboriously throwing up earthworks to guard his front, while all the time he was being subjected to effectual environment. The eastern side of the river, which protected his left flank, was planted with batteries of artillery, and watched by numerous patrols. The heights to the west of the marsh, which protected his right, were occupied in force. Round to his rear there was a still larger detachment sent—one that outnumbered his whole army. Thus cooped up, it soon began to suffer dire distress. The pangs of thirst were more severe than those of hunger, for rations of food were dealt out in small quantity, but water was unobtainable. What was drawn from the marsh could not be drank, while to approach the river was almost certain death. In these circumstances, Peter had no option but to try whether he could not break through the circle which girdled him. On two successive days he made the attempt It was made with a strength that had all the fury of despair. Nevertheless, it failed; and on the evening of the second day he gave orders that the camp baggage should be destroyed, preparatory to a final effort at getting away. He then retired to his tent, and wrote this letter to the Russian senate, entrusting it to a messenger who, in the confusion that ensued, got through the Turkish lines :—" I announce to you that, deceived by false intelligence, and without blame on my part, I find myself here shut up in my camp by an army four times larger than mine. Our supplies are cut off, and we momentarily expect to be taken prisoners, unless Heaven come to our relief in some unexpected manner.

Should it happen to me to be taken captive by the Turks you will no more consider me as your Tsar and Sovereign, nor will you pay any attention to any order that may be brought you as from me, even should you recognise my handwriting, but you will wait for my coming in person. If I am to perish here, and you receive well-authenticated intelligence of my death, you will then proceed to choose as my successor him who is most worthy among you."

Nothing could more strikingly illustrate either the magnanimity and patriotic feeling of the man or the gloomy forebodings by which he was oppressed. The alternative which stared him in the face was that of annihilation or surrender. The conception that his antagonist would be such a fool as to accept any compromise never entered his clear and decided mind. Most fortunately for him his peremptory sense was reinforced, or rather was superseded, by a wisdom which he must have deemed irrational. Catherine wrung from him a reluctant consent to try an expedient which had occurred to her. Having obtained permission, she dictated to the chancellor a letter suing for terms of peace, and entrusted it to General Scherematoff for delivery. At the same time, she gave him all the jewels and money she could gather, to be distributed as he chose, in order to further an accommodation. Scherematoff fulfilled his mission with great tact. He was lucky in the persons with whom he had to deal. The steward of the Grand Vizier was greedy and influential. The Grand Vizier himself was greedy and timid. Applying first to the steward, Scherematoff got him to smooth a way to his master, who was induced to grant an interview. A favourable reception being obtained, Baltadji allowed himself to be persuaded that he could win without bloodshed all that the most complete victory would secure. The conditions imposed were very hard, and the language used to express them was galling from its haughtiness; but anything was preferable to the destruction that must otherwise have befallen. Accepting "the royal and infinite goodness of the thrice powerful and gracious Padishah," Peter gladly agreed, provided he was allowed to withdraw with his army, arms, colours, and baggage, to surrender Azoff with its artillery and stores, to give up interference in Poland and the Crimea, paying the Tartars an indemnity for what they had endured, to allow Turkish goods free entrance into Russia, to liberate all Turkish prisoners, and to provide King Charles with a safe-conduct. That night the Russians got supplies of food. Next day they were on the road home, starting sixteen thousand men fewer than when they came to Jassy. Thankful as he was for his escape, reflection did not tend to reconcile Peter to the terms on which it was bought. He circulated a garbled version of them throughout Europe. He strove to evade their fulfilment. More than once his excuses and delays made a fresh rupture imminent. Mainly through the mediation of Sir Robert Sutton, the British ambassador, this was obviated, and a settlement was drawn which subsisted for a quarter of a century.

This was the last of Peter's great European wars, though for years on end he maintained with growing success his steady pressure on Sweden and Poland. That employment, however, was not enough to engross his energetic nature. He gave heed as well to the eastern side of his dominions. His anxiety for commerce made him look back with envy to the old days when the trade of India and the farthest East made its way through Central Asia, and when that of Central Asia itself was better worth having. To restore that trade to its ancient channels became one of his great objects. Security he knew was indispensable to restoration, and for the enforcement of security he knew but one method. It was his idea that every state and realm, from the Dardanelles to the Indus, from the Volga to the wall of China, from the Euphrates to the North Sea, should pass under his paternal and ameliorative sway.

Movements in Asia.—In 1717 he despatched an expedition against Khiva—a hundred years before diplomatic communications had been opened with that distant khanate. More than once bands of marauding Cossacks had penetrated to it in quest of plunder. These incursions all ended disastrously. Either the invaders were cut off on their encumbered retreat by the Khivese, or the rigours of winter fell upon them with a severity more fatal than the arms of the inhabitants. Peter made vast preparations for avoiding a recurrence of failure. Detachments were posted at all suitable places between Astracan and the operating army. It consisted of 3500 men, with six guns, and a train which comprised 200 camels and 300 horses, under the command of Prince Bekovitch-Cherkasky. He was still a hundred miles from the Khivan capital when he had to give battle to the army of defence. The fight lasted three days, and ended in a Russian triumph. The Khan, owning himself beaten, entered into negotiations and readily assented to the terms the victor dictated. He was invited to the capital, though with the suggestion that he should bring on his army by detachments. The proposal was accepted without any suspicion of ulterior designs. But no sooner was the force split up into fractions than the Khivese, in reinforced numbers, fell upon them separately, and put every man to the sword. The corpse of Prince Bekovitch they flayed, stuffing the skin with hay, and then sending it as a present to the Emir of Bokhara.

Strangely enough, however deeply Peter resented this treacherous check, he took no immediate steps for punishing it. Instead, he contented himself with setting to work nearer home on behalf of the project he had in view. He had formerly made acquaintance with the Caspian Sea, and entertained the notion of linking it with the Euxine by running a canal betwixt the Volga and the Don. He now resumed this idea on a more extended scale, labouring at it for several years. In 1720 he became aware of a design promoted by Austria for disturbing his friendly relations with the Porte. It happened at the same time that Persia had been pitifully misgoverned for years, the Shah being a weak man, at variance with a powerful rebel named Mahmoud, who was sustained by Affghan support. Peter circumvented Austria by calling Turkish attention to these circumstances, and proposing an alliance for composing the distractions of Persia in a manner advantageous to the allies. The league was formed in 1720, and eighteen months later Peter, accompanied by his wife, led an expedition into Persian territory. A force of 45,000 men, of whom 9000 were cavalry and 3000 sailors, were conducted through the defiles of the Caucasus, suffering great hardships on the march. They came out at Derbent, which the governor was keeping against Mahmoud. It was immediately surrendered to Peter, t e terror of whose name had spread far in advance. He abstained, however, from following up his victory with his accustomed resolution. He saw that the country would yield little, and would be difficult to keep, unless it should be found accessible by some other route. He was satisfied, therefore, in the meantime to annex the Persian provinces bordering on the Caspian, stipulating also that the Porte should receive a large accession of territory—a gift which soon drew upon Turkey the vengeance of the famous Nadir Shah.

Second Visit to the West.—Some years before this Peter revisited several western countries. He went first to Denmark, then to Holland, and next to France, returning from Paris to Amsterdam and Copenhagen. His object now was mainly to study political systems rather than useful arts. In the French capital, though he more than once gave way to outbursts of passion, he displayed a politeness which astonished those who came in contact with him. At the tomb of Richelieu he uttered (or is said to have uttered) the exclamation—"Great man! I would have given half my empire to learn of thee how to govern the remainder." He charmed Madame de Maintenon, the widow of Scarron, the farce-writer, and of Louis XIV.; though it may be doubted whether he thought her a woman to vie with his own Catherine. She joined him at Amsterdam, whither she came after having given birth to a son, who only lived a few hours. There he was hugely delighted to find that his former visit was well remembered, and that the cottage where he had lived was preserved under the name of "The Prince's House." All through his journey he was in high spirits. At Nymogen he arrived one night with only one attendant. He made his supper upon a poached egg, with some bread and cheese added. In the morning he was presented with a bill for a hundred ducats. "Eggs must be scarce hereabouts," remarked he. "No, sire," quoth the landlord, with a ready wit which mollified the man he was thus cheating, "but emperors are." Nothing could mollify him, however, in respect of a grievous trouble that came to him at Copenhagen, giving rise to one of the most obscure and repulsive incidents of his life.

Sad Fate of his Eldest Son.—He had a son by his first wife, Eudoxia Lapuchin. This lad of course was his heir. The education of the boy had been conducted in a singularly irregular fashion. He had been indulged, at times, to an extent that really became an education in vice. At other times he had been restrained with a severity that provoked a rebellion against what would have been for his good. He grew up a callous, selfish, brutal being. It is the curse of most monarchs that the heir-apparent is drawn to the headship of an opposite party from that which is in favour at the court. At St. Petersburg there was little room for such opposition, but Prince Alexis openly did his best to provide standing-ground and incitement for such a party. He had been married to an amiable young woman, who died of heart-break from his cruelty. He had been threatened with deprivation of rank and prospect, but was forgiven on the promise of better behaviour. The report now came that in his father's absence he was vapouring about what he would do in the event of his father's death. The system Peter had established was to be overthrown. The favourites he had honoured were to be dismissed. The new-fangled practices he had instituted were to be done away, and the ancient habits of Muscovy were to be re-introduced. When Peter heard this he summoned the youth to attend him at Copenhagen. Instead of obeying, Alexis went off on a continental tour. He visited Austria, the Tyrol, and Italy, waiting till the storm should blow over. When he came back, it was much too soon, for he had to encounter no mere gust of passing wrath, but a white heat of indignation. He was arrested. He was made to sign a paper declaring that his scandalous conduct rendered him unfit for the succession to the throne. A confession of conspiracy was extorted from him. Even after this he was impeached before the senate of high treason, when his father appeared as the chief witness against him. Of course he was condemned, and was adjudged worthy of death, though a recommendation to mercy was added. He died in prison next day after an interview with his father. Russian historians say the death was caused by weakness, fatigue, and remorse; other chroniclers hint at poison having been administered.

Character of Peter.—Seven years later, soon after his return from his Persian campaign, the Tsar himself died in the great capital he had reared. He was then only fifty-three; but into the years of his active life there had been crowded ten times the amount of work and of dissipation that would have killed any ordinary person. He stands out one of the most prominent yet nondescript figures in all history, whether taken as man or as ruler. As a man his bad qualities were numerous and strong. He was sensual, fierce, untruthful, even to his innermost nature. Yet he was capable of what seemed pure affection, of fast friendship, of downright candour, of the most magnanimous generosity. He was always stubbornly self-willed; but it was often an even chance which way his inclinations would fall. He was sometimes cruel with the insensibility to suffering of one who is strong for endurance; but at many great crises in his career he showed himself placable and easy to be entreated, chiefly because he was so self-reliant as to scorn the feebleness of revenge upon those who were powerless. A habitual drunkard, he was capable of abstemiousness for long periods; yet, while his intoxication often served to give a new force and cunning to his moral obliquities, his friends were most afraid of him when he was most himself. As a ruler few men have exerted an influence so wide, so varied, so thorough, or so enduring. He created a new Russia. In domestic affairs the change effected was peremptory, radical, and extended. It swept away the constitutional guarantees to which the Romanoffs were pledged, in order to set up an absolutism of the most imperious cast. It touched not only the framework of administration, but penetrated to the inner spirit of society, elevating its character in many respects, yet producing a strange compound between the fantastic splendours of Tartar domination and the modes of western life. In foreign affairs the change was even more notable; for to Peter there may be traced the groundwork of that policy of intrigue, encroachment, and incorporation, which has been pursued with such an unswerving steadiness of decision, and such an astonishing continuity of success, as to have trebled since his time the extent of Russian territory, and enabled Russia to profit by every considerable event, either in Europe or in Asia.

CHAPTER VII.

THE PERIOD OF FEMALE SOVEREIGNTY.

From the death of Peter till the accession of Paul I., a period of seventy years, the sovereignty of Russia was in the hands of women. It is true that this course of female sway was thrice broken, but the interruptions were brief, lasting only a few months at the longest, and were little more than nominal, for two of the intervening monarchs were children, and the other was an imbecile.

Catherine I.—Peter's heir was his grandson, the child of the unfortunate Alexis. The lad's rights were superseded in favour of Catherine, his grandfather's widow. A strong body of partisans, headed by Menschikoff, took prompt action on her behalf. Despite considerable opposition, she was proclaimed on the day that Peter died. Her title was vindicated on the score that she had been crowned thirteen years previously, when the late Tsar himself set the diadem upon her brow; and that though he had left no specific will directing that she should succeed him, he had often expressed a desire that such an arrangement should take place. Catherine, while firmly asserting her claim, judiciously propitiated her opponents by declaring that she would hold the crown as a sacred deposit for the young Grand Duke. Her elevation was popular, for it was well known with what heroism she had sustained her husband in many of his most arduous enterprises, and with what perseverance and effect she had tempered to clemency his savage disposition. Nevertheless there were murmurs of discontent among the old nobility, who were scandalised that, as they phrased it, "a pastry-cook should make a waiting-maid Empress of all the Russias;" and, unfortunately, her conduct gave some justification to their dislike.

She began well. The capitation tax was reduced. Many exiles were recalled from Siberia. The brave Cossacks, who thought it shame to serve a woman, had their loyalty ensured by a restoration of privileges which had been harshly withdrawn. In fulfilment of a design Peter had long entertained, she established the Academy of Sciences at St. Petersburg, on the plan of Leibnitz. A wise discretion governed all her early activity at home. At the same time the bounds of the empire were extended eastward by the voluntary submission of a Georgian prince, who brought with him a province of that fertile land. A commercial treaty was concluded with China, which contained a stipulation that a Russian hotel, two churches, to be served by an archimandrite and four ecclesiastics, and a seminary for the education of Russian young men, who might afterwards act as interpreters on the frontier, should be established at Pekin. In Europe she entered into an alliance with Charles VI. of Germany, by which it was mutually agreed that, in case of necessity, each should assist the other with a force of 30,000 men. Her only failure was in the case of Denmark, whom she was anxious to dispossess of the duchy of Holstein. The Duke was married shortly after Peter's death to her daughter, the Princess Anne, and about the same time Denmark appropriated his dominion. Catherine was eager to avenge this insult and wrong, but her senate, looking on it as a personal affair, contrived to thwart her, and refused to fire a shot.

Her great mistake was the unlimited confidence she reposed in Menschikoff. She trusted him in everything. She loaded him with honours. His arrogance, no longer held in check either by the kindly satire or the stern reproofs of Peter, became intolerable. He domineered over everybody in a style that excited the keenest repugnance, while the pomps and splendours in which he delighted were provocative of envy in some minds, and of contempt in others. The hatred of which he was the object soon bore fruit. It began to be whispered that he was as absolute with the Empress as with others. The tale of their early connection was raked up, and hints of its renewal were circulated. These calumnies seem to have shaken the mind of Catherine. She was suffering from cancer and dropsy. She gave way to the habit of intemperance she had learned from her husband, affecting particularly the wine of Tokay. That her irregularities hastened her end is certain. She expired in May, 1727, having reigned little more than two years.

Peter II.—From the time of his father's trial and death she had shown herself very fond of the young Grand Duke. She had placed him under the care of a Lutheran pastor's son, Count Ostermann, who rose to be chancellor of the empire. The scheme of education Ostermann drafted was singularly enlightened and complete. By her last testament Catherine directed that the boy, who was then twelve years of age, should continue to be instructed according to it till he was sixteen. Her two daughters, Anne and Elizabeth, with the Duke of Holstein, Anne's husband, were appointed his domestic guardians. Menschikoff was named as Regent. In that capacity he soon showed himself more insolently overbearing than ever. He so flouted the Holsteins that they were glad to leave the kingdom. He then took the young Tsar home to his own palace. Soon after he had him affianced to his daughter, while for his son he planned a marriage with another member of the imperial family. During a few brief months his haughty career was one of unchecked prosperity; but the opposition he had raised during the late reign soon grew more intense and vindictive. The powerful family of the Dolgoroukis took the lead in the cabal formed against him. A scion of that house was foisted upon the Tsar as a companion. In a short time the mind of the royal pupil was alienated from his imperious master. The lad learned to chafe at the degrading restrictions imposed upon him. He resiled from the marriage into the promise of which he now conceived himself to have been trepanned; and having gone out to hunt one day, he not only refused to return, but signed an order for the Regent's banishment. It was executed forthwith. Menschikoff had no idea of the peril by which he was menaced. He had for some time busied himself with plans for becoming Duke of Courland. From this prospective elevation, which overtopped the marvellous height at which he had long stood, he was in a moment hurled to a depth of misery more abject than that from which he sprung. He was stripped of his honours and of his wealth, which is said to have amounted to well-nigh three millions of roubles, or a million sterling; he was exiled to the frontiers of Siberia, where he and his children had to toil hard to keep body and soul together; and he died wretchedly in 1729.

After his departure the Dolgoroukis had things their own way. They grievously abused their trust. The boy Tsar was encouraged in a course of conduct which disinclined and unfitted him for any care about public business. His tutors took that into their own hands, managing it in a fashion as despotic and offensive as Menschikoff had done. Hating St. Petersburg, they shifted the capital back to Moscow. The monarch was never seen there. His absorbing passion was the chase, which he pursued with an avidity injurious to his health, for he was a weakly lad. In the winter of 1729 he was attacked by small-pox, and in January, 1730, he died. With him the direct male line of the Romanoffs became extinct.

The Succession of Anne.—The will of Catherine was at first appealed to as a guide in regard to the succession. By it her daughters were nominated as next in order to Peter II. The eldest, Anne of Holstein, was now dead, and though she had left a son, the senate objected to him both as a foreigner and as a minor. The second, Elizabeth, was offered the crown, but she was then greatly dejected by the recent death of her intended husband, and she resolutely refused it. In the end the honour fell to Anne, Duchess of Courland, the daughter of Ivan, the imbecile half-brother of Peter the Great. Though young, she had been long a widow. Her chances of the throne were so slender that, in making a proffer of it, the senate deemed it a favourable opportunity for enforcing conditions. The proposals submitted were: that she should renounce the right to make peace or war, to impose new taxes, to alienate crown lands, to marry or nominate an heir, without the consent of the senate and council. An additional stipulation was, that a low-born favourite, one Biren, should not accompany her to Russia. When the senate's deputation, headed by Prince Dolgorouki, waited upon her at Mittau, they were astonished to find a mean-looking and shabbily-dressed fellow waiting with her to receive them. The Prince signed to him to leave, and when he refused to stir, forced him out. The man was Biren. The insult he had received rankled in his mind, and bitterly did he avenge it.

Anne demurred to the terms suggested, but finding the deputation inflexible, she subscribed the pledge they sought, cherishing, there can be no doubt, the purpose of throwing it off as soon as she dared. The time came speedily. She was crowned in the spring of 1730. Ere summer was half through Biren was installed in the palace Menschikoff had occupied. He soon collected a party who complained of the favouritism exerted by the Dolgoroukis, and Anne was approached with a representation that her people would rather obey one than eight masters. "What!" she exclaimed, "is not the deed I signed at Mittau in accordance with the desires of the nation?" Producing her copy, she read the articles one by one. At each there came from the throng a shout that it was contrary to their wishes. Thereupon she tore the document in shreds, declaring that she would reign with the same power as her predecessors. The applause evoked by this well acted scene was re-echoed outside, and an oath of fealty to her as an unlimited sovereign was obtained before the gathering dispersed. Swiftly thereafter befell the fate of those who were obnoxious to her and to her minion. Four of the family who had been for some time all-powerful in the State were hurried off to Siberia, while other four—father and uncle, son and nephew—were cast into prison, where they languished for years, ignorant of each other's doom or existence, till they were brought forth to meet at the rack and the scaffold.

The New Reign.—Anne reigned for ten years. Apart from her infatuation for Biren (as he called himself —originally a groom, he took a French title of nobility), she was a person of superior capacity. She had just instincts; she had a clear discernment; she had a firm mind. Wherever her evil genius did not interfere, she did most things well. During her residence in Courland she had acquired tastes and accomplishments which were strange at St. Petersburg. The alteration in the manners of society carried through at the instance of Peter the Great fell far short of what she desired. An imperial ukase, published soon after she came to the throne, ordered that all young gentlemen should learn to read, to write, and to dance. She encouraged a ruinous degree of extravagance A courtier who did not spend two or three thousand roubles a year upon dress made no figure. Sometimes there arose the most odd and offensive blending of pomp and refinement with barbarism and nastiness. The style of life might be gorgeous, but it was incredibly foul. A typical instance is given by Macaulay. In describing the appearance of the Russian ambassador to Britain and his suite at a State ball, he tells that they came dropping pearls and—vermin!

In various respects, however, substantial improvements were made. The new capital was greatly embellished. The canal from Lake Ladoga was completed. Silk and woollen manufactures were instituted and brought to considerable perfection. The mines of the Ural mountains were explored. A voyage of discovery was made to Kamschatka, in order to determine whether Siberia was connected with North America. The territory upon the frontiers of China inhabited by the Kirghises was annexed. With China on the one hand, and with Britain on the other, fresh commercial treaties were concluded, both being very advantageous to Russia. The merit of these things mainly belongs to Count Ostermann, who had now become prime minister.

Marshal Munich, a German, who made his first appearance in the field under the renowned Marlborough, and who had greatly distinguished himself at Malplaquet, was at the head of the army. Through his intervention Augustus III. was established upon the throne of Poland, and the dependence of that country upon Russia was greatly enhanced. Attention was then turned to the affairs of Turkey. For years a desire to wipe away the humiliation endured at the Pruth, and to recover what was then lost, had occupied the national mind. From the memoirs of General Manstein it appears that in 1725 a descent upon the coasts of the Black Sea was planned, though the death of Peter caused a postponement of the enterprise. In 1730 General Keith was sent to inspect the stores that had been collected, and conduct such reorganization as was requisite, when the Polish troubles again caused delay. In 1735 the resolution was definitely taken that Turkey should be attacked, the aim being to reconquer Azoff, annex the Crimea, and make Russia mistress of the Black Sea.

Invasion of the Crimea.—The predatory habits of the Crimean Tartars afforded a pretext for interference, and in 1736 the Crimea was invaded. The Tartars withdrew, drawing on their antagonists, but clearing the country in advance. Terrible sufferings ensued. The invaders lost ten thousand men and gained nothing. Next year, however, the enterprise was renewed, and the war was widened. Munich revisited the Crimea, marching through it in its length and breadth, devastating and pillaging wherever he went, though its occupation he found an impossible achievement. At the same time Lascy, an Irishman in the Russian service, captured Azoff; Leontieff, another foreigner, took Kilburn; and eastward of Yenikale the Kuban Tartars were induced to throw off their allegiance to the Turk. It was not till Azoff had been assailed that the Turkish Divan were roused to consider the war as serious. Their preparations for resistance were very formidable. At the outset, however, they made an effort to avert hostilities by soliciting the mediation in turn of France, Sweden, and Austria. Russia rejected the intervention of the two first-named powers; and while she pretended to accept that of Austria, it was with the secret understanding, which it was sought to justify under the treaty made with Catherine, that Turkey was merely to be amused till it should suit the sham mediator to strike in as an active belligerent. The Austrian motive for this scandalous treachery was a desire to obtain, at the expense of Turkey, some equivalent for the losses Charles had sustained in his last Bourbon war. The unprincipled greed thus shown was signally disappointed. In two successive campaigns the Austrian troops were beaten far back upon their own territory; and in the autumn of 1739 their main army capitulated in a fashion more humiliating than anything known at that time in the history of modern Europe. In the peace that followed, the condition of things established in the last Austro-Turkish war was reversed. All that Prince Eugene gained in 1716-17 was given back; Belgrade became a Turkish town; and the Danube, the Saar, and the Unna were made the boundary of the two empires.

Russia was not much more fortunate. In the campaign of 1738 Munich had sulked and done little, being unable to agree with his Austrian allies. Nevertheless a proposal to make peace then he vehemently opposed. He went to St. Petersburg, where he busied himself as an apostle of what has become the traditional creed of Russia. He counselled the seizure of Constantinople. He pointed out the weakness of Turkey consequent upon the predominance of a ruling caste over outnumbering millions of a different faith. He showed how easy it would be to stimulate the discontent of the rayahs. In short, he inculcated doctrines which have been steadily kept in view for a century and a half after his time. His energy was conspicuous in the campaign of 1739. At Stavatchav and at Khoorim he gained brilliant victories. He then crossed the Pruth, took possession of Jassy, proclaimed Prince Cantemir the Hospodar of Moldavia, and, wheeling round into Bessarabia, was about to strike at Bender, when news of the Austrian pacification arrested him, and he was himself recalled. Much to his chagrin a Russian peace was soon afterwards concluded. It stipulated that Azoff should not be occupied by either of the belligerents, that the conquests made by Munich should be restored, and that no Russian fleet should enter the Euxine, Russian commerce finding transport in Turkish ships. Thus all that Russia had gained by a war which cost her 100,000 men and an enormous sum of money, was the devastation of the Crimea. Even that devastation, ruthless as it had been, did not repress the Tartars, nor keep them from harassing the Russian frontier and insulting the Russian power.

The Biren Regency.—A chief reason for the recall of Munich was the illness of Anne. There was a prospect of quarrels over the succession, and it was deemed desirable to have on the spot the general who had most influence with the troops. In the latter days of the Empress the supremacy of Biren became more assured than ever. His cruelties and excesses were so appalling that even his royal mistress went on her knees entreating him to forbear, and supplicated in vain. In 1737 he was elected, through Russian dictation, Duke of Courland. About the same time he made love to the Princess Elizabeth, the daughter of Peter by Catherine, with the intention of asserting her claim to the throne when it became vacant, and so of obtaining it for himself. His suit was disagreeable to the lady, and the course of events altered his plans. In 1739 a niece of the Tsarina was married to Ulric, Duke of Brunswick. Next year a son was born of the marriage. Anne at once adopted the infant, and named him her heir, choosing Biren at the same time as administrator of the government till the boy should attain his seventeenth year. Two months later she died. The Regent had thus before him a long stretch of uncontrolled authority. The arrogance of his nature rose to a greater pitch than ever. The grinding character of the domination he exerted had never been exceeded even in Russia. No rank nor station afforded any security against his imperious mandates. The parents of the young Prince were threatened with expulsion to Germany, should they interfere with him in any way, and were put under virtual arrest in the winter palace. He had the temerity to insult Marshal Munich, when he thought he could dispense with his services. The marshal thereupon turned against him, forced a way to the Duke and Duchess of Brunswick, induced them to sign an order for his arrest, and had him seized in his bed at two o'clock next morning. The same day he was arraigned before a commission of senators and military men, who had no difficulty in determining that he was guilty of crimes which, " by the laws of God, of nature, and of the empire, merited death." The sentence was commuted, however, into exile to Siberia, whither he was at once despatched, his regency having lasted only twenty-two days.

The Brunswick Regency.—The Princess of Brunswick was now proclaimed as Regent, and guardian of her son. Her rule was at once accepted. It did not last fourteen months. Of a mild disposition, and incorrigibly indolent, there was the utmost difficulty in getting her to pay any heed to state affairs. With a maid of honour, whom she made a confidant, and other female friends, she would seclude herself for weeks together. Thus she became estranged from her husband, and from her ministers— Munich taking part with the Duke, though Ostermann rather sided with her. In this manner the way was prepared for another palace revolution. The Princess Elizabeth had overcome her repugnance to the crown; ambition stirred within her; she shared the aversion entertained by the old nobility to having foreigners at the head of affairs; and her physician, Lestocq, a born intriguer, got up a conspiracy in her favour, which was easily successful. Lestocq was a native of Hanover. He had learnt surgery in Paris, where he so interfered in politics that he became for a time an inmate of the Bastile. On his release he made his way to St. Petersburg. He had not been long there ere he was deported to Siberia. He was speedily recalled, however, was attached to the household of the Princess, and at once became the centre of a camarilla by whom she was surrounded. It was with difficulty he could get her to move, even after he had bribed many of the guards to espouse her cause, and the whole scheme was divulged before it could be put in operation. The Princess Anne sent for her, upbraided her with ingratitude, and accused her directly of having conspired against the young Emperor. With much seeming ingenuousness and many tears she denied the charge, was believed, embraced, and sent home. She was now resolved to abandon the undertaking; but Lestocq felt that he was compromised, and induced her to change her mind by the exhibition of a card showing her on one side with crown and sceptre, on the other as a nun in a convent cell. On the night of her interview with the Regent, that lady, her son, and her husband were seized as Biren had been, and the revolution was accomplished without a drop of blood being shed.

The Reign of Elizabeth.—Elizabeth reigned without molestation for twenty years. She was a strong-minded woman, with much of her father's temper. She was profligate—for she kept a succession of favourites; she was cruel and whimsical—the combination sometimes giving to her conduct a horrible grotesqueness; she was grossly untruthful—never hesitating over a lie where it would serve her purpose; yet she was far-sighted, prudent, prompt, and firm. Till the day she was brought before the public to be proclaimed as Empress, she had lived in seclusion; but at once she displayed a masculine vigour, haranguing the troops, issuing eloquent manifestoes, exhibiting a sleepless vigilance, an amazing courage, and a high degree of political sense. She told her people that the late Regent, her son, and her husband had been sent back to their own country, with the honours that befitted their rank. The facts are that they were kept in confinement as long as they lived, the Princess Anne dying in 1746; the poor little Tsar two years later, when he was aged eight, being moved to Schlusselburgh, where he was murdered in 1764; while his father lived on till 1780, long after Elizabeth herself.

Her Cruelties.—All the men who had held power before her accession were seized, thrown into prison, and condemned to die—the eminent colleagues and rivals, Munich and Ostermann among them. They were brought out to the scaffold together, where a list of their crimes was read over to them, followed by an intimation of their sentences. Munich was to be quartered; Ostermann was to be broken on the wheel. Proceedings commenced with Ostermann. He was undressed and led forward, when at the last moment, intimation was made that his doom had been commuted into one of perpetual banishment. "Pray," quoth he, unconcernedly, "give me back my wig and cap." So saying he buttoned up, smoothed his beard, and resigned himself to life. Munich, neatly shaved, and trimly dressed, as if for a review, heard of his reprieve without deigning to utter a syllable. He was trudged off to Siberia, where he was allowed twelve copecks a day for his maintenance. This sum he eked out by selling milk and opening a school, whence he sent up many expert mathematicians. Six years later he found a companion in Lestocq, who had set the crown upon Elizabeth's head. He had an overweening sense of the value that belonged to his services; he waxed arrogant and dictatorial; and he quarrelled desperately with the chancellor, Bestuchoff, who had ingratiated himself most thoroughly in the good graces of his royal mistress. She gave her old friend up to the resentment of her new minion, by whom he and his wife were exiled—much to the satisfaction of the latter, who, when she found things going against her, fervently entreated the judges to "spare her skin," that is, to absolve her from the torture of the knout. In this she was more fortunate than others. Elizabeth conceived herself the handsomest woman in her dominions, and regarded with a vixenish jealousy all who had any pretensions to vie with her. Among them was one of the Lapuchin family. She was accused of a treasonable correspondence with the Prussian ambassador, and was knouted, before being exiled. From behind a curtain the Empress witnessed unmoved the horrible flagellation, by which the flesh on the back of her fair rival was cut into strips, and parted from her bones. Besides the knout, which was plied with a tremendous vigour, other forms of torture were much in use. Yet the Empress had a great dislike of taking life. In the course of her reign capital punishment was abrogated, and she had medals struck in honour of herself, with the motto "Elizabeth the Clement!" Verily her tender mercies were cruel. She set up a species of Inquisition, called the Secret Court of Chancery, where the vilest cruelties were practised on suspected delinquents in order to extort confessions of guilt. This tribunal had the lives and fortunes of every one in the land at its mercy. Accusations were invited by granting to the accuser a share in the estate of a condemned person. Bestuchoff presided over the court for years, till at last he fell under the displeasure of his royal mistress, was transformed from judge to victim, and was deported to Siberia whither he had sent off many crushed and broken-hearted people.

Character of Her Rule.—The despotism Elizabeth exerted was most minute and inexorable. No one dared pass her palace without taking off his hat, upon pain of being imprisoned. To write her name in small letters was an offence of a heinous kind. She insisted upon the clergy fasting most rigorously upon all appointed days, to eat flesh on such an occasion being accounted a far worse sin than any breach of the decalogue. Drunkenness she abominated and sternly repressed. Her own life was exceedingly impure; but she was inflexibly severe towards those who erred in the like fashion. In her later days she was haunted by a dread of assassination, and durst never sleep except in daylight, and under the protection of a strong guard. Yet she was in many respects a great ruler. Without any very costly effort, she managed to uphold the dignity and to advance the interests of the empire. The population was largely augmented in her reign. She patronised literature. She founded and endowed several scientific institutions. An excellent musician, she strove to make music a part of common education. The war with Sweden, which was in progress when she ascended the throne, was brought to a brilliant close by Lascy in 1743, when the peace of Abo was concluded, under which Russia obtained another large slice of territory, her boundary being advanced to the Kymene river, and Sweden being reduced almost to the condition of a Russian province. In the war of "the Austrian succession," impelled alike by sympathy with Maria Theresa, and deep dislike of Frederick, she took part against Prussia. Under successive commanders, Apraxin, Fermer, and Soltikoff, the Russian troops gained divers notable successes. They were not followed up as they ought to have been; yet they provoked from Frederick a hearty acknowledgment of the bravery displayed. "These fellows," said he, of the Russian troops, "may be killed, but they cannot be conquered." The long-drawn contest was still raging when Elizabeth died in 1762, and her successor at once adopted a complete change of policy.

Peter III.—This successor was Charles Peter Ulric, Duke of Holstein-Gottorp, the son of her eldest sister, who, by their mother's will, had a right to the crown before herself. She had three children by a clandestine marriage with a Cossack to whom she took a fancy from his musical performances in the chapel of the palace; but she would never hear of any proposal to promote them instead of her nephew. He was invited to St. Petersburg at the age of fourteen, was received with great distinction, nay, persuaded to embrace the Greek religion, was rebaptized by the name of Peter, and was thereupon proclaimed as Grand Duke and heir of the empire. From the first he was a cause of surprise and scandal to the people he came to govern. In personal appearance he was mean and ill-favoured. His mental capacity was small, and it was oddly warped. The education he received was in no respect of a sort to amend either his intellectual or his moral defects. Though fractious and self-willed to an extraordinary degree, he was capable of generous conduct when the suggestion was spontaneous, but he disdained advice, and was apt to become vehemently resolute in contradiction. He cherished great objects, but he looked at them with childish views, and pursued them by ridiculous means. Even in early youth he showed himself ambitious without wisdom, rash without courage, obstinate without firmness, and social without sympathy, while he grew up depraved and immoral without shame. Uniting the blood of the great rivals Charles XII. and Peter I., he had to choose between the thrones of Russia and Sweden. He transferred the monarchy of Sweden to his uncle; yet he was prouder far of his little German duchy than of the great empire to which he was invited. As all his early recollections were German, so all his likings continued to be. He made Frederick of Prussia his idol, speaking of him as "the king my master," and even while his adopted country was at war, boasting of how differently he would act when he got the power. At his palace of Oranienbaum he was surrounded with his Holstein guards, whom he drilled and dressed in Prussian fashion, appearing himself in a Prussian uniform. Such perverse eccentricities were not his worst faults. He learned to drink hard; he had a decided talent for mimicry, which he cultivated by association with buffoons and flatterers; an indescribable coarseness came to characterise his amusements; and while yet a young man he had become as sensual, as profligate in every mode of his profligacy, as his grandfather had been. His aunt was not easily scandalised, but even she began to see that his excesses must be checked.

His Wife.—With the view of reforming him, she chose a consort on his behalf: she selected Sophia-Augusta,

Princess of Anhalt-Zerbert, who was wedded to him in her seventeenth year, having been previously received into the Greek Church, and rebaptized by the names of Catherine Alexeyna. In the marriage contract it was stipulated that, should the Grand Duke die without children, she should succeed to the throne. It is said her mother had long intended her for this destiny, and trained her in the hope of attaining it. Certainly ambition had more to do with the match than love, for on being first presented to Peter, who was then recovering from small-pox, his extreme ugliness so impressed her that she fainted. It was an ill-assorted union in every respect. Catherine was one of the most beautiful women of her time—noble in figure, graceful in deportment, with features which made her profile a copy of Minerva, fascinating hazel eyes, and a profusion of extremely fine chestnut-coloured hair. She was highly accomplished, had a keen intelligence, and soon developed a dauntless spirit as well as an ardent desire for power and fame. For a brief while she exerted a complete ascendancy over her husband, and it seemed as if the purpose of her advent was to be completely realised. Soon, however, the boorishness of his nature broke out, causing quarrels, in which the semblance of cordial affection was exchanged for resentment and fear on the one side, for contempt and hate on the other. Peter returned to his low society and his dissolute life, and Catherine, after a time, revenged herself for his infidelity by entering upon that astounding career of vice which earned for her the name of the modern Messalina. Her first favourite was Count Soltikoff, who, upon their intimacy being discovered, was despatched to Sweden on a special mission to announce the birth of an heir to the throne, Paul Petrovitch, born eight years after her marriage. Her next was an accomplished and well-born Pole, Stanislaus Poniatowski, who came to St. Petersburg as an *attaché* to the British embassy. When he was sent back to Warsaw she asked permission to go home to Germany, but the Empress refused it, from an apprehension that the interests of her infant Paul, of whom Elizabeth had become very fond, would suffer. Catherine, therefore, gave herself up to seclusion, and to a fresh lover—Gregory Orloff, whose four brothers were soldiers in the Guards. At this time it was deemed not improbable that Elizabeth, who was slowly dying, would cancel the will by which she declared Peter her heir; and Catherine busied herself in preparing for such an event. It did not occur, for on her deathbed the Empress confirmed him in the rights that had been settled upon him. On the 6th of January, 1762, he ascended the throne without opposition, the Archbishop of Novgorod publicly thanking God that a prince had succeeded so likely to imitate his illustrious grandfather.

His Reign.—His self-will was speedily exhibited in a remarkable manner. At first his action was highly popular, even in cases where it was questionably prudent. He immediately abolished the Secret Chancery. He recalled from banishment about 17,000 persons who had been exiled by its decrees. Lestocq, Munich, and even Biren, were among those brought back; and he amused himself greatly by having the three at the imperial table, their embarrassment at the unexpected meeting being, no doubt, ludicrous enough. He abolished various severe and tyrannical impositions, especially a tax upon salt, the pressure of which was very galling. He propitiated the nobles by abrogating restrictions on their power which Elizabeth had established. He sought to please the army by lessening the number of offences which entailed corporal punishment. He ingratiated himself with the common people by openly receiving petitions and making personal inquiries into causes of complaint. His activity, however, became mere fussiness; and if in some respects he consulted the interests of his people, in others he cut recklessly athwart their prejudices. He was as good as his long-promised word in regard to his relations with the King of Prussia: no sooner did he grasp the power of doing as he liked than he hastened to inform Frederick of his wish to stop the war, and to return all that Russia had gained! He disgusted the army by insisting upon the introduction of Prussian tactics and discipline. He gave dire offence, and roused much suspicion, by trying to disband the Guards, who, since the time of Catherine I., had always been engaged about the palace. He insisted upon the secular clergy cutting off their long beards, which his grandfather had not dared to meddle with; he ordered the removal of what he called idols from every national church; and he set up a Lutheran chapel at his own favoured home. While he thus stunned the people, irritated the army, incensed the clergy, and left every one in doubt what he might next attempt to do, he anew affronted his wife by taking the Countess Woronzoff as his mistress, and announcing his intention of having Catherine divorced and shut up.

Her beauty, her talent, her ill-usage, had won for her a wide-spread admiration and pity, such as even her misconduct could not abate nor chill. She had been most attentive to the late Empress during her long illness. She had charmed the populace by her affability and grace. She assured the heads of the clergy that she utterly reprobated her husband's sacrilegious interference with their privileges, and they seemed to believe her. The brothers Orloff had been very successful by various means, including extensive bribery, in diffusing through the discontented army a sentiment favourable to her. Count Panin, the foreign minister, once the tutor of her son, was one of her fastest friends, and influenced the nobility in her behalf. In addition, through the Countess Daschkoff, the sister of Peter's mistress, she had a full knowledge of all that went on in the imperial court from which she was exiled. Thus, while the Tsar vapoured about what he was to do, she made ready to counteract him whenever the time came; and when the people— ignorant of what was being contrived—began to suspect him of incipient madness, they grew to respect her as a woman deserving of confidence and esteem, who might have sinned, but had been grievously sinned against. Nevertheless the issue of this strained situation was accidentally precipitated. Peter, who ten weeks before had made an appeal to the courts of Europe, entreating them to follow his example in giving up all he had gained from Prussia, so as to restore peace, now intimated that he must fight Denmark for the recovery of Schleswig, which he held ought to go with his duchy of Holstein. He further intimated that he meant to lead the expedition. This greatly disconcerted the conspirators, who felt it of paramount importance to secure his person.

Accession of Catherine.—Catherine was at Peterhoff. The Tsar was to join her next day to celebrate the festival of St. Peter and St. Paul, preparatory to his meditated expedition. He set out from Oranienbaum at the head of a gay party, with the Countess Woronzoff as a noted member of it. When they arrived at Peterhoff all was confusion and dismay. It turned out the Empress had been privately summoned by one of the Orloffs at four o'clock in the morning, that she had hurried off, accompanied only by her waiting-maid, and that no one knew what had become of her. Information speedily came, the sender being one Bressau, a Frenchman, originally a hair-dresser, whom Peter had taken into favour, and who seems to have been the only man in all the capital who cared what became of him. While the court party were traversing the gardens, haunted by a vague presentiment that something important was about to befall, a messenger handed a billet to the Tsar, who read —" The regiments of the Guards are under arms; the Empress is at their head; nine o'clock strikes; she is entering the church of Kazan; all the people appear to follow this movement, and the faithful subjects of your majesty do not appear." It was even so. Catherine had driven straight to the barracks at St. Petersburg, and called out the soldiery, saying that she had come to them for protection, since the Tsar had given orders to put her son and herself to death. She was received with immense enthusiasm, the men shouting that they would die in her defence—a pledge they readily ratified by an oath in presence of a chaplain who held aloft a crucifix.

Accompanied by a strong guard, she then repaired to the winter palace, had her little son sent for, and taking him in her arms, dressed in his night-clothes as he was, presented him from a balcony to the military and to the people, who had by this time assembled in large numbers and in high excitement. They hailed her with cries of "Long live Catherine our mother." A proposal to have her proclaimed Regent was defeated by Gregory Orloff, who insisted that things ought not to be done by halves, and produced a ready-made proclamation in her name as "Empress of all the Russias, by the style and title of Catherine II." Forthwith she went to the cathedral of Kazan, when the Archbishop of Novgorod, clad in his sacerdotal robes, and attended by an immense array of priests, waited at the altar to greet her. Having sworn to respect the laws and religion of the realm, she was formally crowned, immediately after which she rode round the grand square, telling the troops she meant to be their general, and evoking the plaudits of the multitude who thronged to kiss her hand. Later in the day she received the allegiance of numerous grandees who crowded to the palace, among them the Chancellor Woronzoff. He who had been one of the imperial party in the morning, set off as soon as the news of what was taking place arrived, upon the pretence that his presence might avail to check the revolution. In the course of the day a proclamation was issued, in which Catherine was made to say that, in obedience to the decrees of Divine Providence and the approving suffrages of her countrymen, she had ascended the throne. She continued —" We assure our faithful subjects that we will not fail, by night nor day, to invoke the Most High to bless our sceptre, and to make us to wield it to the maintenance of our orthodox religion, the security and defence of our dear country, and the equal administration of justice, as well as to put an end to all miseries, iniquities, and violence, by strengthening and fortifying our heart for the public good, not entertaining the least doubt that all our loving subjects, as well for the salvation of their souls as for the honour of religion, will invariably observe the oath they have taken in the presence of Almighty God; and we hereby assure them of our imperial favour." In the evening she started for Peterhoff at the head of an army 20,000 strong, with intent to seize her husband Learning that he had fled, and that the place was left undefended, she was persuaded to repose for a few hours in a castle on the road, but her impatience hurried her forward, so that within twenty-four hours of the time she had left the palace as a fugitive, she re-entered it as a sovereign. The revolution had been swift, bloodless, and irresistible.

Peter's Murder.—From the moment Peter received Bressan's note he behaved like one demented. Now he gave orders that Catherine should instantly be put to death. Then he proposed an advance to the capital. Anon he resolved to stay where he was, and with the aid of his Holstein troops to defend Peterhoff. These troops he ordered up. It was about the only rational thing he did, except to consult old Munich as to what he ought to do more. The wise advice given he disregarded till too late. It was to push on at once to Cronstadt, where there was a strong garrison and a fleet lying equipped. The imperial party did not set out till the tidings came that Catherine was on the march. Then, when Cronstadt was reached they found its guns turned against them, and in answer to a demand for admission to the Emperor, were informed that there was no Emperor. Again appeal was made to Munich, who replied they should row to Revel, take a ship of war and sail to Prussia, where the army was eighty thousand strong, at the head of whom the empire might be subdued in six weeks' time. This counsel was opposed by his mistress, and the plan decided on was a return to Oranienbaum, whence he sent a request to Catherine that he might be allowed to retire to Holstein with the Countess, her rival. The answer was a formula of abdication sent to him to sign. When the signature was obtained he was sent as a prisoner to Robschak. In a short time afterwards he was murdered. When the first excitement of the revolution had abated, a feeling of pity on his behalf sprang up, such as the conspirators who had dethroned him dreaded might become hazardous. The commander of the castle was one of them. He was joined by two of the brothers Orloff and another officer, who were introduced to the fallen Tsar. They recommended themselves to him by abusing the Empress, and then the four sat down to drink. Poison was poured into Peter's glass. He quickly suspected what had happened, loudly exclaimed against the baseness, and called for milk. The governor of the prison entered, and, to silence his outcries, threw a napkin round his neck, which Alexis Orloff immediately pulled tight, so strangling the unhappy victim. The balance of proof is against the conjecture that Catherine was privy to this foul deed. Orloff reported it in a letter which implies distinctly that there was no preconcert with her. She carefully preserved this document; and its perusal five and thirty years after convinced her son, who had no liking for her, that in regard to this affair she was innocent. Still, no punishment was inflicted upon the perpetrators; physicians were found to certify that the death was natural; and the people were asked to believe it by a public exhibition of the corpse, carefully dressed.

Catherine I.—From July, 1762, till her death, in November, 1796, Catherine ruled over Russia with a splendour and success that have very rarely been paralleled. There are respects in which her private conduct had a depth of vileness that would shame and appal the most degraded of her sex. There are also respects in which her public behaviour was marked by a vigour of mind, a consistent elevation and width of purpose, a self-reliant capacity for coping with the possibilities of events, that have won the admiration of all who are able to recognise intellectual superiority, and have exalted her to a first rank among great rulers. Apart from her gross licentiousness she had, both as woman and sovereign, many attractive qualities. To strangers she was always courteous and kind, even when most dignified. To enemies she was often frank and placable, not so much from motives of policy, but because she could not retain resentment against those who were not actively opposing her. To friends she was ever open, true, and nobly indulgent. Throughout her long reign she almost invariably triumphed over the immensely varied difficulties she set herself to face; and yet this uniformity of success was sometimes gained by the most dishonourable methods, for, where ambition and resolve were conjoined, never was any monarch more thoroughly unscrupulous.

Her first business after she was seated on the throne was to reward those who had helped her ascent. This she did with a lavish liberality which always continued one of her prominent characteristics. Her next care was to seek out capable and trustworthy advisers. This she did without any regard to their antecedents. Bestuchoff, whom her husband could never forgive, she recalled and endowed with a big pension. Biren, who was a childless man, she reinstated in his duchy of Courland. Prince George of Holstein, the uncle of her husband, the commander of the German troops, though arrested by the Orloffs, she at once released, creating him a field-marshal; and he ever afterwards served her with a loyal devotedness. Even the stout old warrior, Munich, she overmatched and outshone. When he, a man of eighty years, was introduced to her, she said, "And you wished to fight against me!" His reply was, "Madam, could I do less for a prince who redeemed me from captivity?" Instead of being offended, she at once took him into her confidence; listened with patience and appreciation to his long-meditated ideas about Turkey, which had grown stronger during his exile; honoured him with many signal honours; and appointed him governor of Livonia and Esthonia—which office he held for five years, till his death in 1767, aged eighty-six.

The early years of her reign were, however, disturbed by the existence of many malcontents, and the appearance of many pretenders. The nobles, the clergy, the soldiers, the people, all expected that she would do more for them in a direct way than she saw meet to attempt; and each of these classes grumbled over the disappointment. The storm grew so high and fierce that it is said she visited the fortress of Schlusselburgh, where the wretched Ivan, the legitimate Tsar, was confined, in order to see whether her title to the crown could not be confirmed by making him her husband; but his appearance was as sorry as that of her first spouse, and his doltishness was even more painful. Soon afterwards, when she was in a distant part of the country, an attempt at his release was reported, accompanied by the intimation that he had been slain in the scuffle. The incident suggested many suspicions, one effect of which was that five or six impostors appeared, asserting his identity, and claiming his rights. Some two or three deceivers waxed even more bold—alleging that Peter had not been murdered, and claiming all the benefits of survivorship. With them Catherine dealt very summarily. They were put to death in the most public manner—each successive victim weakening the claim of those who came after. Meanwhile, the Tsarina used all her acts to conciliate those who sympathised with them; and did so with that effect which seldom failed any of her great purposes.

Domestic Reforms.—In four years' time any thought of opposition to her had died out. During the interval she had shaken her government clear of the Prussian complications into which Peter had rushed; and, while she kept a very keen eye upon the course of foreign politics, she particularly bent her regards upon the improvement of domestic administration. She entered with zeal upon a series of reforms which in great measure changed the face of Russia. Great daring was evinced in many of her actions, both private and public. An epidemic of small-pox, like that which raged shortly before she came from Germany, broke out soon after she was crowned. The preventive of inoculation was derided by some as useless, was dreaded by others as hazardous, was denounced by many as impious. Catherine sent for

Dr. Thomas Dimsdale, an eminent London physician, by whom she and her son were vaccinated. The performance was wholly successful, and the fortunate doctor received a fee of £10,000, with the addition of a pension for life amounting to £500 a year, payable in London. He was a frequent guest at the imperial table, and he has left a record of the entertainment, which states that, "what enlivened it most was the unaffected ease and affability of the Empress with each of her guests (not more than twelve). We all had a share of her attention and politeness; the conversation was kept up with a freedom and cheerfulness to be expected rather from persons of the same rank, than from subjects admitted to the honour of their sovereign's company." Equally enlightened and advanced was her conduct otherwise. In 1766 she convoked an assembly of deputies for consultation as to framing one code of laws for the empire. They reported that the diversities of race, custom, and civilization were too manifold to permit of a compilation being made, such as could be put in use with any good result. Thereupon she issued a commission to a company of learned men, charging them to traverse her vast dominions in order to report upon the geography, the climate, and the productions of the different provinces, as well as upon the manners and customs of their people. This great survey—an enlarged Domesday Book—would alone have sufficed to immortalise her name. She followed it up with great assiduity and aptitude. She encouraged agriculture, striving to attract skilled German colonists towards fertile regions, and planting out among them many sober, thrifty, and hard-working families. She founded numerous towns and villages, and wherever one of them was set down, a school was established in the midst. She patronised the higher education—extending the Academy of Arts, and assigning a sum of sixty thousand roubles a year for the maintenance of an Academy of Sciences, to the supervision of which she invited a learned German professor, giving him a house and a life-pension. And in 1776 she promulgated a code of laws she had herself prepared, certainly one of the most remarkable performances that ever owned female authorship.

A New Code of Laws.—No doubt it was drawn in large part from such masters of jurisprudence as Beccaria and Montesquieu, but there was great co-ordinating power in its arrangement, and it was brightened by many gleams of original sense and dexterous adaptation. It comprised five hundred and twenty articles, and contained an apology, perhaps as good as could be offered, for the absolute power which it ascribed to the sovereign. Its author was highly complimented over it both by the King of Prussia and by Voltaire. Frederick wrote to her that "the ancients would have placed your imperial majesty between Lycurgus and Solon." In answer to the French philosopher she gave expression to very enlightened sentiments. "These laws," she said, "about which there has been so much talk, are not yet finished, who then can tell whether they are good for anything? Posterity, not ourselves, must decide that question. They are made for Europe and for Asia. What a difference of climate, of customs, of persons, even of ideas! Still I must make them a dress which will serve them all. I have nearly an universe to form, to unite, and to preserve. . . . Laws are made for all persons, and all are obliged to conform to them; they should therefore be drawn up so that all may understand them; still, they should be simple and concise, and should admit no latitude of interpretation. . . . It is better to prevent crimes than to punish them. Would you prevent crimes, take all possible means to enlighten the people. Punishments should be speedy, proportioned to the crime and to the public. The most efficacious preventive is not the severity of punishment, but the certainty of it."

Literature and Religion.—Mention may here be made of the facts that Catherine shared the sceptical opinions of her distinguished correspondents; that she maintained a brisk interchange of opinions with them upon many subjects, philosophical as well as political; and that her literary activity led to the production of a drama, founded on the story of her predecessor Olga, which was acted, of course with great applause, on the St. Petersburg stage, as well as of a volume entitled "Pieces from Russian History," which is really a model piece of writing. Her sympathy with the French encyclopædists naturally led her to despise the mediæval extravagances of the Greek church. Yet, as a matter of policy, she conformed to its rites, and kept friends with its clergy, though she established universal toleration. The only exception to the complete liberty of conscience she conceded was in the case of Roman Catholicism, of whose encroachments upon the civil power she was exceedingly jealous. At intervals during her reign she issued ukases regulating the relations between the state and the professors of that faith. Mohilow was fixed as the seat of their archbishop, a right of veto was claimed upon the appointment of all ecclesiastical functionaries, foreign priests were debarred from settling in her dominions, and she prohibited the reception of any bull from the Pope, or other writing sent in his name, "ordering that the same shall be sent to our senate, who, after having examined their contents, and particularly anything that may appear contrary to the laws of this Russian empire, or to the rights of the ecclesiastical power which we have received from God, shall be obliged to communicate to us its opinion, and to wait our permission or prohibition before rendering any such bulls or writings."

Civil Administration.—A like energy was infused into every department of public affairs. The empire was divided into forty-one provinces, over which governors and sub-magistrates were appointed by the senate, subject to the approval of the sovereign. The magnificence of the court eclipsed that of every other in Europe. The army was reorganised, and a conscription was instituted by which one recruit was drawn from every five hundred male inhabitants. A formidable rebellion, headed by an able man named Pougateloff, who aimed at rendering independent the provinces of the Don and the Volga, inhabited mainly by dissenters from the Greek church, was swiftly suppressed, and its leader executed, the Empress writing, very significantly, to the French king concerning him, "I shall keep his depositions secret, that they may not aggravate the disgrace of those who set him on." And all the while a vigilant regard was paid to foreign policy.

The First Partition of Poland Planned.—Catherine's first exploit on the foreign field was performed in Poland. In 1764 the luxurious and apathetic king, Frederick Augustus, died. She resolved that her old friend Count Poniatowski should be chosen in his stead. Quoth she, "I will have him to be king, and king he shall be." By this time he had married the Princess Czartoryski, through which alliance he had become connected with the powerful family of the Jagellons. There was nothing so outrageous, therefore, in her proposal. Still, it certainly would not have been carried but for her decisive action in advancing Russian troops close up to Warsaw. Sent as a friendly contingent, they remained for another purpose. Poniatowski, who took the title of Stanislaus Augustus, became exceedingly popular with his subjects, and he did his best to promote patriotic ideas. It soon became evident, however, that Catherine had ulterior purposes in his elevation. Her representative, Prince Repnan, asserted an absolute sway at Warsaw, where the Diet was distracted by jealousies and alienations. These he fostered and made much of in a manner fitted to lead up to the consummation she designed, even that of extinguishing Polish independence, and dividing the country among its neighbours, seeing she could not hope to acquire the whole of it for herself. For this purpose she required to establish an understanding with the intended spoilators. There seems to be no doubt the project was first broached by Catherine during a visit paid to St. Petersburg by Prince Henry of Prussia, the King's brother, at the close of 1770. All Europe rang with accounts of the splendour which marked the festivities held in his honour. No suspicion was entertained as to the serious nature of the business which was transacted A secret treaty was negotiated by which the respective shares of the partners in this gigantic larceny were determined, and arrangements were concluded for approaching Austria on the subject. Said the Empress to her guest, "Gain you Austria, and let her amuse France; England I will flatter; Turkey I will frighten." This programme was assiduously carried out. Misled by her son Joseph II., now associated with her in the government, Maria Theresa, who had ever spoken of Catherine with a contemptuous hate as "cette femme," was induced to treat with her most intimately; and Austria, scandalously forgetful how, eighty years before, John Sobieski had saved her capital from the beleaguering Turks, was hurried into participation in the contemplated iniquity. The process of frightening Turkey had already begun. Some time before, the Porte had pointed out to the cabinets of Europe the hazards of allowing the predominance at Warsaw which Russia was asserting; but nothing had come of the representation. In 1768, consequent upon a quarrel between the Roman Catholic prelates and nobility with the dissenters of Poland — Protestants and members of the Greek church — the number of the Russian troops had been increased, the Prince-archbishop of Cracow, and three other senators were sent to Siberia, and the Diet was subjected to fresh and more rigorous intimidation. This interference goaded the inhabitants of the provinces adjoining Turkey into revolt. They besought the aid of the Sultan, Mustapha III., which was readily given. He declared war against Russia at once.

War with Turkey — a Russian Fleet in the Mediterranean. — On her side Russia was eager for the fray; and the summer of 1769 saw it begun. Mustapha had been far too precipitate, for his preparations were seriously defective. His armies were beaten all round, though the Russian successes were so inferior to what they might have been that Frederick sneeringly spoke of the campaign as a contest between the one-eyed and the blind. Next season much more vigour was displayed. In Armenia and Transcaucasia great successes were won. The Crimea was invaded, Azoff and Taganrog again coming into Russian occupation. Romanzoff, who had the chief command, speedily cleared Moldavia, receiving in its capital the homage of the boyards to Catherine. After two great battles, he acquired all the Turkish fortresses on the Danube and the Dniester, only two of them—Brailoff or Ibrail, which stood out for three weeks, and Bender, which offered a gallant defence for as many months—giving him much trouble. Further, acting on the advice of the aged Munich, who now saw a chance for the "oriental project" he had recommended thirty years before, a Russian fleet was sent from Cronstadt to the Mediterranean, carrying troops who were meant to rouse the Greeks to insurrection. Little success attended the operations on land, but the Turkish fleet was annihilated. Three British seamen—Vice-admiral Elphinstone, Commodore Greig, and Lieutenant Dugdale—were in command on the Russian side. With only eight sail of the line and seven frigates, Elphinstone attacked a fleet of twenty-six vessels, some of them much bigger than his largest, compelling them to make for safety to the bay of Tchesmé, between Siev and the mainland, where a number of Turkish merchantmen also lay. While a feigned attack was made from one opening, and a rigorous blockade was kept up at the other, Dugdale after nightfall sent a couple of fire-ships in amongst them. The proceeding attained its object. The whole flotilla, numbering about a hundred vessels, was destroyed, only one sixty-gun ship and three half-galleys escaping. Elphinstone would fain have carried the tidings of his victory to Constantinople, proposing to force the Dardanelles, and bombard the city. That the project was feasible can hardly be doubted; but Alexis Orloff, his nominal superior, demurred, and the idea was abandoned. The Turks had indirectly a dire revenge for the loss they had sustained. The crews of the Turkish ships infected the Russian sailors with the plague. It was thus spread over the empire, becoming particularly dreadful in its ravages at Moscow, where it raged for years. It is said that not one-fourth of the dwellings in the city were exempt from the visitation, though the number of deaths was not stated. The behaviour of the government in the circumstances was admirably prompt, wise, and humane.

The Crimea Annexed.—In 1771 Turkey was bereft of the Crimea. A new Khan had lately been chosen, who was objectionable to some of the tribes. They refused to co-operate in the resistance offered to the Russians under Prince Dolgoruki, who forced the famous lines across the isthmus of Perekof with even greater ease than Munich and Lancy had done. At the same time he landed a force in the rear of their defenders. The new ruler was thus utterly disconcerted. In his bewilderment he took to flight, making his way after many wanderings to Constantinople, where he died of grief. Left without leadership, the Tartars everywhere submitted. Dolgoruki showed great discretion in dealing with them. He promised them the appointment of a Khan belonging to their ancient royal house, stipulating only that he should rule under the protection of Russia. The condition was accepted, and while fifty chiefs repaired to St. Petersburg with a tender of allegiance, the Russian troops quietly took possession of the towns and fortresses throughout the peninsula. It was a poor compensation for this heavy and discouraging blow, that the Turks recovered Giurgevo, and otherwise improved their position somewhat throughout the Danubian principalities.

The Partition of Poland Carried Out.— Next year there was much talk of peace. It was started by Austria, who, immediately before her accession to the conspiracy against Poland, had concluded a convention with Turkey, whereby, in return for the promise of a large subsidy, free admission to her commerce, and a guarantee of protection to her merchant ships in the Levant, she pledged herself to an alliance. Instead of fulfilling this compact by helping Turkey to fight, she now pressed her to desist, the urgent recommendations made leading to an armistice, during which a conference of plenipotentiaries assembled at Bucharest to consider terms of peace. Meantime the tripartite treaty for the partition of Poland was subscribed. According to it, Prussia was to acquire five palatinates, and a part of Great Poland, amounting in all to over a thousand square leagues of very fertile land, and a million of new subjects; Austria four divisions of the kingdom, comprising two thousand seven hundred leagues, with two and a half millions of people; while Russia got no less than three thousand four hundred and forty miles of territory, with a population of a million and a half. In the month of September the Austrian minister intimated to the Polish king and senate the meditated robbery, his coadjutors coming forward with corroboration. Prussia found a pretext for her conduct in connection with the ancient rights of the Electors of Branderburgh and the Duke of Pomerania; Austria alleged certain pretences in connection with the Hungarian crown; but Catherine having no antiquated claims to fall back upon, unblushingly declared that she was entitled to compensation for costs she had incurred in defending the republic. Poor King Stanislaus had nothing for it but to convoke the Diet, as he was told, in order to consider the proposed cession. He did so in a manifesto, which plaintively set forth that "there are no hopes from any quarter, and delay will only tend to draw down the most dreadful calamities upon the remainder of the dominions which are left to the republic." Withal, however, he had the spirit to point out that Poland was entitled, under the treaty of Oliva, concluded in 1660, to appeal to the guarantee of protection given by the very powers who now so coolly proposed dismemberment. Of course the appeal was useless. The nefarious aggression was carried through. Surrounded by foreign bayonets the senate, after long debate, by a majority of six, ratified the cession, while in the lower house assent was carried by a single vote. The courts of London, Paris, Stockholm, and Copenhagen remonstrated against the seizure, **but mere remonstrances did not count for much. In the** end the acquiescence of Britain was bought by concessions on the part of Russia to her commerce. France, debilitated by the misgovernment of Louis XV., was in no condition to intervene. Denmark and Sweden were at odds with each other, and were besides racked by domestic dissensions. Turkey was the only power that cared to do anything either to prevent, or to punish, this shameless act of brigandage.

The Treaty of Kainardja.—The Bucharest conference was broken up indignantly, and the war was renewed with greater fury and zeal than before. In this campaign the Turks gained a number of signal successes. Romanoff, who again commanded the Russian hosts, was discomfited with enormous loss at Silistria, at Shumla, at Varna; while at Rustchuk the Ottoman forces assumed the offensive, routed the besiegers, and captured many prisoners, among them Prince Repnin, who was sent to Constantinople. The fortune of the war seemed to have turned, when, all at once, whether from despair of co-operation, or disgust at the attitude assumed by the other European powers, or apprehensive of a great rally on the part of their opponent, the Turks gave in. The Sultan was a valetudinarian; he was impressed by a superstition which pronounced the name of Mustapha unfortunate; and latterly he abdicated in favour of his brother, who made haste to conclude a pacification. Mainly through the exertions of Surwarroff, who commanded at Hirsova, and now first displayed that alacrity and determination which made him afterwards so celebrated, a change was wrought to Turkish detriment upon the aspects of the war; but it was not of such moment as reasonably to account for the arrangement made by the treaty of Kainardja which was negotiated in July 1774, and, through a little bit of manœuvring on the Russian side, was subscribed on the anniversary of the day when the convention of the Pruth was concluded. Russian writers have always dilated with a suspicious earnestness on the magnanimity displayed in this bargain. It is **quite true that its terms were much under what had been**

stickled for at Bucharest. But it is also true that the
Turks were undeniably outwitted. Not one stipulation
about Poland was admitted into the treaty, though the
wrongs of Poland formed the occasion of the war.
Turkey got back Moldavia and Wallachia, but subject to
a stipulation that, "as the circumstances of these principalities may require, the ministers of the court of Russia
at Constantinople may remonstrate in their favour;"
while another article is capable of being construed, as
Russia has repeatedly construed it, into a recognition of
a Russian protectorate over all Greek Christians throughout Turkey. The Crimea was not annexed to Russia;
but it was declared to be independent of Turkey, while
Kertch and Yenikale, Azoff and Kilburn, were given to
Russian keeping. A right to station consular representatives of Russia throughout the Turkish empire was
granted, but there was no provision made for any reci-
procity in that respect. Finally, Russia acquired a title
to the free navigation of the Danube and the Black Sea.
In all these respects she gained not only immediate
benefit, but a potent means of future influence. In this
view Von Hanmer, the Turkish historian, sees in the
treaty a great note of Turkish decadence. He describes
it as "containing the germs of all that followed at
Adrianople." Favourable though it was for them,
the Russians soon repented of their lenity in consenting to it.

On the western side they had almost no trouble.
At home Catherine had no more engrossing business
than to keep up the splendours of her court, and
attend to the domestic interests of her son. In these
circumstances she had ample leisure for activity elsewhere. She intrigued in Moldavia and Wallachia,
encouraging the Christian population to regard her as
their protector. She intrigued in the Crimea, causing
the displacement of the new Khan, who had not proved
sufficiently obsequious, and getting him superseded by a
more pliant tool. Hardly had he been appointed than a
quarrel arose betwixt him and his brother, the governor

of the Kuban. Avail was taken of the dispute to march in a strong Russian force, to constrain both functionaries to resign, and to incorporate with Russia the whole peninsula, a vast territory peopled by a million and a half of inhabitants. Thus fell the last of the Tartar dominations that had played so important a part in Russian story. Turkey fumed and threatened over the annexation; but was coerced into giving formal assent by a treaty executed in 1780, supplemented to that of Kainardja. France was the only other nation that raised a word of demur, and her opposition was merely verbal.

Prince Potemkin.—The agent who conducted this successful movement was the Prince Potemkin. No more extraordinary person figures in Russian annals. He was one of the dozen men who held in succession the post of "aide-de-camp general" to the Tzarina—in other words, who were her recognised lovers and attendants. He filled the disgraceful office only for a period of fifteen months, but for more than twenty years he had a predominating influence in her councils; and, till his death, Catherine deferred to him as she deferred to no one else. He was an astonishing compound of strength and weakness, vanity and reserve, calculation and impulse, energy and sloth, fickleness and resolve, sumptuous extravagance and self-denying austerity—

"A man so various that he seemed to be,
Not one, but all mankind's epitome."

He was omnipotent in the empire, but he never put any restraint on his own passions, however costly or difficult their gratification. When the whim took him, he would send officers a distance of two thousand miles—from Kherson, in the Crimea, to Riga, for oysters—or to St. Petersburg for sterlet soup; yet at other times he would, without warning, start himself on journeys of equal length, travelling like a common courier, and living on the black bread of the peasantry. At times he entered with prodigal zest on the enjoyments of power, pomp, and luxury; but at other times he seemed so utterly sated with them that he would wander about his palace biting his finger-nails in moody abstraction, or chuck about his diamonds, which he could weigh out by pounds upon pounds, as a child plays with peas. He had most of the vices that debase and torment human nature; yet he was a man of grand conceptions and great sagacity. Munich's "oriental project" he patronised with a zealous favour. Catherine was prejudiced towards it, and he made it his business to foster and guide this inclination. In 1779, while the arrangements about the Crimea were in hand, he urged upon her a comprehensive and daring scheme for Turkish extinction. Britain was then at war with her revolted colonists in America. Potemkin proposed that Russia should help her, the assistance to be paid for by the cession of Minorca, which he would have made a station for a Russian fleet, a rallying-place for Greek disaffection, a rendezvous whence there might be repeated on a large scale the Orloff and Elphinstone movement. The scheme miscarried, though its author continued to preach that a British alliance was the surest method to the attainment of Russian success; and its ultimate object filled the mind of Catherine for years. Her second grandson was born at this period. She had him named Constantine. Greek women were procured to nurse him, so that, as was said, he might suck in the Greek language with his milk. In every way he was encouraged to think of himself as destined to fill a Greek throne at Constantinople.

An Austrian Alliance.—As British aid was unattainable, a fresh Austrian alliance was by and by concluded, with the view of realising this design. The bargain was ratified at personal interviews between Catherine and Joseph II. He accompanied her in 1787 on a triumphal progress through her newly-acquired Crimean province, which was named Taurida, where Potemkin received them with prodigious display. They met at Kherson, over the southern gate of which there was inscribed in Greek characters the significant intimation, "By this the way leads to Byzantium." They met again soon afterwards at St. Petersburg, whither Joseph went on a visit, the magnificence of his entertainment being such that he had to beg a release from the festivities contrived in his honour. No pains were taken to hide the motive and end of their deliberations. It was sought to include France in the bargain by a promise of Egypt as her share of the spoil, but she refused the bribe. The Porte having been goaded into a declaration of hostilities, Catherine, on the 8th of April, 1788, issued a manifesto, in which she reproached Turkey with a violation of treaties, protested that she was innocent of all the calamities the war might engender, and declared that she had a right to rely "not only on the justice of God and the assistance of her allies, but on the devout aspirations of the Christian world for the triumph of her cause."

The triumph did not come. It was the boast of Potemkin that he would batter down the Ottoman empire in two campaigns; but he miscalculated. The war lasted four years, and its conclusion was of a nugatory character. At first considerable successes were won by the armies of the coalition. In two years, however, Joseph was tired of the contest. Under Marshal Laudon his troops had captured Belgrade and Semendria, and had advanced into the heart of Servia, when home-troubles put an arrest on their movement. France was at enmity, the Netherlands were in revolt, Hungary and Bohemia were discontented. Soon after Joseph sickened and died. His wiser brother, who succeeded him, made haste to end hostilities. This was done by the treaty of Sistova, according to which Austria relinquished great part of her conquests, and the boundary-line betwixt the two empires was re-arranged much as it had been drawn two centuries before.

The Capture of Ismael.—That Catherine resented this defection is certain, but for a time the contest was continued with renewed vigour by her troops. At the close of 1790 their prospects were of the most reassuring character. A Russian navy rode in the Black Sea, intercepting the supplies of corn for Constantinople.

Throughout the Danubian provinces no Turkish force dared show itself in the field. The strongly-fortified place of Ismael, the key of the Lower Danube, alone hindered a Russian march by the coast road upon Varna. The reduction of this place Potemkin rightly regarded as the indispensable preliminary to a safe advance. It had been invested for months without the slightest impression being made upon it. The story goes that, as the prince began to wax impatient, he was one evening playing at cards, when a lady of the party, pretending that the bits of pasteboard enabled her to divine the future, announced, "In three weeks Ismael will be yours." He replied, "I know how it may be gained much sooner;" and forthwith penned a note to his stern lieutenant, Suwarroff, "Let Ismael be taken in three days, at any cost." No message could have been more welcome to this daring and pitiless soldier. He had the grace to make a demand for surrender, which was answered in oriental style by an intimation that "the Danube must first cease to flow, or the heavens bow to the earth." The response was that, unless "a white flag was hung out that day, the place would be taken by assault and the garrison be put to the sword." This menace being disregarded, because disbelieved, the signal for attack was given at five o'clock next morning, being Christmas day. After a struggle of the most desperate character, which endured for twelve hours, the Russians, who seemed to be animated by the appalling energy of their commander, were triumphant. The garrison were completely overpowered. For the next three days the place was given over to pillage and slaughter. Suwarroff computed that 30,000 persons were slain and 10,000 made prisoners, while, as he phrased it, "the soldiers shared gold and silver by handfuls." His estimate of the loss has been generally supposed to be under the mark. At any rate, the Turkish prisoners were engaged for the best part of a week in throwing the corpses of their countrymen into the Danube, it being impossible to dig pits for their reception with sufficient rapidity, while the hazard of epidemic disease was very great. The pithy despatch in which Suwarroff announced his victory is well known:—" Glory to God and the Empress! Ismael's ours."

The Treaty of Jassy.—The effect of this victory was overwhelming. The Russian strength was launched in full force upon the confounded and panic-stricken Turks. They were driven from post to post, till at length the invaders menaced Varna, the sea-key to Roumelia. Its magazines were cut off from communication with its defenders. Its reduction was imminent. Should it fall, the road was opened to Adrianople, where no stand could be made, and then the capital was exposed to an assault which it seemed hopeless to parry. The Sultan shut himself up in his palace. Consternation prevailed among the people. The body of the Ulemas, as a counsel of despair, resolved on humbly suing for peace. To their own surprise their petition was favourably entertained. In an incredibly short space of time the treaty of Jassy was negotiated. It was subscribed in January, 1792. By it Russia ceded all that she had won in the Danubian provinces, confining her claim of territorial aggrandisement to the country round the northern shores of the Black Sea, where she had Oczakoff on the one side, and where she speedily planted Odessa on the other. There was, besides, a stipulation made for a large indemnity; but this Catherine renounced as soon as it had been formally agreed to.

The motives for this sudden change of resolution were various. There had been in 1790 a short though sharp war with Sweden, whose king, Gustavus III., had been a guest at St. Petersburg a few years before. He seems to have suspected that it was meant to entrap him into undue concessions, and to have left with the notion that he would choose his own time for counteracting the plot. He took avail of the Turkish conflict to try whether he could execute this design. The trial came to an unhappy end. For a brief period a gleam of success brightened his fortunes. A powerful fleet came within sight of

Cronstadt, blockaded the port, and created so much alarm
that terror reigned in St. Petersburg, and the Empress
was advised to seek safety in flight. She refused, calmly
remarking, "If driven hence, we shall find a better capital in the south." Ere the end of the season Admiral
Greig had swept the Swedish marine from the north seas,
and Gustavus was fain to re-establish the treaties of Abo
and Newstadt. Plainly, Russian acquiescence in such a
settlement could only have been granted by a desire to
keep Sweden quiet. Its conclusion was a bitter disappointment to the British Minister, William Pitt, who
had united Holland and Prussia in an anti-Russian
league, had dictated the terms of the Austrian peace at
Sistova, had coerced Denmark into an abandonment of
her Russian alliance, and who (despite the energetic
remonstrances of Charles Fox and the British Whigs)
was threatening to send a British fleet to the Baltic to
do what the Swedes had failed to accomplish, unless
Catherine should consent to make terms with the Porte.
She consented, mainly because of a new incident which
gave an opportunity for carrying out her designs in a
different direction.

Poland again Divided.—On the 3rd of May, 1791, a
new constitution was proclaimed for what remained of
Poland. It contemplated the establishment of a hereditary throne. It contemplated also the abolition of the
famous *liberum veto*, that absurd provision of the constitution which allowed to every member of the Diet the
power of arresting all procedure, concerning which Lord
Brougham has said, "No human contrivance was ever
invented so effectual to tie up the will and paralyse the
judgment of a deliberative assembly;" while Montesquieu
has remarked that, "through the great care it took for
the liberty of every one, it caused the oppression of all."
Other reforms were proposed of a sort which the Prussian
monarch, the nephew of Frederick the Great, heartily
approved, and upon which Mr. Burke, then launched
on the full tide of his rage against French doctrines,
lavished an unbounded approbation. But Catherine dis-

liked them, and saw how she could turn her antipathy to account. Twenty years before she had stood forth as the advocate of the Polish dissenters, the upholder of a free toleration. Now she appeared as the determined enemy of civil reform. The veterans she had recalled from Turkey were marched straight into Poland, once more to overawe the Diet. She wiled the Prussian monarch to become an abettor in this work by the lure of a participation in a fresh robbery. He had approved the constitution; she had denounced it as intolerable; he had bound himself by solemn pledges to make common cause with Poland against any foreign intervention; but what were fidelity and truth that they should bar the chance of filching Dantzic and Thorn, and the rich palatinate of Posen?

With an infamous facility he joined in the representation that, in order to preserve one half of diminished Poland from the contagion of French principles, it was requisite that he and Catherine should divide the other and bigger half betwixt them. This was done by the convention of Grodno, concluded in 1793, by which Russia took 83,000 square miles of Polish ground, and Prussia 22,500, leaving to the truncated republic no more than 40,000, imposing also a stipulation that its army should not exceed 15,000 men. This miserable little state was really allowed no more than a nominal independence. Its vassalage to Russia was so complete that its endurance was only a matter of time. A brief period sufficed to end it. In 1794 the brave and high-spirited Kosciusko, who had served under Lafayette with the insurgent American colonists, was implored by some of his countrymen to head an effort for getting rid of an intolerable tyranny. His intrepid conduct, and the spirit of enthusiasm he aroused, encouraged for a while the hope of deliverance. Three times over he defeated superior numbers of Russians. Three times over the contest ended in a drawn battle, which his tactical skill enabled him to improve. Warsaw, the capital of what was still styled independent Poland, was possessed by

Russian troops, whom a popular rising cleared out.
Everywhere, over the newly-annexed territories, the
armies of occupation were driven back. No doubt the
expulsion was marked by some regrettable severities, but
they were not such as to justify the atrocities that were
perpetrated by way of punishment and revenge. Austrian,
Prussian, and Russian troops were all ordered up. The
fierce Suwarroff was instructed to re-take Warsaw. He
stormed Praga, one of its suburbs, which was garrisoned
by 30,000 men, with a pitiless ferocity and cruel carnage,
that far outvied even what had been witnessed at Ismael.
Only 3400 persons were saved as prisoners. The rest
were slain by sword or bayonet, or were driven into the
Vistula before the eyes of the inhabitants on the other
side. Next day Suwarroff entered the city, which he
treated as a conquered place. On the 1st of November he
ordered a grand "Te Deum" to be sung to the God of
armies in honour of his victory. On the 25th the wretched
Stanislaus resigned his crown, the three allied powers
guaranteeing him a pension. In the following May
Poland was wiped from the map of nations by a third
treaty of partition, in which all the three were participants.

Death of Catherine.—This was the last great achievement which the Empress saw accomplished, if exception
be allowed for the final annexation of Courland, which
followed as a sequel to the swallowing up of Poland.
Other projects she had planned. One was a great coalition
for the purpose of subjugating or overawing revolutionary France, which broke down through the assassination of Gustavus III. of Sweden in 1791. She continued
ambitious, however, of playing a grand part as arbitress
of Europe, and in 1795 she formed a confederacy with
the leading neighbours of France for effecting her restraint, entering at the same time into a special treaty
with Britain, who had so lately opposed her in the matter
of Turkey. That matter she continued to regard with
an eager anxiety, which prompted a sleepless vigilance.
There is some evidence that she entertained a design for

twisting round the part she proposed to herself in European troubles, into an instrument for furthering her cherished project of continuing the Byzantine empire by a Russian sequel. The same motive has been attributed to an invasion of Persia, which she simultaneously undertook. Under the command of Valerian Duboff, a great army had penetrated eastward past Derbend, the commander being empowered to set up a new Shah. The conjecture is that he would then have fallen upon the Asiatic provinces of Turkey, forcing the Ottoman power to denude itself of its European troops for their defence, and so throwing open the way to Constantiple. Whatever truth there may be in these speculations, they all suffered collapse by her sudden death in November, 1796, at the age of sixty-seven.

Undoubtedly the most notable woman of her own day, she has had few compeers in any age. Her ambition was of the loftiest kind, though it sometimes stooped to the meanest artifices. When she mounted the throne only twenty-two millions of people paid her homage. When she died the number had grown to thirty-six millions, one-half the increase arising through territorial acquisitions. The whole of Little Tartary and the Crimea, the island of Taman and the county of Kuban, the principalities of Georgia, Imeritia, Mongrelia, and the passes of the Caucasus, came under her sway. By means more gradual, more gentle, and certainly more efficacious than those which Peter the Great employed, she strove for the security and improvement of her vast empire, and it is impossible to regard without wonder the extent of the resources which were developed during her reign. The splendours of her court, combining, as they did, Asiatic pomp with European grandeur, threw into the shade those of every other; upon occasions of her great winter masquerades she often received upwards of eight thousand guests, who were enabled to enjoy themselves without confusion and without constraint. By extreme luxury, by the wealth she lavished on her favourites, the glory that accrued to her arms, her sedulous attention to affairs, the vast scope of her conceptions, the uniform success of her plans, she compelled both admiration and astonishment. Everything about her was on a large scale; even her vices were so huge as to be appalling in their turpitude, and in their seeming incompatability with the good and engaging qualities she displayed. She exerted the powers of a tyrant in a style that went far to realise her dearest wish, that of figuring as an autocrat at once irresponsible and idolised!

CHAPTER VIII.

THE FIRST HALF OF THE NINETEENTH CENTURY.

The Reign of Paul (1796-1801).—The Grand Duke Paul Petrovitch was proclaimed as Emperor and Autocrat of all the Russias, by the title of Paul I., on the day after Catherine's death. She had never regarded him with much of love or confidence, and he soon showed how greatly he had dreaded and disliked her. She had kept him poor, and at a distance. Partly through this cause, but mainly through the influence of his consort, Maria Feoderowna, a princess of Wurtemburg, his life had been reserved and decent, if not exemplary—a strong contrast in every way to that of his sovereign and mother. Immediately after his accession he had the dust of his father brought from the obscure grave where it had reposed for four and thirty years, laid out in state alongside of his mother's corpse, and buried in the same grave. The bones of Potemkin, who had died on the roadside on his way from Jassy, where he had been assisting to negotiate the treaty of 1792, were raised from their resting-place in the church of Kherson, over which Catherine had intended to build a splendid monument, and were pitched into a hole in the moat of the fortress, so that no one could say, "Here lies Potemkin." Whatever the late Empress had most approved, that the new Tsar most unhesitatingly condemned and annulled. At first there was a disposition to honour his conduct and respect his motives, but as his incessant and unaccountable activity went on it began to work confusion, mischief, and wretchedness, till men learned to note and fear a repetition of the rigours and eccentricities which had made his father's reign intolerable.

Peter and Paul Compared.—The resemblance betwixt the two men was remarkable from the first, and it was soon developed with like dire effects. They were similar in appearance: Paul had inherited the stunted figure, the mean aspect, the Tartar physiognomy of Catherine's husband. Their education had been conducted on a like plan: both had been kept ignorant of public business, and had been treated rather as prisoners of state than heirs to the crown. They exhibited corresponding tastes in their employments and recreations: as Peter had played at soldiers in his fortress of Oranienbaum, so did Paul in his retirement at Pavlosky, and each entertained the delusion that he could rule an empire as he had done his household, ordering thirty millions of people much as he had ordered his lackeys and body-guards. In making this impossible attempt, each ran into a fussy meddlesomeness which became incredibly capricious, harassing, and cruel: to recount the ordinances that succeeded each other in a single month would be to present an amazing recital of foolish enactments directed to frivolous ends, and set forth with perplexing minuteness. The *morale* of both was low: if Paul did not sin as grossly as his predecessor, his provocations were less serious and formidable. That both were mad can hardly be questioned—though the insanity of Paul became the most furious and pronounced.

Shortly after his accession he opened the prison doors of Kosciusko, offering him an estate, with numerous serfs, an offer which was declined. As a counterpart to this, the King of Poland was brought from Grodno, was kept as a prisoner about the court, and was subjected to such indignities as moved universal pity. The most rigorous etiquette was established in all the royal arrangements, and any breach of it was punished with remorseless severity. Wherever the Tsar appeared, those who set eyes upon him were ordered to flop down on their knees, though it were in the mud. Visitors to the royal gardens were compelled to walk through them bareheaded. The philosophy of clothes engaged much attention, and numberless fantastic rules respecting them were ordained. Top-boots were forbidden. To wear trousers instead of knee-breeches was a sufficient cause for arrest. Round hats were decreed to be even more abominable. The uniform of the troops was changed half-a-dozen times in as many months. They were harassed by perpetual drills, and were kept in readiness to turn out at any moment, being often called three or four times in a day. The arbitrary whims of the Tsar were endless, and spared no class. Meeting an officer who wore a long pelisse, and had given his sword to be carried by a servant, Paul was so offended that he immediately ordered the men to change places. Coming upon a nobleman who was looking on at some labourers planting trees, he enquired, "What are you doing?" "Seeing the men work," was the reply. "Strip off his pelisse and give him a spade," was the immediate order. When in good temper his conversation was maundering and silly, but if women were present he made it disgustingly obscene. He was as ready with his stick or his fists as Ivan the Terrible had been. Thus, he rushed upon an officer who fell from his horse at a review, and kicked him viciously. He thought it an excellent joke at a court reception to slap the face of some unsuspicious guest, and then chuckle forth the explanatory remark, "The salutation of me, Paul, with mine own hand!"

War in Italy and Holland.—In foreign affairs his frivolity, his fickleness, his violence, had full scope. At first he detested the French Revolution. His dislike was shown characteristically. He issued an ukase ordering the French word "*magasin*" to be painted out from every shop-front; forbidding students to apply the word "revolution" to the movements of the heavenly bodies; and instructing the managers of theatres that on their play-bills they should print "permission" instead of "liberty." His opposition soon took a more formidable shape, for the victorious march of the French troops to the gates of Vienna thoroughly alarmed him, and he joined with enthusiasm the league formed to drive back the armed apostles of democracy. Hitherto Russian soldiers had never advanced beyond Poland. Now one strong contingent entered Germany, and another was sent south to Italy. After a time Suwarroff, the short, pug-nosed, large-mouthed old man, the idol of the Russian army, was recalled from the disgrace into which he had fallen through his contemptuous criticism of the Tsar's tailoring, and was sent to command south of the Alps. He manifested all his old swiftness and strength. Sweeping like a simoom over North Italy, he routed both Moreau and Macdonald, and at Parma, at Trebbia, at Novi, and elsewhere, taught astonished Frenchmen that they had to deal with a man who despised the formal tactics of Austria, and was as averse as Napoleon himself to regulate his movements by the instructions of an Aulic council. Paul was delighted. He created Suwarroff Prince Italianiski, and ordained that henceforth he should be deemed the greatest general of ancient or modern times. But the Austrian council were terrified by their own successes. They interdicted the Archduke Charles from carrying the war into France. Suwarroff was shifted to Switzerland. He crossed the St. Gothard amid such difficulties that even his men began to murmur and falter, whereupon he threw himself on the ground, beseeching them to trample on him and bury him, for nothing remained for him save to die. Instead, they took fresh heart, carried him forward in their arms, and made the passage in safety. It was only to find that the incompetency of his colleague had sacrificed the forces under him, and wrecked the arrangements for a junction. For the first and only time in his life Suwarroff had to give ground. He felt it would be madness to engage the forces that swarmed around him. His retreat was accomplished in a masterly manner, though his troops suffered much.

This incident, coinciding with the ignominious failure of the Russo-British expedition to Holland under the Duke of York, utterly changed the temper of Paul. He conceived that he had been betrayed. Suwarroff was recalled, degraded, loaded with invectives and reproaches, and so scurvily used that he shut himself up, dying soon afterwards from sheer vexation. Austria and Britain became hateful to the Tsar, whose ministers he insulted, and whose friendship he repudiated. He conceived a violent admiration for Napoleon, who very skilfully played upon his weaknesses, and ingratiated himself into his favour. From being enemies they suddenly became allies. Paul entertained all manner of foolish projects as to how he could help his new-found friend. Some three hundred British ships lay in Russian harbours waiting till the spring should open the Baltic for navigation. He laid an embargo upon them, seized their cargoes, and carried off their crews to prison. He vapoured a good deal about an invasion of British India. He penned a challenge to the other sovereigns of Europe, in which, as a method of "putting an end to the wars by which it had been desolated for eleven years," he invited them to meet him in single combat, "bringing with them, as seconds and esquires, their most enlightened ministers and able generals, such as Thurgott, Pitt, Bernstoff," while he would take with him Counts Pahlen and Kutousoff—the one his prime minister, the other a Turkish valet he had taken into favour. This precious document appeared in the *St. Petersburg Gazette*, and was translated into other languages at its author's request. Nor was this the most distinct token of his insanity. Life in St. Petersburg became unbearable. Domiciliary visits were made at all hours by a secret police who were under the Tsar's orders; midnight arrests were frequent; the road to Siberia was crowded by exiles; and no one knew where the wrath of the capricious tyrant might next alight. He had begun to suspect his wife, whom he subjected to cruel usage. He imprisoned his eldest son, whom he had always kept mistrustfully near himself, his prejudices having been quickened by a report that Catherine had meant to nominate the young man as her immediate successor. At last his two friends, Pahlen and Kutousoff, saw that something behoved to be done in order to curb him.

His Assassination.—The conspiracy which they organised for this purpose was widely ramified. Its head was Pahlen, a grave and self-contained man of irreproachable character, who had made a favourable impression upon Paul when he visited Riga as grand duke, and from whom he never withdrew his confidence. Its hand was Beningsen, who commanded the guard at the grand new palace of St. Michael. Among the most active agents were the three brothers Zuboff, the eldest of whom was the last recognised favourite of the Empress Catherine. The evening of the carnival was chosen for the execution of their design. Paul had spent it with his mistress—his wife and the younger members of their family being confined to separate apartments in the building. At midnight his room was entered, access being obtained by a private way, and a hussar who slept in an antechamber having been cut down. The noise awoke the Tsar, who strove to escape by a secret staircase to his wife's rooms, but he was unable to work the spring. He then hid himself behind a barricade of tables and chairs. When discovered he first threatened, then tried to bribe, and finally besought and adjured. Finding words vain he struck out furiously, with a chair for his weapon; he next tried to jump from a high window, but was pulled back, after having his hand cut by the shivered glass; and then he was knocked down by a heavy blow. All the while he had been pressed to sign a deed of abdication, a form of which was held out to him. He tore the paper and vehemently refused compliance with any request of the kind, even when clinging to the knees of those he besought to spare him. Wearied alike of his stubbornness and of his importunities, Beningsen exclaimed, "We have crossed the Rubicon; if we spare his life, we shall die before the setting of to-morrow's sun; we shall be his victims." Thereupon Nicholas Zuboff undid the sash he wore as a cavalry officer, twisted it round the imperial neck, and gave one end to a fellow-conspirator. They drew tightly, and, after a few convulsive struggles, **the murder was accomplished.** Thus the resemblance to his father, which distinguished his life, was carried out to the end.

Reign of Alexander.—Much controversy has been waged as to whether the Grand Duke Alexander was privy to the assassination. The weight of evidence is adverse to the idea. At most, an indirect and remote connivance is all that can be urged against him with any show of reason. His accession to the throne was eagerly welcomed. Much was hoped for from what was known of his temperament and training. He was naturally a man of clement disposition, amiably sentimental, of a judgment which was rather well-intentioned than strong. At the instance of his grandmother, his mind had been carefully cultivated by a tutor of her choice, Cæsar la Harpe, a Swiss republican and latitudinarian philosopher, whose teachings retained their influence even after he had passed through a period of mystic religious enthusiasm. There was a certain softness in his moral fibre, which made him weak and pliant at more than one great crisis of his life. He did much for his country in a pre-eminently difficult time; but he failed to do all he might have accomplished for her at a less perplexed and anxious epoch, or to win for himself that exalted and enduring respect which would have accrued to a man of more robust decision, or of more consistent integrity.

Enmity to Napoleon.—At once he reversed the course of imperial conduct in relation to foreign affairs, thereby powerfully affecting the issues of the war then raging, and leading up to the treaty of Amiens, subscribed in March, 1802. That treaty proved only a short-lived truce, for the violation of which it is difficult to say whether Britain or France was most to blame. Alexander sought to mediate betwixt them, but his intervention found no favour. After hostilities were renewed he would have gladly acted against Buonaparte, but he could act effectively only through an intermediate State, while both Austria and Prussia held aloof. Whenever Austria threw off her supineness he came promptly to her side. The campaign which ensued was signally disastrous.

Mack was overthrown at Ulm. Vienna opened her gates to the conqueror. The allies were lured by him to Austerlitz, where, in December, 1805, a hard-fought contest, which remained long undecided, was at last crowned by one of Napoleon's most famous victories. Here the Tsar was under fire for the first time, and he behaved with commendable gallantry. His troops retreated in unbroken masses within the protection of their icy clime, while the Austrian Emperor made haste to conclude the humiliating peace of Pressburg.

Alliance with Napoleon.—The year 1806 saw another nation overcome by the French assailant. The flight of the imperial eagles was now directed against Prussia. It was rapid and irresistible. The double conflict at Anerstadt and Jena laid the country of Frederick the Great at the feet of one who had studied Frederick's tactics to greater purpose than his successors. Here again Russia stood forward as an ally of the vanquished. Her conduct was not wholly disinterested, for Napoleon had employed Kosciusko to rouse the Poles, while he had also detached Turkey from the league against him, and was using her to cripple the powers of the Tsar. She exerted herself to such purpose that Napoleon resolved to bring her to a reckoning. The task, however, proved more difficult than he had bargained for. At Pultusk, at Eylau, at Friedland, the Russians fought so well that the results of these engagements were dubious. Both sides suffered very severely, and were rendered anxious for peace. This desire brought about the interview and treaty of Tilsit. A vast raft was floated on the Niemen; the two armies were drawn up on each side of the river; and, in a pavilion erected on the raft, the Emperors made their bargain. Its exact nature has never been authentically divulged, though all the information available concurs in pointing to an arrangement by which Russia was to acquire all Turkey, except Constantinople and the province of Roumelia, while France was to help herself to Spain and Egypt. The plan was not lost sight of for a long while, though nothing came of it. The immediate results were, that Russia did not give up her Danubian provinces, as Napoleon had promised to Turkey she would be forced to do; and that, instead of Poland being revived, the domination of Russia was confirmed, and a slice of territory was added to her portion from that which was allotted to Prussia in 1772.

Another Change of Policy.—This change of sides on the part of the Tsar was followed by swift retribution. Russian trade by sea was annihilated by the vigilance of British cruisers; the gates of the Baltic were closed by a British fleet; a Russian squadron which had been sent to the Tagus was captured; and ere long Alexander discovered that Napoleonic pledges were not altogether trustworthy, any more than Napoleonic policy was altogether wise. Russia had given her aid to carry out the Berlin decrees, those famous edicts by which it was sought to close every continental market against British goods; but the stroke thus directed against the sellers of Britain told with equal effect upon the buyers of Europe. Great discontent was excited throughout Russia, and an extensive smuggling trade, carried on through the European provinces of Turkey, sprang up, although the two countries were still at war. In December, 1810, Alexander promulgated an ukase opening the ports to British produce, provided it did not come direct from Britain. The French ambassador complained. His remonstrances were disregarded. Retorts were made as to French violations of the engagement made at Tilsit. Unsettled relations subsisted all through the year 1811, and when, in the spring of next year, Napoleon seized Swedish ships and marched an army upon Swedish Pomerania, Bernadotte appealed to the northern autocrat, who promised to stand by him. Napoleon was furious. He decided at once that Russia should be crushed as well as her ally.

Russia Invaded.—From Dresden, where he was entertaining the Emperor of Austria, the King of Prussia, and a crowd of minor vassal sovereigns, treating them to grand reviews by day and Talma's acting at night, Napoleon issued orders for the assemblage of a larger army than had met in Europe since the days of the crusades. Austria furnished 30,000 troops, Prussia 20,000, Italy 20,000, the Confederation of the Rhine 80,000, and France no fewer than 270,000. It was after midsummer ere these immense masses crossed the Niemen into Lithuania, then the westernmost province of Russia. The troops of the Tsar retired, carrying off every truss of hay and sack of grain. Long before the invaders reached Smolensk they were sorely bestead through lack of food. Yet, though wasted by sickness, the stragglers that dropped off from fatigue being speared by Cossacks, while the garrisons that were left on their road reduced their strength by nearly one half, they still persevered. Disease was in their midst, famine was left behind, and in front the whole population moved away, the light of burning villages being left to mark their path. At last Moscow was reached. Then the battle of Borodino was fought, ten thousand Frenchmen being left dead on the field. The ancient capital of the Tsars was entered on the 15th of September, but was found deserted by every one but beggars and convicts. From the palace of the Kremlin it was announced that the grand army would winter in the city. Next night the place was in flames, mysteriously kindled, which could not be subdued till four-fifths of its dwellings had been destroyed. The conflagration moved Napoleon deeply. At St. Helena he referred to it as " the spectacle of a sea and billows of fire, a sky and clouds of flame; mountains of red rolling flames, like immense waves of the sea alternately bursting forth and elevating themselves to skies of fire, and then sinking into the ocean of flame below. Oh, it was the most grand, the most sublime, the most terrific sight the world ever beheld!" A month later the invaders started on that retreat, the appallingly tragic incidents of which are unmatched in modern annals, perhaps in the whole history of war. From Moscow to Smolensk, from Smolensk to Wilna—for the now victorious Russians forced the fugitives to take the road they had traversed · the frozen land was thickly strewn with dead and dying men, who were buried where they lay beneath the ever-falling snow, while crowds of mounted Cossacks speared every straggler and broke up every bivouac. Abandoning them to their fate, the guilty cause of all hied swiftly on to Paris, anguish gnawing at his heart, his intellect reeling on its throne. There was drawn from him the sorrowful confession that, except the Imperial Guard, he had no longer an army.

The Fall of Napoleon.—For the means of improving the victory which the elements had given him, Alexander was much indebted to the diplomacy of Britain. At her instigation an advantageous peace had been concluded with Turkey, one article of which contained on the part of the Turks a recognition of Servia as a quasi-independent State. Thus a large force was liberated at the right moment, and in the best position for hanging with fatal effect upon the skirts of the invaders, till "the grand army" which had been the terror of Europe became a feeble and disorganised remnant. Alexander offered to stop his pursuit at the Vistula, if Napoleon would give up all his conquests beyond the Elbe. The proposal was scouted; and then the Tsar, meeting the Prussian monarch at Kalisch, formed a league with him for the liberation of Germany, to which in due time Austria acceded. Meanwhile Napoleon harangued, decreed, and enforced, recalled his veterans from Spain, turned his militia into regular soldiers, insisted upon new conscriptions, and once more found himself in command of three hundred and fifty thousand men, though a large proportion of them were raw levies. The campaign of Dresden was organised with the same genius that planned those of Marengo and Austerlitz. For a moment the star of victory appeared to gleam upon him once again. The victories of Lutzen and Bautzen, gained on May the 2nd, and May the 21st, 1813, brought him back Leipsic and Dresden, while a cannon ball removed his old rival Moreau, and at the same time imperilled the life of the Tsar. But his marshals were badly beaten, and he was forced upon that false strategy which enabled the allies to shut him up in the basin of the Elbe, where his young legions melted away in the Saxon autumn almost as quickly as their veteran predecessors in the Russian winter. On October 16th and 18th there came the two days' fight at Leipsic, in which they were vanquished, followed by his flight to Paris, which was seething with discontent. He was surrounded on all sides. British ships watched every mile of coast; the Russians and Prussians were advancing from the north and east; the Austrians were marching through Switzerland; Wellington was coming up from the south. Still the Napoleonic spell was powerful. Peace was again offered by Alexander, on the condition now that France should retire within her ancient limits: and again it was refused. For two months the adversaries who were pressing upon Paris were kept at bay, though their weight was so overwhelming that a prolonged resistance was impossible. Buonaparte tried to outwit his northern foes by getting behind them. His idea was, that if he could cut them off from the Rhine he would arrest their march upon Paris. The scheme was discovered. A Russian force of 10,000 men was left to deceive him, while the rest of the allied strength pushed on. Marmont was driven back; Paris surrendered; and on the 31st of March the Tsar and Frederick William entered the city. Two months later, Napoleon having abdicated and been sent to Elba, the first Peace of Paris was concluded, pending the assemblage of a Congress appointed to meet at Vienna in the autumn.

The Congress of Vienna.—At the appointed time and place the potentates and plenipotentiaries, most of whom had spent the summer in Britain, met in the Austrian capital. The Tsar attended, as did the Emperor of Austria, the Kings of Prussia, Denmark, Bavaria, and Wurtemberg, and the representative of every European Power except Turkey. Talleyrand came, claiming admission on behalf of France, getting his claim allowed, and forthwith proceeding most artfully to sow dissension. Russia asked, as her reward, for the whole of Poland;

Prussia for the annexation of Saxony. Lord Castlereagh, the British representative, first assented and then refused. Quarrels ran high, when the tidings that Buonaparte had escaped from Elba, and was gathering round him the military strength of France, compelled their abatement. A new coalition was formed, the battle of Waterloo was fought, the second treaty of Paris was signed, and the diplomatists resumed their work in a more accommodating temper. Russia had her Turkish acquisitions recognised; she gained Finland, to compensate Sweden for which she was confirmed in the possession of Norway; while, as regards Poland, a bit of Warsaw was given to Prussia; another bit to Austria; the city of Cracow, with a small surrounding territory, was created a republic; and all the rest was raised into what was called the kingdom of Poland, which was endowed with a parliamentary government, liberty of the press, a national army, the restored use of the national language, and was then placed under Russian sovereignty. By this odd contrivance did the Congress try to conciliate western scruples and to gratify Russian ambition.

The Holy Alliance.—When the territorial rearrangements were settled, the Tsar brought forward a project of his own. He produced a paper in the form of a contract, which he wished his fellow-monarchs to sign. It ran in these terms : " Conformably to the words of Holy Scripture, which command all men to consider each other as brethren, the contracting monarchs will remain united by the bonds of a true and indissoluble fraternity, and, considering each other as fellow-countrymen, they will, on all occasions and in all places, lend each other aid and assistance ; and, regarding themselves towards their subjects and armies as fathers of families, they will lead them in the same spirit of fraternity, to protect religion, peace, and justice." The King of Prussia signed the document off-hand, much to the gratification of its author; the Emperor of Austria took time to consult both his confessor and his chancellor, the latter of whom, Prince Motternich, relieved his mind by the assurance that it was "pure verbiage;" and Lord Castlereagh, on behalf of Britain, quietly evaded the proposal. On Christmas day, 1815, the Tsar issued a manifesto in his own name and that of his two allies, wherein they declared "their fixed resolution in the administration of their respective States, and in their political relations with every other government to take for their guide the precepts of the holy religion of our Saviour, the precepts of justice, Christian charity, and peace, which, far from being applicable only to private concerns, must have an immediate influence on the councils of princes, and guide all their steps, as being the only means of consolidating human institutions and remedying their imperfections." This was the origin of "the Holy Alliance." Alexander was sincere in desiring something more than a political paction. Ever since the burning of Moscow he had cherished serious thoughts about religion. He was now under the influence of Madam Krudener, a clever woman, who, from being the brilliant leader of a Parisian *salon*, had become the devotee of a mystic and high-wrought pietism. The Tsar and she had long communings and Bible-readings. She accompanied him to Paris and to Vienna. If he had any adviser in this business, she filled that place. Their friendship did not endure; but the influence of her teachings never passed away from his mind, and till his death he entertained a vivid sense of the personal obligation he had contracted by this engagement, which suited well with his exalted notions of "the divine right" by which he reigned.

The Closing Years of Alexander.—These ideas told powerfully upon his internal government as well as on his relations with other Powers. At first he gave a sedulous attention to domestic affairs. He addressed himself with much wisdom and energy to various important reforms. One master-evil, however, he lacked courage to grapple with. Every department of administration was corrupt. The fact was well known; but the Tsar shrank from dealing with it, contenting himself with a bitter jest in reference to the most audacious public robberies. He remarked of some highly-placed men : "If they knew where to warehouse them, they would purloin my line-of-battle ships; if they could do it without waking me, they would steal my teeth as I slept." As the Napoleonic conflict went on, the consideration he gained led him to devote his regards more and more to foreign affairs, in relation to which he came under the ascendancy of Metternich. Home matters he left to be managed almost entirely by an all-powerful favourite. He had still a speculative attachment to liberal ideas, and dreamt for a while of conceding, as he saw meet, popular immunities; but he was angered and alarmed by the way in which the Poles strove to work the constitution they had obtained, persisting that it should be put to use, instead of treating it as a thing only for show. His naturally benevolent temper still prompted him to an occasional interference for some worthy object, but his conduct was as capricious as the conduct of despots usually is. The liberal revolt over all Europe which followed the settlement of Vienna he deemed unwarrantable and dangerous; and he went thoroughly along with the action of those congresses held from time to time by which the advisers of those who signed the Holy Alliance devised a system of repression. This rather tied his hands during the Greek war of independence, which Russian agents joined in suggesting and maintaining, and he himself would have liked to aid. In the end of 1823, when the third campaign had closed, he addressed an earnest memorandum to his allies in the interests of peace. He proposed that the country should be divided into three principalities, after the pattern of Moldavia and Wallachia, each being under the suzerainty of the Porte, to whom a certain tribute should be due, but otherwise independent. The proposal ran counter to all the ideas of Metternich, who vehemently opposed it, and was able to tell its author that he ought to look at home, for a conspiracy against himself was spreading fast.

This was true. The revolutionary spirit had invaded Russia. Secret societies formed in the army had obtained the countenance of many nobles, and drew support from large numbers of the lower orders. The conspirators sought to overturn the Government and change the dynasty. How much of the truth came to Alexander's knowledge is uncertain. He certainly learned enough to cause him much uneasiness. For some time before he had shown himself weary and disquieted. He had become exceedingly deaf. His children were all dead. His wife was very ill. Before going south with her to Taganrog in the winter of 1825, he had recurred to arrangements planned some years previously for a renunciation of the throne on behalf of his younger brother. Had he come back they would in all likelihood have been carried through, but in December he died. The event was unexpected, and naturally suspicions of foul play arose. They had no justification.

The Accession of Nicholas.—When the news reached St. Petersburg a little comedy was enacted, the motive for which remains incomprehensible. The Grand Duke Constantine was the next heir to the throne. The prospect of his accession was viewed with universal dread. Unlike his brothers, who were singularly handsome men, he was so ill-favoured as to be repulsive. The mean appearance of his father and of his grandfather was reproduced in him with added traits of ferocity. His aspect did not belie his disposition, which was petulant and vindictive in an extraordinary degree. In his frequent moods of ungovernable temper, his Calmuck physiognomy became so forbidding that people quailed before him as before an ogre or a ghoul. The only human being he ever inspired with affection or trust was his morganatic wife, a Polish lady. To her he was devotedly attached, and he did her bidding with spaniel-like docility. At her instigation he had consented to waive his right to the throne, and a writing to this effect, duly ratified, was left by Alexander in a sealed packet addressed to the senate, with instructions that in the event of his death it should be opened before any business was transacted. Nicholas was privy to this abdication, nevertheless he chose to affect ignorance of it, was conspicuously eager to take the oath of allegiance to the legitimate heir, and insisted on having him proclaimed even after the document had been produced. Great confusion was likely to ensue. It was avoided by the action of Constantine, who forwarded a paper intimating that in no circumstances would he recall his renunciation. Thereupon Nicholas no longer hesitated.

After the comedy there came sundry exciting incidents of another sort. The conspiracy—or, at least, one of the conspiracies—of which Alexander had been warned, burst forth. Its leader was Conrad Ryclieff, a man of many fine qualities, with an ardent devotion to democratic ideas. Nicholas began his reign on the 24th of December. Next day the conspirators met at Ryclieff's house to concert their final measures. The Governor-General of St. Petersburg, a gallant soldier, known as the Murat of the Russian army, and a great friend to the new Tsar, was informed of the assembly, but he made light of the warning. "Bah," quoth he, "they are a set of dreamers met most likely to hear bad verses." Next day, as he rode forth with his sovereign, he was shot by one of his own soldiers. Sympathy with the insurgents was not so strong among the troops as the leaders of the revolt had been led to believe; yet their proceedings created much alarm, and masses of the populace took part with them. The Tsar behaved with courage and consideration. He rallied those of the troops who were faithful. Before ordering them to act he caused appeals to be addressed to the patriotism and the religion of the mutineers; but they were drowned amid scoffs, and jeers, and the roll of drums. Then a cavalry regiment charged upon the throng, but it was not dispersed by this onset. Finally, cannon were brought forward, and by sundry rounds from them, the Senate-house Square, where the muster had been made, was swept clear. The corpses of those who fell were thrust into the Neva through holes in the ice. Many prisoners were made, the majority of whom were treated with leniency. Only the leaders of the conspiracy were executed. Among them was Ryclieff, who was allowed, through the awkwardness of the hangman, to fall to the ground uninjured. On being brought back to the platform he exclaimed, "What a country this is, where they know not how to rule or to plot, to judge or to hang!"

Character of the New Tsar.—Nicholas was a man of narrower mind than his deceased brother, but of more imperious will. Notwithstanding the mingled firmness and clemency with which he met the crisis that signalised his accession, it startled him in a manner, the effects of which never passed away. The noise of the artillery so frightened his wife, a daughter of the heroic Queen Louise of Prussia, that she contracted a nervous twitching of the face which endured through life. In her husband's case, there was produced an unhappy mental impression which lasted as long. An abiding sense of insecurity possessed him. He knew no way to overcome the hazards he dreaded, save that of stern repression. To this task he gave himself with a vigour that was absolutely merciless. It would be untrue to say that he did not succeed surprisingly, but his success was won by the infliction of a tyranny more grinding and punctilious than can well be conceived. Especially difficult is it to imagine the modes by which his tyranny was so tempered as to be rendered anywise tolerable. In his domestic circle, and among his friends, he showed as a man of kindly nature. In all his personal tastes and habits he was very simple, though he had an exalted idea of what his station demanded, and kept up the tradition of splendour in his court to a pitch that almost vied with the magnificence in which his grandmother delighted. That it was his earnest wish and endeavour to benefit his country cannot be doubted; only he could never be brought to see that his methods were false and impossible. He deemed it his mission to uphold the principles of order and faith in a world that seemed to him every day becoming more prone to revolution and unbelief; and, with such an idea of duty, he had little choice of means.

His hatred of liberalism passed into a species of mania. The severities by which he sought to stamp it out were most fell and unrelenting. His activity grew at last to mere restlessness. He became inconceivably self-sufficient and obstinate. Whatever he willed should be done, it behoved to be accomplished at any cost. When the railway line between St. Petersburg and Moscow was planned, there arose a difference as to the proper route, which was referred to him. He took a ruler and drew a straight line between the two cities, saying the railway should be constructed so. Thus it was constructed, bringing a fortune to the Yankee contractor, but avoiding cities, running through wastes, and entailing a permanent burden on the State. The temper which prompted this performance came to have an unchecked sway in every department of affairs. Such things prejudiced outside opinion, which never had long to wait for some fresh fillip to its dislike. Yet, by the mass of his intelligent subjects, he was regarded with a curious blending of admiration and awe.

War with Turkey — The Peace of Adrianople.— Foreign wars have always been a favourite method with despotic rulers for diverting attention from home troubles. Count von Moltke, the German soldier, ascribes to this motive the origin of a Russo-Turkish war which was waged in 1828–9. Almost immediately after the accession of Nicholas, as also after Sultan Mahmud had disbanded the Janissaries, certain claims were pressed upon Turkey which she was in no position to resist. They consisted in the surrender of some Asiatic fortresses which were to have been given up under the treaty of Bucharest, in the restoration to the Moldo-Wallachians of privileges they were said to have forfeited by the revolt of 1821, and in the cession of complete independence to Servia. All this was granted by the treaty of Akerman in 1826, which renewed the conventions of Bucharest and Kanairdji, and gave special emphasis to the Russian right of interference on behalf of members belonging to the Greek church in the Ottoman dominions.

This right was soon stretched so as to justify intervention on behalf of some Armenian Christians at Constantinople, who were subjected to pillage in the form of exorbitant taxation. Complaint was likewise made that Turkey had tried to cause a revolution in the Caucasus, and had closed the Bosphorus against Russian ships. A fiery rejoinder was given to these charges in a proclamation alleging that for sixty years Russia had incessantly been creating pretexts for war, that she had encouraged the Greek insurgents, and that by her conduct in the principalities she had violated both the treaties of Bucharest and Akerman, which the Sultan now repudiated. "Her final aim," said the proclamation, "is nothing less than to destroy Islam itself. We have to fight, not for a province, nor for a boundary, but for our faith. Let every true follower of the prophet obey this call to arms." It was obeyed with much enthusiasm, but the consequences were unfortunate. The Turks fought with extraordinary spirit, but they were outnumbered and out-generalled. The war was carried on simultaneously in Asia and in Europe. The Russian army of the Danube numbered a hundred thousand men. It advanced to that river without opposition. There, the fortress of Ibraila detained one division of it more than a month. When reunited, an advance was made upon Schumla and Varna. Schumla resisted successfully, but Varna was taken, partly by aid of a fleet, containing sixteen ships of the line, under Admiral Greig, partly by the treachery of Yussuf Pasha, the second in command. An attempt was then made upon Silistria, which failed, the invaders retiring for the winter. Moltke, setting their sacrifices against their successes, found it hard to say whether they had won or lost. The second campaign proved decisive.

Marshal Diebitsch was entrusted with the supreme command, unfettered by home instructions. He defeated the Turks in a well-planned scheme for opening a road to the recapture of Varna and the relief of Silistria. Then, by a stroke of Napoleonic strategy, while he made a feint against Schumla which caused such alarm as to induce many of the troops employed in the Balkan passes to be summoned in order to aid in its defence, he penetrated one of the valleys which run through that mountain-range, and came out with twenty thousand men on its southern side, advancing rapidly upon Adrianople. The panic thus excited was extreme. It enabled him to dictate a peace. Had his real circumstances been known, he would never have obtained the terms given him. The truth is, he made a narrow escape from destruction. A fourth of his troops were speedily in hospital, victims of the plague. He might easily have been overwhelmed. But the *prestige* of a success which was deemed irresistible attached to him. The representatives of Britain and Austria, as the friends of Turkey, pressed the necessity of an agreement, in order to avoid destruction. The Sultan was very unwilling; but in the end he ratified a compact, consenting that Russia should guarantee the separate administration of Moldavia and Wallachia, that the stipulations of Akerman should be renewed in regard to Servia, that the independence of Greece, as defined by the treaty of London, should be recognised, and that a large pecuniary indemnity should be paid. Besides this, the protectorate of Russia over the Greek church was renewed, the whole eastern coast of the Black Sea was ceded to her, and she acquired a right to navigate the Straits, as well as command over the mouths of the mouths of the Danube. Some compensation was obtained on the Asiatic side. There, throughout his two campaigns, Paskewitch, who in 1827 had distinguished himself in a Russo-Persian war, had pursued a steady and brilliant career of success. Great part of his conquests was restored, however, the idea being to obtain a welldefined frontier for those provinces of the Caucasus which Russia intimated she had annexed in perpetuity.

Insurrection in Poland.—No sooner had this settlement been concluded than work was found for Prince Zabalkansky—that is, the Balkan-passer—as Diebitsch was now called, upon the plains of Poland. A national rising took place in 1830. Some students had drunk the memory of Kosciusko in one of their clubs. The incident came to the ears of the Grand Duke Constantine, who was the governor. He had the lads severely flogged. Out of this, riots ensued in which the authorities were worsted. The Grand Duke was respectfully conveyed to the frontier, while a deputation was sent to St. Petersburg to explain the origin of the revolt, and to supplicate the concession of those constitutional guarantees which had been repeatedly promised. Of course the request was spurned. Absolute submission was demanded. Then resistance was resolved upon. A *levee en masse* of the people took place, and for many glorious months the Russian masses were kept at bay. The Balkan-passer died suddenly in June, 1831, some say of cholera, some of poison, some of chagrin. A fortnight later Constantine was removed with a like mysterious suddenness. Prince Paskewitch was now entrusted with the task of crushing the insurrection. He accomplished it by the help of Austria and Prussia, while the other Powers who had subscribed the treaty of Vienna looked on idly impotent. In September Warsaw was taken. Soon after the Tsar proclaimed that "order reigned" there. The chiefs of the revolt were sent to Siberia. Noble ladies were forcibly married to common soldiers. The common people were drafted into regiments serving in distant parts, or were sent as serfs to cultivate estates that were not well-stocked with labourers. The use of the national language was forbidden. The constitution was formally abrogated, and in July, 1832, Poland was declared an integral part of the Russian empire. Nicholas thus created a bridge for the entrance into his empire of the democratic ideas he dreaded. At the same time thousands of Poles scattered themselves over all lands, becoming, wherever they went, the missionaries of revolution.

Russia and Turkey in Alliance.—A little later, in 1833, Russia unexpectedly appeared as the friend and protector of Turkey. Mehemet Ali, the Pasha of Egypt, had gradually made himself almost independent of the Porte. His increasing power was viewed with great jealousy at Constantinople. When he was checked he arrogated all the rights of an independent sovereign, made war against his fellow-pasha of Damascus, conquered Syria, and threatened to overturn the Ottoman throne. At this juncture the Tsar offered to his friend and brother the Sultan any amount of force, by sea or land, that might be necessary to sustain him. Outside Turkey the proffer excited much suspicion and remonstrance. Britain and France combined in opposing the movement. For a time the negotiations consequent on it were delayed, but new alarms soon terrified the Sultan into a request that it should be carried through. The supplication was promptly complied with. A Russian fleet appeared in the Bosphorus. A Russian army was stationed in Constantinople. They went under the stipulation that when peace was restored they should return. There was great scepticism in many quarters as to whether their mission was to make peace or to hinder it, and the idea was very generally entertained that in no case would they go back. Both notions were speedily falsified. The Russian interference brought the rebellious Pasha to a speedy pause. No sooner had an arrangement been concluded than the Russian troops, who had been feted, feasted, and decorated at a great rate, took their departure. The explanation was that, while they were present, the secret treaty of Unkiar-Skelessi had been negotiated. By this instrument Russia bound herself to help Turkey whenever need should arise, in consideration of a pledge that Turkey should close the Straits of the Dardanelles against the ships of all other nations, whenever called upon to do so by her ally.

Complications with the Western Powers. — This stipulation was very distasteful to Britain and France, who combined in order to render it null. Nevertheless, it was not formally repealed till eight years afterwards. Fresh troubles then arose betwixt the Sultan and Mehemet. Syria was again the subject of dispute and the field of conflict. The Sultan deposed his rebellious vassal. Mehemet responded in a style that made it likely he would annihilate his master, whose numerous innovations had provoked the rage and mistrust of all strict Mohammedans, without bringing to the country the regeneration he sought. The five great Powers—Britain, France, Russia, Austria, Prussia—intervened to bring about an arrangement. M. Thiers, then premier of France, began this work; but, as it proceeded, differences of opinion sprang up betwixt him and Lord Palmerston, the British foreign minister, and it was concluded without French participation, in a manner contrary to French wishes. Mehemet was coerced into submission, though his hereditary title to the government of Egypt was recognised. At the same time the treaty of Unkiar-Skelessi was rescinded. Throughout these proceedings the Tsar acted heartily with Britain. During the next six years, when her relations with France were frequently strained to a violent degree, he made ostentatious professions of his sympathy with her. In 1844, while one of these minor quarrels was at its height, he paid a visit to the Queen at Windsor, which was universally credited with a political significance. The tales current as to his domestic administration prevented him from acquiring any great popularity among the British people, while the course of events abroad soon made him the object of an extreme dislike.

In 1846 he concurred in extinguishing the republic of Cracow, the last fragment of independent Poland, its territory being handed over to Austria, though Lord Palmerston, who, after half-a-dozen years' exclusion, was again back at the British Foreign Office, protested against the act. The protest was sustained by both Houses of Parliament; and a proposal by Mr. Joseph Hume, to withhold an annual payment to Russia in connection with a Dutch loan, which was guaranteed by the same treaty which set up Cracow, received a large measure of support. The revolutionary year, 1848, excited Nicholas to much apprehension and activity, his principal exploits

being to help the young Emperor of Austria to put down
a rising of the Hungarians, which was done in a perfidious and cruel fashion, and then to quarrel with Turkey
for the asylum she gave to the beaten patriots—a quarrel
which led to a diplomatic rupture between the two
countries, and threatened, for the best part of a year, to
embroil Great Britain, who took the Turkish side with
ardour. In 1850, despite his regard for his brother-in-law, the Prussian King, he persuaded him, or rather
compelled him, to forego the headship of Germany, with
an imperial title, then within his grasp, and forced back
the rising Prussian state upon a species of vassalage to
the house of Hapsburg. In 1852 he was again at variance with Turkey. She meditated the subjugation of
Montenegro. Austria disliked the project. The Tsar,
seemingly unable to forget the spirit so favourable to
Russia often displayed by the inhabitants of the Black
Mountain, joined in energetic remonstrances against it.
The Western Powers could not support a scheme for
reducing a self-governed community to the rank of
tribute-paying rayahs. So Turkey was obliged to give
in; but while the difficulties connected with this matter
were in process of adjustment, the causes that led up to
the Crimean war were growing to a head.

The Crimean War—Its Origin.—Louis Napoleon was
the author of that great conflict. From being President
of the French Republic he had got himself recognised as
the third Emperor of his line. It was natural, perhaps
it was essential for him, that he should find means to
engage and dazzle the attention of France. Without doing
him any injustice, it may be assumed that he had canvassed various expedients for that end. The expedient
chosen was undoubtedly felicitous. To please the Romish
church, the strength of which in France had been disclosed in a manner that surprised him; to incense Russia;
to attract Britain to his side as an ally; and so not only
to turn away regard from domestic questions, but to
establish a position among the confraternity of sovereigns—
all this he had the wit to accomplish by one stroke. The

weapon he used was an old dispute between the Latin and Greek churches regarding the custody of certain so-called "holy places" in Palestine. It goes back to the time of the Crusades. A firman granted by Mahmoud I. in 1740, which restored to the Latins an authority which the Greeks were said to have usurped, was presented, and its re-issue asked for. This document was doubly null. It was obsolete, for there is no proof that it ever was acted upon. It had been superseded, for since its date the Greeks had received repeated confirmations of the rights they were accustomed to exercise. At first little heed was given to the demand preferred in respect of it, but the French ambassador took care that its importance should be magnified. He insisted on an immediate compliance; and when delays were interposed, spoke loftily about sending a French army to occupy Jerusalem, as a method of securing what he wished. As if to show this was no empty menace, a French fleet appeared before Tripoli with a threat of bombardment if two deserters from Algiers, who had turned Moslems, were not at once sent back. The effect was that the vigilance and pride of Russia were aroused. She conceived that she must be humiliated if France was to be gratified. The Sultan and his advisers saw the dilemma. They took the worst way out of it. First they procrastinated; then they prevaricated. Russia was confidentially assured that the *status quo* would be maintained. France was at the same time told she would get what she wished. This secret pledge M. de Lavalette, her ambassador, made haste to proclaim in token of his success. He was recalled in triumph for promotion. Hardly had he left Constantinople when Prince Menschikoff arrived as a special envoy from St. Petersburg, charged with a mission to undo his work.

The Tsar had strong ideas as respects both France and Turkey. The French revolution of 1848 he detested with an abhorrence even more violent than his abhorrence of its predecessor in 1830; and the contempt with which he had also regarded Louis Philippe, the citizen-king, was intensified in its application to the new Emperor. As for Turkey, it was his firm conviction that no power could arrest her decline or avert her destruction. Twenty years before he had stated as much to Prince Metternich, describing the country under the figure of "a sick man," who might at any moment slip away, and for whose dissolution it were well to be prepared. Ten years before he had discussed the same subject in London with the Duke of Wellington, Lord Aberdeen, and Sir R. Peel, insisting upon the probability of a speedy collapse, and the wisdom of being prepared in such an event to pursue a common policy. He now reverted to these ideas in his intercourse with Sir George Hamilton Seymour, the British ambassador at St. Petersburg. "We have on our hands," quoth he to Sir George in the early part of 1853, "a sick man, a very sick man, who may suddenly die, and I put it to you whether it is not better to be provided beforehand than to incur the chaos, confusion, and certainty of an European war, if this should occur unexpectedly." The danger he subsequently described as threefold, arguing that an external war might precipitate an overthrow, or that it might be caused by a Christian rising, or be brought about by the feud between the old fanatical Mussulman party and the party of what he called the new and superficial French reforms. The arrangements he desired were lightly sketched. He repudiated any wish to obtain Constantinople, saying he had not inherited the dreams and visions of Catherine in that respect—a style of remark which was habitual with him; but he added that he would not let Britain, nor any other great state, have it. Servia and Bulgaria might be constituted, he thought, independent states, under his protection, after the pattern of the Danubian Principalities, while he saw no reason why Britain should not have Egypt and Crete. All this Sir George was asked to lay before the British ministry for their consideration, with the remark that he wished for no treaty nor protocol, but only for a general understanding, as between gentlemen. In reply to the representation, Lord John

Russell, then at the Foreign Office, wrote that no crisis had arisen to render such arrangements requisite; that they were wholly without precedent; that, as they would soon become matters of common knowledge, the enemies of Turkey would be stimulated to activity by the assurance of success, so that thus "there would be produced and strengthened the very anarchy which is feared, and the foresight of the friends of the patient would be the cause of his death." At the same time, his lordship intimated that the British had no wish to hold Constantinople, and would never think of entering into any engagements as to the future of Turkey unknown to Russia. With this the Tsar was greatly pleased, so far as it went. In a memorandum drawn by himself, under date July, 1853, he equally renounced any desire to hold the Turkish capital, and promised to do nothing in the event of a Turkish collapse without consulting Britain. He added that now "he regards with less apprehension the catastrophe he still desires to prevent and avert, as much as it shall depend on him to do so."

By this time affairs at Constantinople had become extremely perplexed. Prince Menschikoff had borne himself very haughtily. His conduct had the ill effect of causing his proposals to be sadly misjudged. No difficulty was found now in settling the trumpery quarrel about the holy places. The Greeks got undivided charge of the church at Bethlehem, and of the silver star on the altar of the Nativity; nay, the Turks consented to wall up the harems that look out on the sanctuary of the Holy Sepulchre; but they refused to make the Greek patriarch at Constantinople irremovable, or to embody in definite language a recognition of that protectorate over Greek Christians which Russia claimed. Lord Stratford de Redcliffe was foremost in counselling refusal. His conduct was generally praised as tending to defeat a subtle scheme for establishing Russian influence. The mistake was pardonable in the western public, but he ought to have known better. Hitherto, the right both to appoint and to degrade Greek bishops had rested with

Q

the Sultan. It was only the right to degrade it was proposed to take away. Instead of strengthening Russian influence, this would have weakened it. Outside Russia, every orthodox Greek, however willing to recognise the Tsar as a protector, refuses to acknowledge him as pontiff. To the patriarch of Constantinople there belongs hierarchal supremacy. To give him an enhanced measure of security was therefore to make him more independent of Russia. In the end this claim was withdrawn; but an *ultimatum* was presented in the form of a "Note," demanding a convention guaranteeing the maintenance of the ancient usage respecting "the holy places, and of all the rights belonging to the Greek church, including the Russian protectorate, as also the concession of a title to share in every immunity and advantage that might be granted to other churches." It was replied, that to come under such a contract was incompatible with the sovereign authority of the Sultan. Thereupon diplomatic relations were broken off, and the question hitherto argued between the two disputants was carried before the tribunal of the great Powers.

Appeal to the Great Powers. — Redshid Pasha, the new Turkish vizier, a *protege* of Lord Stratford's; and the veteran Count Nesselrode, the Russian chancellor, each stated his case with consummate plausibility. The leading answer was returned by the French minister, M. Drouyn de Lhuys. Each pleading was in some degree partial and fallacious. The Turkish circular erred by hiding the fact that a precedent, for all that was asked, existed in the concessions made to Austria as regards the Roman Catholics by the treaties of Carlowitz, Belgrade, and Sistowa. The Russian circular erred by its contention that the claim which Count Nesselrode rightly described as traditional and inevitable, a thing of facts, not words, was likewise covered by the treaty of Kanairdji, for neither that instrument, nor the treaty of Adrianople, could be construed with any precision as carrying a sense so wide. Finally, the response of the

French minister, however sound as an abstract argument, was vitiated by the fact that over and over again France had exerted such an influence as Russia claimed. Louis Napoleon himself, as President of the Republic, had a few years before, as "Protector of the Roman Catholic faith in Turkey," coerced the Porte into supporting the strict Romanists against the Gregorians, who are the much larger body. But the controversy was not now to be settled on grounds of reason. Other influences had been called into play, and every week that passed gave to the stern arbitrament of war more and more of the severe aspect that belongs to the inevitable.

Warlike Movements.—The British and French fleets had been advanced to Besika Bay, at the entrance to the Dardanelles, before Menschikoff left Constantinople—a decidedly menacing step. In accordance with the intention Nesselrode had announced, two divisions of the Russian army were, immediately after the ambassador had departed, sent across the Pruth into the Principalities, not, as it was explained, to make war, but to take possession of a "material guarantee." This distinction between an armed invasion and a war was not very comprehensible; but Turkey was not ready to resent it, and the Powers joined in representing that she should not try. There came a brief pause of anxious uncertainty, during which a last effort was made to avert hostilities. Austria offered to mediate, suggesting that a plan which had been devised in Paris, of embodying in a "Note" all the points upon which the disputants were agreed, and leaving over those upon which they differed, might be accepted as the basis of a settlement. Asked if he would accept the proposal, the Tsar said "Yes;" but, instigated by Lord Stratford, the Sultan said, "No, not without certain changes." At the same time, upon the strength of a report that it was intended to massacre the Christians in Constantinople at the feast of "Bairam," the British and French ambassadors ordered up four vessels from their fleets into forbidden waters, in order **"to protect their compatriots, and, in case of need, to**

give aid to the Sultan." The movement was ludicrously inadequate for its professed purpose, but it served to complicate affairs as cleverly as if designed for that end. It incensed the Tsar, who was rendered more stiff than ever in his repugnance to any modification of the Vienna Note. To a renewed demand for its unconditional acceptance, Turkey replied by a declaration of war, dated the 5th of October. Omar Pasha, her commander-in-chief, warned Prince Gortschakoff that he must withdraw his troops from the Principalities. The Prince replied that he would evacuate as soon as the Tsar got the satisfaction to which he was entitled; and, three weeks later, Russia announced that she was reluctantly compelled to take up arms in order to avenge insults, and to enforce respect for treaties.

Hostilities Begun.—Before this, the Turks had fired on a Russian flotilla sailing up the Danube. Immediately afterwards, the Turks crossed that river in force at four places. One division, 18,000 strong, advanced upon Oltenitza. The commander at that place had less than half their strength; but, deceived as to their numbers, he went forward to stop their march. The encounter took place in the most favourable circumstances for the Turks. They fought under cover of the guns in the fortress of Turtukai, and they gained a decisive victory. It is supposed that, had their success been energetically followed up, they might have wintered at Bucharest; but the season was late, and Omar preferred to sit down in Schumla. As an offset to this defeat, the Russians were soon able to report three great successes in Asia Minor. They were followed up by a terrible blow—the destruction of the Turkish fleet in the Euxine. Its existence was a great point of pride with the Sultan. It consisted of seven frigates, three corvettes, and two steamers, which lay in the roadstead of Sinope under the protection of four coast batteries. Six Russian ships sailed right into the bay, silenced the batteries, destroyed the whole squadron, with the exception of a small steamer which escaped in the confusion, and bombarded the town, from which the Turkish authorities had fled. The bombardment might have been spared, though in the course of the war worse things were done on both sides; but the main portion of the exploit is now admired by naval men, as illustrating the critical operation of an attack with sailships on a squadron off a lee shore. It was performed almost within ear-shot of the British and French fleets, which had entered the Bosphorus some weeks before. This circumstance excited great chagrin in London and Paris, prompted a rather ridiculous outcry about treachery and massacre, and undoubtedly hastened the action of the allies. In the spring a collective Note was sent to St. Petersburg by the four Powers, intimating upon what terms the Sultan would make peace, to which the Tsar deigned no response. On the 12th of March a treaty of alliance was signed betwixt Britain, France, and Turkey; and, on the 28th, the two first-named Powers declared war against Russia, forthwith reinforcing their naval strength in the Black Sea, despatching troops to Gallipoli, and sending a fleet to the Baltic.

Though war was declared by the western powers, they were not ready for its prosecution. The summer passed while almost nothing was done. The Baltic fleets bombarded and destroyed the petty town and fort of Bomarsund, but shrank from any more hazardous enterprise. The Black Sea fleets bombarded Odessa, the granaries and merchant shipping being so greatly injured, that the Russians complained of the proceeding as a violation of civilised warfare. The Turks made a gallant defence of Silistria, from before which the enemy, hearing that the allied troops were being sent on to Varna, and dreading a junction between them and the Turkish garrison of Schumla, retired precipitately. Nothing more was attempted till autumn. The British and French armies were kept idling for months in the vicinity of Lake Devna, where they suffered dreadfully from cholera and fever. Then, to the surprise of their commanders, they were ordered to the Crimea in order to attack Sebastopol.

Invasion of the Crimea. — A landing was made at

Old Fort, some thirty miles north of Sebastopol, on the 14th of September. Six days later, the battle of the Alma was fought. Prince Menschikoff, desiring to bar the advance of the allies, awaited them on the southern slope of the little valley so named. He was beaten back mainly by the gallant onset of the British against his centre and right, for the French, advancing by the shore, had little to do. Instead of pushing on at once for the city, which would then have fallen an easy prey, the invaders recoiled from the appearance of defences on the north side, which were undermanned and useless, made a march round it, and took up position on the south, the French communicating with their ships in the harbour of Kamiesh, the British with theirs in the harbour of Balaklava. The garrison expected a simultaneous attack by sea and land. To guard against the first, seven ships were sunk in the harbour so as completely to block the channel. To repel the second, energetic preparations were made under the directions of Captain Todleben, an engineer officer in attendance upon Menschikoff, and of Admiral Korniloff, who was left in command. They were allowed more time than they had hoped, for again the allies, instead of making a sudden dash, resolved upon proceeding by way of regular siege. Till the 17th of October, they drew lines and cast up parallels, the other side being at least equally active. They made their assault on that day, and were repulsed. From that time onward the contest became mainly one of engineering skill. The attack and the defence were almost on a par as regards the amount and weight of artillery, while the allies not being able to invest the place, Todleben could draw supplies and reinforcements from the open country behind with little less facility than his opponents could bring them across the seas. So the contest proceeded for weeks, the besiegers ever pounding away at the fortifications and entrenchments towards which they were working themselves forward; the defenders, while replying to this fire, ever strengthening damaged places, or throwing up new entrenchments in front of menaced points. The monotony of this toilsome work was varied by two incidents, in which the Russians assumed the offensive. On 25th October, they made a furious attack upon Balaklava, with the object of cutting the British off from their base and depôt. On 5th November, a still more formidable and desperate attack was made on the British position at Inkerman, intending to drive the defenders back upon their ships, or into the sea. Both efforts were defeated, through the valour and tenacity of those assailed. They were successful, however, in so far as they prevented any renewal of the assault upon the citadel, and compelled the besiegers to winter on the bare and wind-swept heights they held.

For this no preparations had been made. The season proved one of terrible severity. The three armies endured straits and privations of the most grievous cast —though reporters were allowed only in the British camp. An enforced pause of well-nigh four dreary months ensued. Avail was taken of it to try whether a peace could not be arranged. For this purpose a conference was held at Vienna. Complete agreement was readily arrived at on every point but one—the restriction of Russia's naval power in the Black Sea. Some half dozen, projects of limitation, counterpoise, and appeal to the other Powers were successively considered and rejected, sometimes by one side, sometimes by the other. In the end the conference broke up without result. While it was sitting Nicholas died, but events for a time went on as before. The new Tsar hastened to proclaim that, as regards the conflict, he recognised two great obligations—to defend Russia with all his might, but to further any peace founded on the bases his father had sanctioned. These bases were defined as being — to confirm the freedom of worship among the Christian peoples of Turkey; to place the immunities of the Principalities under a collective guarantee; to secure the free navigation of the Danube for all traders; to put an end to the rivalries of the great Powers respecting the East; and, specially, to arrive at an understanding as to the principles of closing the Dardanelles and the Bosphorus.

SEBASTOPOL.

The Fall of Sebastopol and the Peace of Paris.—The war was renewed in March with greatly augmented forces, the strength of the allies having been increased not only by fresh recruits, but by a contingent from the little kingdom of Sardinia. New defences had been reared in the interval, and old ones had been made very formidable, especially those immense works which were named the Great Redan, the Little Redan, and the Malakoff. The last, an insignificant construction at first, was now a formidable affair, and occupied a site which made it the key of the position. All through the summer much desultory fighting went on. Thrice the allies subjected the works to a furious bombardment, as a preliminary to an assault, but each time the attempt at capture was frustrated. As the autumn waned, Prince Gortschakoff, now in command, made a resolute effort to shake off the besiegers. His plan was a repetition of that tried at Inkerman. A great battle ensued, known as that of Traktir, the brunt of which was victoriously sustained by the French and Sardinians. A month later, on the 8th of September, after another dreadful bombardment, the French got inside the Malakoff, though they were repulsed from before the Little Redan, as were the British in assailing the companion work. At once Gortschakoff, carrying with him whatever was transportable, crossed to the north side of the town by a bridge, which he immediately afterwards destroyed, and established himself there before his departure was known. No serious attempt was made to molest him. The war came to an end for the winter, save in Asia, where, on the 28th November, Kars was taken by the Russians, after a prolonged defence by the Turks, under the British General Williams. It soon became evident that France was averse to its renewal. On 15th December a trusted French authority wrote: "All that the Eastern war could give to France—in moral or political results, in strength, in consideration, or in influence in the councils of Europe—it has granted; why, therefore, not agree to a peace on the terms proposed since the commencement of hostilities?" The road to an agreement was smoothed by the proclamation at Constantinople of a firman, named a "Hatti-Hamayoum," which gave to the Christian subjects of the Porte a wider toleration than had hitherto been conceded—giving them, indeed, co-ordinate civil rights with the Mohammedan population throughout the empire; and this firman, it was understood, the Sultan was willing to submit to the cognisance of the Powers. On the Russian side, the Tsar accepted the proposal made at Vienna as to the Black Sea, with an interpretation which did not sensibly affect its meaning, Britain and France likewise recalling their scruples. The rule finally adopted was that Russia and Turkey might each have six war steamers, not exceeding 800 tons each, in addition to four light vessels; but that the arrangement of 1841, according to which the Sultan was empowered to prohibit the entrance of all other ships of war, should be renewed.

Peace was signed at Paris on the 30th of March, 1856. Napoleon III. lauded its terms as "honourable to all, humiliating to none." The Tsar gave his opinion in a manifesto which expressed much satisfaction at the close of the struggle; declared that Russia did not begin it; described her object as having been to protect her co-religionists in the East from persecution; asserted that her arms had triumphed everywhere except at Sebastopol, where "the heroic defence of the fortifications, erected under the eyes and the fire of the assailants, will live in the memories of the most distant posterity;" and explained that "Providence having prepared, in an unexpected way, an act which realised the object of the war, inasmuch as the future condition and rights of the Christians in the East were to be guaranteed," he could with a good conscience stop the efforts and sacrifices Russia had been called to make, and welcome the invaluable blessings of peace. The reference was, of course, to the "Hatti," which embodied the principles that Britain, France, and Austria had combined to press upon the Porte, which was then promulgated as a spontaneous act on the part of the Sultan, and of which the Paris Conference declared that "the contracting Powers recognise the high value;" while the Turkish minister, in a representation to all the Powers, though speaking of it "as only the confirmation and development of the Act of Gulhane [issued in 1839], which solemnly decreed the regime of equality, and opened the era of reform in the Ottoman empire," also pointed out this difference—that "the Act of Gulhane was merely the acknowledgment of a right and the promise of a reform which might remain barren, but this would convert promises into facts, and introduce them into the institutions of the country."

CHAPTER IX.

THE REIGN OF ALEXANDER II.

The Death of Nicholas.—The death of the Tsar Nicholas, on the 2nd March, 1854, was ascribed throughout western Europe to heart-break and chagrin. The truth is that, contrary to the advice of his physicians, he attended some military exercises while suffering from a severe influenza; that the exposure aggravated his malady; and that, while it ran a fatal course with unexpected suddenness, he behaved with the greatest calm. No doubt his equanimity was the covering of a spirit sorely smitten and chafed. Equally certain is it that, though the mass of the Russian people looked up to him with a superstitious veneration and pride, his decease enabled them to breathe more freely. In his later years the prerogative of absolute power, which no man can safely wield, had developed in him an overweening arrogance which was distinctly fanatical. At the same time, the sense of insecurity by which he was haunted had rendered him incredibly suspicious and severe. He condescended to a detestable espionage; policemen and spies swarmed everywhere. He exerted a grinding tyranny; no one could guess who next would be struck down, or to what abasement he might be doomed. Before the Crimean war, which would have been avoided save for the combination of strength and weakness in his character, there existed a deal of latent discontent; and the progress of the conflict did much to further its spread and to enhance its intensity. He had not wished to fight; like others of the combatants, he drifted into the strife; but he was not so weak as to shrink from a chal-

lenge, nor so strong as to win a victory that would have
made fighting superfluous. However loath he may have
been to enter upon the struggle, it is certain that he
hoped to come out triumphantly. He thought his army
invincible. This delusion was played upon to their
own profit by the servile crowd who surrounded him.
When news came of swiftly-occurring defeats and disasters, he and they were confounded. The truth was
jealously concealed from the people; perhaps the whole
of it did not reach himself. Enough was known, however, to beget universal mistrust and uneasiness. The
autocrat grew more and more morose, inaccessible, and
impatient of contradiction. The people filled up their
defective knowledge by the most unfavourable conjec-
tures, and eagerly welcomed the violent statements and
criticisms which found expression in a widely-circulated
manuscript literature, and still more in such publications
as the *Kolokol* (the Bell), a journal printed in London for
Herzen, a refugee, which was smuggled into the country
by hundreds of thousands.

Accession of Alexander—Sects of Russian Agitators.
—The new Tsar, Alexander II., was thirty-seven when
he ascended the throne. Little was known of him, yet
he was generally credited with the clement and liberal
temper of his uncle, after whom he was named. This
idea received countenance from the immediate dismissal
of certain obnoxious officials, and a general relaxation of
the stringent police system. The liberty thus conceded
was not only received with delight, it was used without
stint in a manner that horrified the few persons who now
professed belief in the wisdom of the old rule. The
country seethed with debate upon projects of reform,
many of them tremendously radical and comprehensive.
Three classes of agitators may be discriminated. There
were the aristocrats—who had been hurt by the scornful
isolation of Nicholas in standing so far apart from them
and above them, and conferring only with his chosen
councillors—who, despite their pretensions to rank with
the richest, the most brilliant, and most accomplished of

European nobles, had been shut out from the political influence that falls to their western compeers—and who now sought to find place and play for the dispositions of an oligarchy. There were the Pan-Slavists—a sect originated outside Russia by John Kollar, a Bohemian clergyman, poet, and historian, who, with certain likeminded associates, had sought to elucidate the affinities of the Slavonian dialects, and to establish a common literature; whose patriotic and ethnographical ideas had, with the connivance of Nicholas, been transferred to the region of politics—the notion of a great Slavonic empire, gathered round Russia, and spreading over the East, being one to fascinate him; which notion, however, taken up by the students of Moscow, then under the influence of Schelling and the German Romanticists, had been carried much farther back, till it prompted a special regard for whatever was native and indigenous, found the golden age of the country in the days anterior to Peter's so-called reforms, or even to the Mongol domination, and was transmuted into the doctrine that the last and best result of Slavonic development would consist in a recurrence to its primitive types. There were the ultra-democrats— led by Herzen and his associates, levellers of the most extreme breed, who made much of the ancient communal institutions of Russia, but only in order to graft upon them the teachings of French socialism; for to them an historical basis was a thing of wind, national partialities were unwarrantable, and the gospel of political reformation was comprised in the principles of liberty, equality, and fraternity, as preached by the adherents of red republicanism. It says much for the Tsar, that at first he was neither dizzied nor alarmed by the hubbub which was raised by the advocates of these and other theories. It appeared that he was thinking out plans of wide reach and grave consequence.

Withdrawal of Russia from Foreign Politics.—For some time Russia held aloof from all concern in foreign politics, at least on the European side. Shortly after Alexander's coronation, which took place with great splendour in September, 1856, Prince Gortschakoff, who had succeeded to the office of chancellor, addressed a circular to the European Powers, in which he complained of what he called violations of the European compact on their part, but added that Russia did not charge herself with interfering, and explained why. "Russia," he wrote, "is reproached with isolating herself, and remaining silent in presence of facts not accordant with right or justice. Russia, it is said, 'sulks.' Russia does not sulk : Russia is collecting herself [*se receuille*]."

Abolition of Serfdom.—The first result of this withdrawal appeared in a measure which will make the reign of Alexander ever memorable—a re-modelling of the agrarian laws. To abolish serfdom was one of the schemes that engaged the mind of Catherine II. Her grandson, Alexander I., had dreamt about it. Even Nicholas had appointed committee after committee to inquire; but after 1838 all action had been dropped. At the time of his coronation, Alexander II. mentioned in presence of the nobles that he had an earnest desire to effect the object; but they scouted his design, and refused to believe he had the independence or ability to make anything of it. In this they were mistaken. He persevered, and the announcement of his purpose brought to him such an accession of strength that their attempts to resist, or to weight his policy with extravagant demands for compensation, were rendered futile. Much inquiry and thought led to the issue, early in 1861, of a decree which effectively secured the main object aimed at, while it included a great number of most ingeniously contrived adjustments to make the scheme fair and workable.

The rule had been that a portion of every estate, generally about two-thirds, was reserved for the use of the *mir*, or village community, who possessed it in common. A new division was made every nine years. Account was taken for the most part of the size of the family in making the allotment. According to Godunoff's law, no peasant could sever his connection with his *mir*, or escape the thraldom of servitude to the owner of the estate where it was situated. These serfs were of two classes—household and agricultural. The first were entirely dependent on their lord. The second had to till his land, without wages, for three days in the week. Runaways were punished with great severity; but any peasant, desiring to settle in the towns, might arrange with his lord, if he could, for leave to do so, either by buying his own freedom or paying a yearly tax. Many proprietors derived in this way large revenues from serfs who had become rich merchants or tradesmen. By the new scheme household servants were bound to serve for two years at a fixed wage, after which they could do as they liked. The town settlers were also to retain their old condition for two years, but it was decreed that the tribute payable by them should not exceed thirty roubles for a man (about £4) and ten for a woman. The crown peasants, who formed more than a third of the whole number, were dealt with very generously. Possessions were assigned to them for which they are to pay rent at the rate of the poll-tax previously exigible during forty-nine years, after which the land is to pass as freehold property to them or their children. The case of the remaining serfs was the most complex and difficult. It was dealt with in an elaborate manner, which has proved substantially successful. Precautions were taken that the proprietors should not encroach upon the territories requisite for the self-sustaining completeness and further development of the village communities, while the gratuitous cession of the area which was marked off under the superintendence of officials called peace-mediators, was rendered as palatable as it well could be. Counter-precautions were also taken that the peasantry should not lapse into idleness nor vagabondage, while facilities and inducements to self-elevation were supplied. The *mir* was dealt with as the unit recognised by the law in regard to the land. The system of common husbandry and periodical re-allotments to which the emancipated serfs had been accustomed was retained, except they could themselves agree to an alteration, though, when such an agreement was arrived at, then any individual who desired to exchange his position of copyholder for that of freeholder got help by means of a government loan. The communal system was thus fitted to become the cradle of a peasant-proprietary; but the existence of a stable *mir*, or of a stable peasantry, was ensured. At present all the three forms of proprietorship—large estates, peasant-ownerships, and communal holdings—subsist side by side, and they are likely to supply an instructive comparison in modes of agricultural life. By the law now described, 23,000,000 of people were restored to personal freedom.

Further Reforms.—Eighteen months later two other great reforms were introduced. The administration of justice had become unspeakably corrupt, dilatory, and hap-hazard. The judges had frequently no legal knowledge. The law books were antiquated and unpractical. Bribery was practised on a great scale. Cases were hung up from year to year by interminable appeals. Very often the final decision was dictated by high-placed officials outside the courts. The fundamental law of September 29th, 1862, abolished all privileged jurisdictions; the interference of the executive with the law courts was prohibited; their transactions were ordered to be public and oral; the number of appeals and the time for making them was limited; it was decided that criminal charges should be determined by a jury; and (six months later) corporal punishment was abrogated. Simultaneously with these important and salutary changes, which at once gained the confidence of the people and raised both their sense of right and their respect for law, there came the institution of a new local government by boards of administration, appointed by, and responsible to, district and provincial assemblies. The district assembly comprises delegates from landed proprietors, from the inhabitants of towns, and from the elders of the peasant communities. It chooses the board for its own district, as also representatives to the district assembly, by whom in its turn a provincial board is chosen. To these authorities are entrusted the supervision of all matters connected with the maintenance of highways and public buildings, the material requirements for civil and military administration within their bounds, and the collection of local taxes, but general politics are peremptorily excluded. The members of the boards are paid. It is alleged this experiment has not been so successful as the other, and the reason given is that the large landowners have been excluded by the boards in favour of poor men, to whom the salary is an object.

Another Polish Insurrection.—The course of beneficent legislation thus entered upon was arrested and turned by an unhappy event. Fresh troubles broke out in Poland, which were not, in the first instance, very wisely managed. The Poles were excited by what was then happening in Italy. They persisted in thinking that what Napoleon III. was doing for the Italians he would be willing to do for them. They were misled into the belief that, if the government at St. Petersburg was not inherently weak, it would be found anxiously compliant. Accordingly, they resolved to hold a patriotic celebration on the scene of their overthrow in 1830. The governor foolishly thought the wisest plan to prevent this, was by occupying the ground beforehand for a review in honour of the victory then achieved. Naturally enough a collision ensued, blood was shed, and ill-feeling was aroused. The populace carried the corpses of those slain on their side to the French consulate, where they invoked justice and revenge in the name of Napoleon. At this juncture the nobles who remained in Warsaw intervened, and for a time it seemed as if the disturbance would be allayed. They mollified the populace, getting the honour of a public funeral for those slain in the riots. They compounded with the Tsar, obtaining from him the pledge that all his decrees should run in the name of the Polish King; that a Council of Notables should be called, having as its head Count Zamoyski; that full municipal government should be given to cities and communes, and that the system of national education should be revised. Moreover, he appointed his brother, the Grand Duke

Constantine, who had loyally stood by him in his various Russian reforms, as Viceroy. Hardly had the Grand Duke set foot in Warsaw when two attempts were made to assassinate him. He remained at his post, adopting as his prime adviser the old Marquis Wielopolski, who had been the envoy of the revolutionary government to Great Britain in 1830. Meantime the ferment spread. Lithuania caught the infection. True to his democratic principles, Herzen, who had become the tribune of the Russian people, advocated the movement with his customary fervour. It was a movement, however, that involved not merely questions of abstract right but of national position. Herzen's appeals were contradicted in that sense by another journalist, Katkoff, with an eloquence and fervour equal to his own, and with an effect which not only destroyed his ascendancy but dictated the governmental procedure. Stern Russians were appointed to administer Lithuania. Wielopolski, hoping to avert the like appointments for Poland proper, at the usual conscription devised a scheme by which he proposed to have all the dangerous youths chosen and drafted off. This project was revealed, and it aggravated the difficulty, leading to eighteen months' hard fighting. In the course of it, Generals Mouravieff and Berg behaved very ruthlessly. At its close a decree was passed which, for a trivial sum payable to the government, made the Polish peasant the proprietor of his rented land, thus ruining the nobles, while most of the monasteries were abolished, the estates of the clergy were confiscated, and means more efficacious than had ever been before resorted to were employed to stamp out everything distinctively Polish. This was the work mainly of the minister Miluytin, an enthusiastic Pan-Slavist, who had been a prime adviser in the task of serf emancipation, and who now found an opportunity for carrying out his theories more boldly than was formerly possible. The policy tended in so far to discomfit and weaken the democratic partisanship of Herzen, but it created much jealousy among the Russian nobles, who could not but descry in it a menace to themselves. At first the European powers looked coldly on at what was done. Napoleon III. desired to intervene, but could not make up his mind when or how. He joined with Britain in offering remonstrances, which Prince Gortschakoff at first accepted in principle, though in the end, after he had concluded an alliance with Prussia, he refused to give them any practical application. Talk of war he then disregarded, and Napoleon, who fell back upon the proposal of a General Congress, wherein various shattered schemes he had thoughts of might be re-pieced, had his suggestion negatived by a curt refusal from the British minister.

A Conservative Reaction.—The extension to Russia of such measures as had been introduced to Poland never made any way. Instead, after the 4th of April, 1866, a distinctly conservative bias was given to the domestic policy of the empire. On that day the Tsar was shot at by a Moscow student named Karakosoff. He was neither aristocrat, German, nor Pole, but one of the extreme socialist and democratic party, who had assumed the name of *Nihilists*, because they would accept nothing, proclaimed their intention to overthrow all existing order, and sought to annihilate church, state, property, marriage, and society. Immediately after the revelations that followed upon the inquiries prompted by his crime, an imperial manifesto was issued, stating that dangerous intrigues against the principles of right, property, and religion had been discovered; that these must be held sacred; and that, in so far as the doings of the government had been held to militate against them, the intention of the Tsar had been misapprehended. At the same time, certain significant changes were made in the administration. Count Schuvaloff was brought from being governor of Livonia to be director-general of the political police in the capital, and other men of conservative tendencies were promoted to office. A little later, some extreme journals were suppressed. There was no recurrence to the terrorism that marked the later days of Nicholas, but the license that distinguished the early days of Alexander was never again tolerated.

Russian Advance in Asia.—During the first decade of the Tsar's reign, abstinence from voluntary action in Europe was compensated by much activity in Asia. The pacification of the Caucasus was effected, the Mohammedan tribes in the Transcaucasian portion of the empire being thoroughly subdued. In 1859 the mountain-hero Schamyl, who for well-nigh half a century had waged an adventurous war for the independence of his country, was captured, and with his seizure all resistance collapsed. He was taken to St. Petersburg, where he was well received and well treated; but those of his people who did not at once submit were driven down to the shores of the Black Sea, where the Turks gladly received them, assigning thousands of them free quarters, not in Asia Minor, but in Bulgaria—an arrangement productive of much evil afterwards. Beyond the Caucasus further conquests have since been made with a rapidity comparable only to the development of the British empire in India. By a concentric movement, proceeding from Siberia and the Caspian, the Khanates of Bokhara, Khiva, and Khokand have one after another been reduced to a state of vassalage. Much complaint was raised about an alleged breach of faith in connection with the Khivan expedition of 1873, and the cruelties perpetrated by the invaders. The expedition was undertaken to overawe the marauding population of Turkestan, who were in the habit of pillaging the Russian and Persian caravans, and capturing those who conducted them, who were then sold in Khiva as slaves. The British government took alarm at how far retaliation might be carried, and received a general pledge that Khiva would not be annexed. Even before the upshot, eminent Anglo-Indians, notoriously hostile to Russia, such as Sir Henry Rawlinson, declared that this engagement could not be observed fully without loss and peril. The extent to which it has been infringed is that General Kaufman, after liberating thousands of slaves, took over territory up to the line of the Amu

Daya, where Russian gunboats can protect the navigation. As to the alleged cruelties, it is noticeable that the witness whose testimony is adduced to substantiate them, Mr. Eugene Schuyler, a representative of the United States, distinctly says, on a general review, that the movement was marked by "great discipline and humanity."

Russia and Turkey.—Even from the first the withdrawal of Russia from the field of European politics was not so complete as to prevent vigilant observation and occasional interference. This was especially true of her conduct in regard to Turkey. She took the part of the Servian Assembly when it deposed the son of Czerny-George, and recalled old Milosch to the throne. In conjunction with France she diligently protected the little state of Montenegro in its frequent squabbles with the Sultan. She championed the union of Moldavia and Wallachia, and helped to nullify the compromise of separate administration by promoting the election of Prince Couza for each province, greatly to the wrath of both Austria and the Porte. In 1860 she convened the ambassadors of the great Powers to examine "the painful and precarious position to which the Christians of Bosnia, Herzegovina, and Bulgaria are placed," and afterwards issued a circular in which that position is described, asking the other Powers to verify her accusations. The consuls of the various European states were thereupon instructed to report upon the subject. Their answers supply the materials for one of the most terrible indictments ever laid against a government. They showed that the property, the honour, the lives of the Christian populations, were at the mercy of the Mussulmans; that the benefit of the law was scarcely obtainable in any case except through bribery, while, where Moslem prejudices were concerned, it was not obtainable at all; and that the vaunted Hatti Hamayoum had remained a dead letter. When the Turkish massacres took place in Syria immediately afterwards, Russia instructed her naval force off the Syrian coast to co-operate with that of Britain in whatever mode the commander of the British squadron might deem best for the behoof of the Christians and of the European residents; and though she had not a single soldier in the country, remonstrated against ending the Anglo-French occupation till efficient protective measures had been established. When like massacres were perpetrated in Crete, during the winter of 1866, she cordially adopted the proposal of Austria, which gained also the assent of France, that it had become needful for the safety of the Christian populations of Turkey to put them under the protectorate of the whole of Europe, endowing them with independent institutions, in accordance with their varied religions and races—Prince Gortschakoff arguing that "the only escape from the course of expedients and palliatives, which had served but to increase difficulties," was to encourage "the gradual development of autonomous states." In 1870 she pressed for, and obtained, from a conference held in London, release from the clauses in the treaty of Paris by which the Black Sea was neutralised. The settlement arrived at was nowise distasteful to Turkey, who regarded her own expulsion from those waters as humiliating, was full of confidence in certain new "iron-clads" she had obtained, and was pleased by having her command over the narrow straits revived and strengthened.

Troubles in Bosnia.—Such had been the course of the relations betwixt Russia and Turkey since the time of the Crimean war. During the autumn of 1874 disturbances broke out in the Herzegovina. The harvest had been scant and poor. Many of the population were reduced to dire straits. Nevertheless, the Mohammedan tax-farmers made no abatement of their oppressive exactions. Their rapacious cruelty provoked a general movement for resistance and redress. The Herzegovinians appealed to their Montenegrin brethren, who gave them effective help in withstanding the robberies to which they were subjected. They appealed to the Austrian Emperor, then making a tour in Dalmatia. They even appealed to the British government through a memorial drawn up by one of their Roman Catholic bishops. The stir they made led to the appointment of a consular commission of inquiry. It was presided over by Servir Pasha. Its report confirmed many of the worst charges that had been advanced, and recommended sundry important reforms. An "irade" was issued from Constantinople, ordering that they should be made; but, amid the throes that attended a declaration of national bankruptcy, no heed was given to their execution. The rising assumed larger proportions, and attracted the notice of the authorities at Berlin, Vienna, and St. Petersburg. What they thought of it was explained in a Note drawn by Count Andrassy, the Austrian minister. It described the Herzegovinian and Bosnian Christians as reduced to a state in which they felt themselves slaves. It proposed reforms much more extensive than the scheme of the consular delegation, such as, in addition to the establishment of religious freedom, the sale at a cheap rate to the peasantry of waste lands, and the expenditure within the province of all the direct taxes. Further, it represented that, as the peoples had been so often deceived that they could not trust the Sultan's word, it was requisite that the Powers should receive from him a formal acceptance and adequate pledges for its fulfilment. The propriety of this course was enforced by a hint that the governments of Servia and Montenegro had found difficulty in keeping their populations quiet; and that, if the spring passed with nothing done, it might be impossible to prevent the rebelliously-disposed peoples all about from revolting. The British government demurred to this Note, giving a final consent to its presentation in a form that robbed it of its practical value. The Porte bettered this example, so that nothing came of the proposal. Meantime the insurrection became more determined and sanguinary. In May, 1876, the representatives of the three Powers met at Berlin, and drew up a memorandum containing a fresh set of expedients for restoring peace. France and Italy cordially endorsed them. The British government refused to do so, and the document was never officially transmitted to the Porte. In all these deliberations Russia had played a secondary part; but in June she came to the front. Prince Gortschakoff invited the London cabinet to propose whatever solution it might favour, adding that the necessity was urgent, if they would avoid a conflagration in the East, perhaps even a war of extermination. The answer was, "Nothing remained except to allow a renewal of the struggle, till success should declare itself more or less decisively on one side or the other."

The Bulgarian Atrocities.—While these negotiations were in progress the area of the struggle was greatly widened. The Turks say they had information of a conspiracy, having its headquarters at Outloukien, in Bulgaria, the object of which was a general massacre of the Mussulman population. The action taken by the governor upon this report provoked a riot, which speedily grew to the magnitude of an insurrection. To quell it the resident Circassians, and the irregular soldiers whom the Turks call Bashi-Bazouks, were let loose upon the Christian inhabitants. They conducted themselves with a ferocity that would have disgraced the following of an Attila or a Tamerlane. The story of the atrocities they committed stirred and thrilled the opinion of Europe. Whatever exaggerations there may have been in some of the reports, there is ample evidence that ruthless and heart-sickening cruelties were perpetrated upon a scale of astounding magnitude. Rapine, carnage, and every evil passion characteristic of a savage and irresponsible soldiery, were allowed free scope. Districts of large extent were swept utterly desolate, the dwellers being plundered, tortured, and put to death. Mr. Walter Baring, the secretary to the British legation, who was sent to make an independent inquiry as to the facts, and whose report goes to minimise the statements of unofficial investigators, nevertheless says, "The manner in which the rising was suppressed was inhuman in the last degree, fifty innocent persons suffering for every guilty one;" and he computed that "no fewer than 12,000 persons perished in the Sandjak of Philippopolis alone."

Servia declares War.—The Servian government was awkwardly placed during these troubles. Its obvious interests prompted to the maintenance of peace. Yet it was difficult to suppress the rage which the treatment of the Bulgarians excited. A taste of it was occasionally brought nearer home, for the Bashi-Bazouks were not careful in regard to boundary lines, and sometimes crossed the border to burn, and slay, and terrorise among the prosperous farms and villages of Servia. Representations made at Constantinople on this subject were contumeliously spurned. Thereupon a strong measure of patriotic feeling was aroused. Upwards of 70,000 men volunteered for service against the Turks; and there was a great display of liberality in offering war contributions for their support. Enthusiasm is a strong force, but it could not render a levy of ill-armed peasants a match for the Turkish hosts. The Servians had some successes at first. They penetrated a considerable way down the Morava Valley. Discomfiture befell them, however, when they encountered the Turk in force. In a few weeks after their declaration of hostilities, the remnant of their army was back in disorder at Deligrad. A few weeks more saw the road to their capital laid open, while the Turks were pressing upon their government very humiliating conditions. They escaped its acceptance through a combination of the great Powers to enforce an armistice, which speedily became a peace.

Conference at Constantinople.—This was the work of Britain. The news of the Bulgarian atrocities led to a brisk interchange of views between the European Powers. All those of the Continent agreed that the misrule of the Porte must be brought to an end; that some measure of self-government for the disturbed provinces was a *sine qua non* of any settlement likely to last; and that if Turkey should refuse to be counselled, she ought then to be coerced into obedience. For effecting this purpose Russia proposed that her troops should occupy Bulgaria; that the Austrians should occupy Bosnia; and that the British fleet should enter the Bosphorus and dominate

Constantinople. The British government objected to any armed demonstration, but proposed an armistice, and a conference of the Powers as to what should be done. The bases of agreement suggested were—the *status quo* as regarded Servia and Montenegro; the grant of local and administrative self-government to Bosnia and Herzegovina; and guarantees against continued mal-administration in Bulgaria. These suggestions were accepted; but, while accepting them, Russia also called out a portion of her army, not, as she explained, because she wished for war, or was averse from the purposes laid down by agreement with the other Powers, in the mode they contemplated, but because she was determined to have these purposes made secure.

The conference did nothing to secure them. It met at Constantinople on December 18, 1876. A month was spent in the consideration, first of counter-proposals with which the Turks tried to stop the plenipotentiaries, and then of Turkish objections to the plans they came to urge. These plans were gradually lowered to what the Russian representative termed an "irreducible minimum." The Turks would not consent to the appointment by the Powers of mixed commissions charged to superintend the execution of needed reforms. Consequent upon this obstinate refusal, the conference broke up—Lord Salisbury, the British representative, declaring with much emphasis, that his government stood clear of all responsibility for what might ensue, and that it "must rest solely upon the Sultan and his advisers." At the same time, he wrote home, "The principal object of my mission, the conclusion of a peace between Russia and Turkey, has failed."

The Protocol of London.—Still, Russia did not undertake hostilities. Instead, she pointed out to the other Powers that the conduct of the Porte had brought the Eastern crisis to a new phase. They were all concerned, she said, to vindicate and enforce the advice they had proffered. For herself, she could not withdraw her troops without having obtained some substantive improvement in the condition of the Christian peoples; but, before sending them forward, she was "desirous of knowing the limits within which the cabinets with whom she had endeavoured, and still desired, so far as may be possible, to proceed in common, are willing to act." The issue of this inquiry was a protocol, signed at London on the 31st of March, in which the six Powers invited the Porte to carry out its promises in its own way, merely adding that they "proposed to watch, by means of their representatives at Constantinople and their local agents, the manner in which they are carried into effect." Even to this Turkey objected. It was an abrogation of the independence guaranteed by the treaty of Paris; to let it pass in silence would be to surrender all she had fought for as regards freedom from foreign intervention; rather than acquiesce, she would face the risk of an unsuccessful war and the loss of one or two provinces.

War Begun—The Objects of Russia.—War was thus made inevitable. On the 20th of April the Tsar left St. Petersburg for Kischenoff, the headquarters of his army in Bessarabia. On the 24th an order was given his troops to cross the Turkish frontier. It was explained this was done in order to obtain that which the unanimous efforts of the Powers had failed to acquire by means of an understanding, and so to end a state of things incompatible with their welfare and that of Europe. Britain alone intimated that the course had not her concurrence or approval. At the same time, she gave a pledge of neutrality in the contest, provided there was no interference with British interests. The conditions were frankly accepted. A pledge was given that, although the Khedive was sending troops to Turkey, Egypt and the Suez Canal would be excluded from the operations of the war; that any new arrangement as to the Straits would be submitted to the decision of the Powers; and that no attempt would be made to acquire Constantinople permanently, though the right of occupying it for military purposes, if necessary, was reserved. The Tsar went farther, for, in a memorandum dated June 8th, he explained on what terms he meant to insist. They included the freedom of Bulgaria up to the Balkans; guarantees for administrative reform in its southern portion; an increase of territory to Montenegro and Servia; local self-government for Bosnia and Herzegovina; and the independence of Roumania. For Russia he wished nothing but to retain the part of Bessarabia taken away in 1856, and the cession of Batoum, with adjacent territory. If Austria deemed herself entitled to compensation, she might have it partly in Bosnia and partly in the Herzegovina. This statement was corrected in a few days by the remark that the separation of Bulgaria into two provinces would be impracticable, and therefore that it ought to be emancipated throughout.

The Contest in Asia.—The war opened in Asia with a Turkish success. The port of Soukum-Kaleh was taken, whence men and arms were sent to foment an insurrection in the Caucasus. The attempt did not grow to much, but it afforded employment for more men than the Russians could spare. Their chief object was to capture Erzeroum. For this purpose they marched southwards in three divisions, which it was proposed afterwards to concentrate. One was directed by the coast road upon Batoum; another went by a parallel line towards the old fortress of Ardahan; the third and strongest took a route farther to the east, throwing out a force which invested Kars. Ardahan was taken on the 17th of May; Bayazid was captured by the left wing a few days later; and the combined divisions inflicted a severe defeat upon Mukhtar Pasha at Zaidikhan on the 15th and 16th of June. Then the tide turned. Their command of the sea enabled the Turks to ward off the attack upon Batoum, and to supply Mukhtar with reinforcements. He had taken up a strong position covering Erzeroum. When assailed, he not only stood his ground, but retaliated so forcibly that the invaders were driven back along their whole line. Bayazid was retaken; Kars was relieved; the Russians retired within their own frontier; and for two and a half months the two armies lay watching each other, being content to act on the defensive.

The Contest in Europe.—Disaster had begun in Asia before the Russians really took the field in Europe. It is true that no sooner had war been declared than the railway bridge over the Sereth, which was dangerously near the Danube, was seized, protection being thus secured for their communications, as also that by means of torpedoes (the first instance given of how efficaciously this new engine of war might be used) they destroyed some of the Turkish "Monitors" set to guard the Danube, and paralysed others. Yet it was not till the night of the 21st June that they crossed the river. It had been swollen to an unusual height by the spring rains, and there is no recollection of a time when it was so late in falling. To build pontoon bridges was impossible, and nothing remained save to wait. The passage over was first made from Galatz, the forces that crossed capturing in succession Matchin, Toultscha, and Hirsova, establishing themselves in the Dobrudscha, laying hold on the valley of the Jantra, and threatening the communications of the Quadrilateral with the sea. On the 27th of June another crossing was made at Simnitza farther up, and the town of Sistova was captured. General Krudener was sent to the right to push forward by way of Nicopolis, which he took early in July; the main army, under the Grand Duke Nicholas, took first Biela and then Tirnova, the ancient capital of Bulgaria; while General Gourko, with a force of a few thousand men, chiefly Cossacks, forced a difficult way through the Balkans, and then assailed the Turkish defenders of the Shipka Pass, which had been deemed the only practicable route, in the rear, while they were simultaneously attacked in front, forcing them to flee by side valleys from a position which might have been held against the most tremendous assault. Gourko then descended into Roumelia, made the people of Adrianople believe he was at their doors, and produced a panic in the capital which led to a ministerial revolution and a change of Turkish commanders.

The change brought a gleam of good fortune to the **Turkish** cause. The **new commander** was Mehemet Ali, by descent a French Huguenot, who had received a German training, and had been for five and twenty years in the Turkish service. He put himself at the head of the main Turkish army, and, manœuvring with considerable skill, drove back the Russians from the line of the Lom, and threatened their positions on the Jantra. His action was not so prompt, however, as his designs were ingenious, and he was plagued by a wilful lieutenant. Sulieman Pasha had been recalled in hot haste from warring with the Montenegrins, to check the advance of Gourko. This he did effectually, and then resolved at all hazards to regain the Shipka Pass. He spent almost a fortnight in essaying that impossible task, sacrificing the lives of twenty thousand men in the fruitless struggle, and turning a deaf ear to the orders and entreaties of Mehemet, that he would seek a practicable route and join him at once. Thus the concert upon which the Turkish generalissimo relied was frustrated, and his opportunity passed away. The Russians, however, made no progress. They were checked by an obstacle on their extreme right. Early in the campaign Osman Pasha had issued from Widdin, intent upon the defence of Nicopolis. He came too late; but his opponents carelessly allowed him to settle in Plevna, which had been in their possession. He quickly discerned the strategical importance of the place, and set himself, with amazing fertility of resource and doggedness of resolution, to hold it. Krudener thought contemptuously of the improvised fortifications, and misjudged both the strength and the purpose of his enemy. An attempt, made four days after the fall of Nicopolis, to dislodge him failed. A more determined effort, made a fortnight later, led to a bloody and disastrous repulse. Six weeks passed, during which the Russian army was driven to concentrate, and the conviction grew that, however reinforced, it could not move southward till Plevna was subdued. A third attack was therefore resolved upon. The nominal command of the besieging force was given to Prince Charles of Roumania, whose parliament had declared their country independent of the Turks, and who had joined the army at the head of a considerable contingent. The place, however, had now been converted into a huge fortress; and the attack, delivered on September 11th, after a fierce bombardment of four days, was repelled with heavy loss at all points except two —on the south, where a couple of redoubts were taken, which had to be relinquished next day; and in the centre, where the Roumanians seized and kept a formidable work. The acknowledgment was now made that Plevna could not be carried by storm, and Todleben was sent for to superintend the measures for its regular investment.

While steps were taken for that end, the supineness of the Russian cavalry commander allowed large convoys of provisions and ammunition to get into the place. Mchemet Ali was also displaced in favour of Sulieman, who was relied on to show more energy. The change was useless. The circle of investment was completed. Sulieman was kept at bay on the east. An army of relief, despatched from the south, was intercepted and forced back. By the beginning of December the garrison were sadly straitened, through lack of provisions and the number of their sick and wounded. On the 11th, the half-starved and tattered force made a supreme effort to break out in the direction of Widdin. The ring of fire and steel was too strong; when Osman fell back it was to find the town occupied from the other side; and so a heroic resistance of five months' duration ended in his surrender.

Close of the Struggle.—A month previously an equally striking and more unexpected success had been achieved in Asia. In the beginning of October Melikoff, the Russian general, having been largely reinforced, resumed his activity. For some days there was severe fighting among the range of hills to the east of Kars, where the Turks were strongly posted. They kept their ground well; but their enemy having contrived to turn their right flank, they were defeated and dispersed. Some of them found their way to Kars. A large number fled to Erzeroum. Both places were promptly reinvested. On the 10th of November Kars was subjected to a heavy cannonade. The response was so feeble that encouragement was given to try an assault. This daring feat was put into execution on the morning of the 13th. The dispirited garrison, attacked at many points, became confused and gave way, surrendering a fortress that had been counted almost impregnable. With the least possible loss of time all the forces that could be spared were sent on to aid in the reduction of the companion stronghold. The idea was that it also might be carried by a swift and powerful stroke, but the severities of an early winter prevented its delivery. Snow blocked the passes; stores and ammunition could not be sent on as expeditiously as men; and it taxed the utmost energies of the besiegers for a while to keep themselves in food and shelter. Notwithstanding, they were able to announce, soon after the new-year, that Erzeroum, Batoum, and Trebizond were each isolated and environed, while throughout all Armenia the Turks had no footing save in these places.

Meantime their commander had been recalled to aid in concerting measures for the defence of Constantinople. This had become prudent, because of the rapid successes which followed the fall of Plevna. Gourko had been brought to a standstill by Mehemet Ali in the Etropol Balkan, on the road to Sophia; but Mehemet was again displaced by Sulieman, who brought with him the major part of his troops from the Quadrilateral. Again he failed. His forces were insufficient to guard all the Balkan passes. Gourko came through one from Orchanie, mid-winter as it was. Skobeloff and Mirsky came through another, named Trajan's Gate. The Turkish forces in the Shipka Pass, numbering thirty thousand men, were shut in and forced to surrender. Sophia, Ichtiman, Philippopolis, and Adrianople, were in succession abandoned and taken. The army of defence was scattered among the Rhodope mountains, whence the fugitives made their way to the coast, and were transported by sea to Constantinople. All round, the Turks had to face either the experience or the threatening of discomfiture. Todleben had laid siege to Rustchuk. The Roumanians were encamped before Widdin. Servia had once more asserted herself, and had cleared her old territory. The Montenegrins, who had behaved with great gallantry all through the contest, had entered Albania. What marvel was it that a great and exceeding bitter cry for an armistice should have been raised?

The Treaty of San Stefano.—On the 31st of January, 1877, by which time the Russian forces had been advanced to Rodosto, so obtaining command of the Eskene valley, and of the direct railway to Constantinople, preliminary conditions of peace were signed, and an armistice, terminable on three days' notice, was agreed to. The conditions were a transcript of those as regards the European provinces of Turkey, which were communicated to the British government before the war, and were received with an announcement of satisfaction that they were so moderate —with the addition of a proviso that the Porte was to compensate Russia for the losses and cost she had incurred. Lines of demarcation were drawn for the two armies, establishing betwixt them a neutral zone of seven miles in width; but the Turkish line was behind the last outlying defences of the capital, so that practically, should the turn of events have demanded it, the Russians might have taken military possession of Constantinople in a few hours' time. After a month of anxious negotiation and tormenting delay, the preliminary conditions of peace were expanded into a definite treaty as between Russia and Turkey, which was subscribed at San Stefano on the 3rd of March.

The Peace of Berlin.—The bargain was precise and formal enough; but, inasmuch as it affected the treaties of 1856 and 1871, it needed the sanction of the European Powers. Ere it was given a long controversy ensued, which was represented on the one side as turning merely upon the terms in which the invitations to the congress should run; while, on the other, the contention was that it powerfully affected the authority of the assemblage. "Europe is asked to register the decrees of Russia," said the British government, who evinced great jealousy on the subject. "A congress is not a judicial tribunal," was the answer, "and Russia does not come as a suitor, but as an equal; she has communicated the treaty to all the Powers; they may examine and discuss every part of it; but she does not surrender the same liberty of appreciation and action as belongs to them." During the progress of the dispute the British fleet was sent into the Sea of Marmora, was recalled, and sent again; the forces of the British reserve were embodied; a vote of credit for six millions was passed by the House of Commons, to be ready for emergencies; seven thousand sepoys were brought by the Suez Canal to Malta; a disruption took place in the British ministry; the new foreign secretary indited a despatch condemning the treaty as fraught with danger to British interests and to the peace of Europe, and as depressing the independence of the Porte to a degree that made its continued existence almost impossible. For a while the hazards and probabilities of a war were seriously dreaded and keenly canvassed. At length, simultaneously with an adjustment of the formula of invitation to the congress, the conclusion of secret agreements between Britain and Russia, and between Britain and Turkey, smoothed the way for an accommodation. A congress met at Berlin on the 13th of June, and, after deliberating for a month, gave its sanction to the San Stefano treaty in almost every essential particular.

The upshot of the war, so far as settled by this arrangement, may be thus described. Russia, while retaining a claim against Turkey for about fifty millions sterling of an indemnity, which she consented to postpone to "anterior hypothecations" of revenue, kept Kars and Ardahan, which she had conquered, while she got Batoum in Asia, and Bessarabia in Europe. Bosnia and the Herzegovina were denied the independence proposed for them; but, instead of being continued under Turkish sway, were handed over to Austria, in accordance with the suggestion contained in the Russian memorandum of the preceding June. The lesser powers of Roumania, Servia, and Montenegro, obtained an acknowledgment of their independence, and an extension of their boundaries. Northern Bulgaria was erected into what is virtually a free state. The wishes of Russia in respect of Southern Bulgaria were overruled, the arrangement adopted being that, under the designation of Eastern Roumelia, it should remain a Turkish province, but with a Christian governor, whom the Powers approve, immunity from the presence of Turkish local officials, and a native militia. Finally, Turkey was anew brought under engagements to the great Powers to amend her administration; the right of interference in case of her failure was vindicated; while Britain, in exchange for the acquisition of Cyprus at a rent of £110,000 a year, undertook the obligation of securing good government in Asia Minor.

Renewed Internal Agitation.—The pacification was favourably received; but soon the revolutionary parties again asserted themselves. They strove to produce a state of feeling intolerable to the ruling classes. The life of the Tsar was repeatedly attempted. In April 1879 four shots from a revolver were fired at him from the distance of a few feet, the assailant missing through extreme agitation. Soon after, when landing at Odessa, a man tried to stab him. Journeying to Moscow in December, his baggage train was wrecked, in mistake for that which carried himself, by an explosion of nitroglycerine. In February 1880 the dining-room of the winter palace at St. Petersburg was blown up at the usual hour of its occupation, he and his guests, whose arrival had caused some delay, being on its very threshold. No one can suppose that thus his dynasty would have been ended. The more likely conjecture is that many of the populace in the cities, who have no sympathy with the revolutionists, expect salutary changes from the accession of his eldest son, a strenuous hater of the German bureaucracy —the term German (*Naümet*) has now become one of reproach—who favours what is called "The National Party," the party of progress from within. A national assembly is a great object of longing; and it is understood the Tsar has been brought to approve the scheme of an Advising

Council—partly nominated, partly elected—charged with watching the administration, but destitute of legislative powers.

CHAPTER X.

EXTENT OF THE EMPIRE—RELIGION—EDUCATION—MANNERS AND CUSTOMS.

It is computed that the Russian dominion extends over one-sixth of the earth. Many parts of this enormous space are sparsely peopled. Accurate knowledge as to its area or the number of its inhabitants has not been obtained. Even as to the European provinces the figures given are in some degree conjectural, though topographical surveys of nearly all have been made, and a census has been taken at various times. The most recent statement gives their superficial area (Finland and Poland being included) at 98,837 geographical square miles, and the population at something over 82,000,000. A return issued in 1874, taking in the vast reaches of Asiatic territory, makes the extent of the whole empire over four hundred thousand geographical square miles, or eight and a half millions English. More than a hundred tribes, with as many different languages, own the sway of the Tsar. For the most part they dwell upon the far-off frontiers. The heart of the empire is occupied by a homogeneous race—numbering in all well-nigh sixty millions, the Poles and Lithuanians, the Fins and Letts, make up the major portion of the remainder.

Like the Athenians of old, the native Russians are in all things very religious. Not only has every village, however small, its fane; every dwelling, from the noble's hall to the peasant's shed, every place of resort, be it shop or eating-house, is consecrated by the presence of a sacred picture, the *icon*, hung in an honoured place upon the wall, with a faintly gleaming lamp before it, to receive the adoration of all who enter, and to turn the building into a temple; while every child has a guardian angel, and a baptismal cross, which is carefully treasured as long as life endures. Throughout the journey from the cradle to the grave the claims of religion meet one at every turn, and are acknowledged with gladsome loyalty as well as punctilious care. A Russian of the true type prays much. He fasts often. He pays an immense respect to sacred days, places, and things. "Slava Bogu" —Glory to God—is a phrase ever on his lips. Religious exercises are the concomitants of his every action, however common-place; they mingle with the most ordinary transactions of every-day life; and they generate a settled habit of devotion which no one would think of violating, even could it be done with impunity, which it cannot. In this respect an oriental spirit animates the mass of the people.

Undoubtedly much of this devoutness is merely formal. It prompts to a multitude of ceremonial observances which do not necessarily connect themselves with moral influences nor constrain to virtuous conduct. This does not imply that their practice must be hypocritical. Moral iniquity combined with a high degree of religious fervour is a phenomenon of perpetual recurrence in history, and it would be idle to suppose that there are no modern specimens of a like incongruous union elsewhere than in Russia. That his religious habits have told powerfully for good upon the character and disposition of the Russian peasant, rendering him pre-eminently gentle, patient, and tolerant, is the verdict of all competent observers. There is no denying, however, that his ideas and feelings are largely superstitious. The pre-Christian faith of his remote heathen ancestors has been assimilated with his conception of the divine revelation, and holds him with a strong grip. Everywhere the old Slavonic gods may be detected lurking behind the sacred pictures, and looking out through their eyes. Thus the attributes of the golden-whiskered Perune, the thunder-god, have been transferred to the prophet Elijah. Volos, the ancient god of cattle, has scarce changed his name in becoming identified with holy Vlas (our St. Blaise), who still has pats of butter set before his picture as offerings on his anniversary, when the flocks and herds are duly driven to church in order to get his blessing and protection for the coming year. The millions of Russia, while devoutly receiving Christianity, have not discarded the wild nature-worship which preceded their knowledge and reception of it; and so they continue to justify the epithet of an old ecclesiastical writer, who called them " a two-faithed" people.

The clergy of the State-church are very numerous, and very poorly paid. They consist of two classes, called secular and regular. The seculars are the parochial clergy, who must marry before they are allowed to perform any spiritual function, who are scandalously ill-educated, and whose position is one of great debasement. Towards their bishops they are abjectly subservient. Upon their flocks they are largely dependent; and, notwithstanding the importance attached to their services, very scant respect is extended to themselves. The prohibition of celibacy is carried so far that the death of a priest's wife disqualifies him for continuing in office, though it is open to a person thus unhappily placed to enter a convent, so becoming eligible for promotion to the higher grades of clerical rank. There are probably ten thousand monks in the empire. In Great Russia, especially, they swarm; the whole land being thickly dotted with cloisters. These " black clergy," as they are called, are regarded with much dislike by many of the educated and higher classes, though those taken from among them to recruit the hierarchy are generally held in high esteem, while, for the most part, they display creditable abilities. Their appointment comes from the Tsar, who can transfer or dismiss as he chooses, and who claims absolute supremacy in all the external affairs of the church; but he has never meddled with dogma. The understanding is that any innovation which would part the church from her sisters under the Patriarchs of Constantinople, Jerusalem, Antioch, and Alexandria should be judged of by a Synod; or, if need be, by a General Council of the five churches, to whose decision the Tsar would be bound to give effect.

Save for sundry restrictions imposed upon the Jews, freedom of faith and worship is allowed to other recognised sects; and there are a good many of them. It is a rule, however, that they shall not proselytise, except among themselves. No member of the national church is permitted to renounce his creed. An avowal of heresy, or a lapse into schism, is counted equivalent to treason. A very strange and hazardous condition of things has arisen under this detestable law. It dare not be enforced: such is the magnitude of the supposed evil against which it is directed that its application is arrested. In the view of the Tsar and his advisers it cannot be safely repealed: they conceive that to annul it would be a sure method of enhancing the mischief they dread. That mischief consists, not so much in the aggrandizement of recognised sects, as in the encouragement of splits within the orthodox church, and in the separation from it of independent communities. It is notorious that the nominal conformity which now prevails covers a large measure of varied and envenomed difference. The general name of "the Raskol" is applied to a mass of hidden dissent, curiously diversified in its complexion—some of it being very old, some the growth of recent years; some being staid, rational, and harmless, some full of the maddest apocalyptic ideas.

By much the most considerable body among these dissenters is the class of "the Staroveri," or "Confessors of the Ancient Belief." They date their origin from the revolt against the revision of the Liturgy carried through in 1657 under the Patriarch Nikon. It is now generally admitted that the work was needful, and was well and regularly done. Nevertheless the publication of the new volume excited much commotion and resentment. This might have speedily subsided had not Alexis, the second of the Romanoff Tsars, prohibited the use of the ancient written Liturgy. Six prelates, many priests, and probably a half of the laity, refused obedience. The cause of the dispute was trivial, but the dispute itself, as the manner of such things is, at once hardened and widened, till reconciliation grew well-nigh impossible. The mass of the "old Believers" in the great towns are marked by the severity of their morals, the superiority of their culture, and a striking measure of worldly success. Their great difficulty in the perpetuation of their sect has lain in the fact that their founders suffered the episcopate to die out; and as they strongly hold that only bishops can ordain, they were thus left without priests save those whom they could induce to desert from the State-church. At various times they have been subjected to dire persecution. The soothing system has likewise been tried upon them. Catherine II. applied her strong mind to an adjustment of the quarrel. In 1789 she published an ukase granting them equal rights with the members of the State-church and liberty to pray as they liked, provided they would adopt the prayer for the Tsar contained in the ritual they preferred (which they had dropped from it), and consent to accept the services of priests whom the State should choose. This brought over some of them, though not many, and the few who came were nowise hearty in their allegiance, being very suspicious of the prelacy, who have of course all along been against them. The present Tsar has likewise pursued a conciliatory course, giving them the greatest latitude in every point of their contact with the State, short of formal toleration. There is a possibility that the more solid and reasonable portion of them may be incorporated with the church upon their own terms. The re-union, however, will not be complete. Many of the "old Believers," accustomed to do without priests, have learned to deem them non-essential, and have either allied themselves with some of the extreme and fantastic schools about them, or have developed on their own account a creed and ritual equally wild. In Russian phrase, they have from being schismatics become sectaries.

It is difficult to describe this motley crew according to any system of classification. The leading characteristic of some is the practice of asceticism and self-torture. Among them are the Pilgrims, one portion of whom wander through the world without home or employment, while others, when illness or old age comes upon them, break up their homes to live in the open air their salvation depending upon death finding them in the guise of strangers and travellers. Another class is the Dumb, who, from the time of their conversion, refuse to speak, though otherwise they maintain their former habits towards the outer world. Then there are the Flagellants, who strive to win heaven by every description of self-scourging; the Skopzi or Eunuchs, who call themselves the White Doves; and the Self-burners, who regard voluntary death by fire as the sole means of purification from sin. Of a different stamp are the Sabbatniki, founded by a Jew from Kief in the fifteenth century, who look upon the Mosaic law as the one divine revelation, Christ being merely an inspired reformer—who, therefore, observe the Jewish Sabbath (hence their name) —and who look for a Messiah yet to come; the Milk-drinkers, who set up obedience to the laws of nature as their religion, and whose title has been thrust upon them from their use of milk-food on fast-days, an indulgence prohibited to the orthodox; and the "Duchoboizi," a word that may mean champions for or against the light, for or against the Spirit, who assign a divine origin to the Bible, but give to its contents a figurative, mystical, and recondite meaning, such as is disclosed only to the initiated. This enumeration does not by any means exhaust the medley of sects. Some of the others go to strange lengths of fanaticism and vagary, cherishing the dream of an imperishable empire, to be ruled from Mount Ararat, or of a reappearance of Napoleon I. as a deliverer, or other whimsies to the full as absurd. Their importance does not spring from their numerical strength so much as from the inconceivable power and influence they derive from the concealment they are forced to observe What might prove a miserably mean and ridiculous affair were the light of day let in upon it, looms portentous and terrible through the mists by which it is surrounded. One potent excuse for retaining a policy of repression has been found in the belief that, among the extreme sects, socialistic theories find eager welcome and strenuous support. If the conjecture be correct, it only aggravates the unwisdom of the treatment that has been pursued.

Perhaps, had the enlightened ideas of Alexander I., as regards the education of the people, been carried out, a more effectual check than now exists might have been interposed to the spread of what is irrational and mischievous. He planned a great system of national instruction. The outlines have been scrupulously adhered to, but they have not been duly filled up. The plan is perfect in its way: the empire is divided into districts, each of them being intended to have an university; a certain number of "lyceums" (mainly for the education of civil servants); with middle schools and elementary schools, according to the area and population. The whole scheme reads like a reminiscence of the project devised by John Knox for Scotland. The two had a like fate, in that they both were dwarfed and maimed. Great progress was made of late years as regards the higher education, till the unfortunate demonstration of the students in 1866 led to a curtailment, not only of the liberties enjoyed by students, but of the free speech accorded to professors as a right.

Very fabulous ideas have been circulated as to the numbers and the wealth of the Russian nobility. They are numerous, and a few of them are rich; but of the great majority it may be said that, being in honour, they do not abide. A very low rank in the government service gives personal nobility; employment in the higher grades carries a title to hereditary distinction; but, unless the patent be renewed by fresh service, it does not endure beyond three generations. It is only in a select number of the highest families that primogeniture is recognised either by law or custom. Similarly, it is only the heads of a few great houses that possess extraordinary wealth. The great body of the upper classes are comparatively poor. Out of St. Petersburg and Moscow, it is said, £2000 a year would be deemed a large income.

Spite of the efforts made by Peter the Great and

Catherine II. to create towns and a *bourgeoisie*, Russia has hitherto retained its rural character, and the numbers of the thriving, thrifty, pushing, mercantile class are small. Moreover, there is a vast preponderance of testimony which goes to show that the Russian merchant is scarcely qualified to take a high place. He has no culture. In some cases he cannot sign his name. In many more he practises a notation which is peculiar and original. He makes no attempt to emulate or copy the manners of the upper ranks. It is in keeping with all this to find him credited with an offensive sharpness. Mr. Mackenzie Wallace compares his style of doing business with English horse-dealing. Nevertheless, of late years a great advance has been made in the prosecution, on a large scale, both of trade and manufactures. Private enterprise has been largely substituted for governmental supervision. The mineral wealth of Russia is inexhaustible, and both coal and iron are now extensively wrought. The products of her cotton looms find a ready sale in eastern markets; woollen stuffs are made up of excellent quality; and it is alleged that her home-made silks vie with those of France.

After all, however, the "mujik," or peasant, remains the most notable figure in Russian society. A change may have begun to pass over him, but in the main he still exhibits the lineaments with which many travellers have made us familiar. He has fidelity and affectionateness for those above him, and yet he is often tempted to cunning devices for cheating them. In most things he shows a child-like docility, but as regards some he is invincibly obstinate. He can originate nothing, but if his prejudices are overcome he will deftly imitate whatever is set before him. Amiable, polite, and inspired by a simple religious zeal; he is also idle—his laziness being an inheritance from the days of enforced labour; he is addicted to certain kinds of theft—which he excuses by saying that "God gave wood, land, and water, to all men alike;" and he is fond of strong drink—this crave being fostered by the number of saints' days in the calendar, and by the encouragement given to intoxication because of the revenue derived by the government from the turn-over in the "vodka" shops. He clings with an unfaltering loyalty to the system of village rule he has inherited, meekly submitting to let the Patriarch choose a wife for h:m, and flog either himself or her. Only one sentiment is stronger—that of boundless confidence in the semi-divine Tsar, whose "child" he is proud to proclaim himself. Amid all the turmoil and confusion that prevail elsewhere, amid the gradual decline among the city population of the extravagant loyalty which once prevailed, the deep devotion of the peasantry continues unabated—a sentiment so widespread and earnest that it forms the surest basis and safeguard of the throne.

More than a thousand years have passed since Rurik, the Varangian, established himself at Novgorod, and laid the foundation of that empire which, through many vicissitudes, has grown up so huge and strange a thing. Yet little more than a century has elapsed since Russia could claim a place in the comity of European nations. From the time of Charlemagne to the time of Peter she had no share in any of the struggles, moral or military, that convulsed Europe. Her friendship or her hostility was no more thought of than that of the wandering Tartars, who had made her wastes their hunting-fields. Peter, like Epaminondas, won the fame of lifting his country from contempt. With a happier fortune than Thebes it fell not by his death. Whether it is likely to last, upon the system he devised, is another question. He swept away the liberal and constitutional guarantees, to which the Romanoffs were pledged as the condition of their title to rule, replacing them by an absolute despotism of a novel type. He found, as his successors generally have done, his instruments in foreigners, and in foreigners belonging to small countries, who concerned themselves only with particular departments. Switzerland has given to Russia, Euler, the Bernorillis,

La Forte, and La Harpe; Scotland, General Gordon, Marshal Keith, Admiral Greig, and others; Greece, Pozzo de Borgo, Capo d'Istrias, and many astute diplomatists; while the minor states of Germany were wont to send hosts of adventurers, who gained the orders of St. George or St. Vladimir. Thus, a grinding despotism associated with itself an alien bureaucracy, both tending to overbear, while they stand aloof from, the life of the nation.

Two inquiries arise. It is true that in the past the machinery of government has wrought without complication or reaction, save for the occasional murder of a sovereign; but can it be imagined that, with the growth of knowledge and opinion, fostered by increased intercourse with western Europe, the liberal ideas of which cannot be kept out by any *cordon sanitaire*, or checked at any intellectual custom-house, the mass of the nation will be content to remain inert, without will, and without influence? Marvellous powers of assimilation have been shown; but is it likely that a dominion spread so far beyond all natural limit will hold together? Some very intelligent and sagacious men (such as Baron von Haxthausen, with whom there agreed the great Chancellor Nesselrode, who guided the affairs of the empire during forty years) seem to have had no doubt it would, though they counselled that Russia should turn her face eastward, and dared to infer that " the time is probably not far distant when St. Petersburg will be only the great port of Russia to the north of Europe, as Odessa is her great port in the south, and both of them be no more than powerful commercial cities on the European side of the empire." But the European side is menaced by hazards of the gravest sort. At present it would appear as if the liberal inclinations and conduct of Alexander II., in the early years of his reign, had only enhanced the probabilities of a violent explosion. A very different temper now prevails from that which marked the demonstrations held in 1862, to celebrate the millenium of the national history. The *Nihilists* may not be numerically powerful, yet they have adherents in all the great towns, who are possessed by a fanatical earnestness, are united by a skilfully-contrived organization, and practise the most unscrupulous methods for advancing ends alike wild and detestable. With uncompromising audacity they have made absolute socialism correlative with absolute democracy, and have linked both with the negation of religion and philosophy, so that they might re-echo the phrase of the German Fuerbach: "No religion is my religion; no philosophy is my philosophy!" To overcome this party of conspirators and assassins, who confound anarchy with the rights of man; to slough off the sillinesses and superstitions that pertain to her religious creed and ritual; to subdue the venality and corruption of her official class; to open up her system of bureaucratic administration; and in some way to substitute representative rule for the despotism of a solitary will,—these are the mighty tasks that lie before European Russia. However she may deal with them, whatever the issue to which she is conducted, the event must, to all the friends of rational freedom and well-ordered government, be fraught with interest and instruction in regard to the fundamental principles, and the necessary conditions, of that great problem that ha~ for them a perpetual and ever-renewing vitality.

INDEX.

Adrianople, treaty of, 201.
Andrussoff, treaty of, 101.
Alexander I., his accession, 188; relations with Napoleon, 189; Napoleonic invasion of Russia, 191; the congress of Vienna, 193; the Holy Alliance, 195; death and character, 197.
Alexander II., succeeds to the throne, 220; disturbed state of the country, 221; serfdom abolished, 223; further reforms, 225; Pan-slavism and other forms of agitation, 225; another Polish insurrection, 226; advances in Asia and in Europe, 228; rupture with Turkey, 232; Turkish war, 236; treaty of San Stefano, 240; peace of Berlin, 241; attempts upon the Tsar's life, 244; condition of the empire, 245.

Balaklava, battle of, 215.
Baltic, expedition to, by British and French fleets, 213.
Berlin, peace of, 241.
Biren, the Regent, 142, 146, 154.
Borodino, battle of, 191.
Bosnia, disturbances in, 231.
Bulgaria, Turkish atrocities in, 232; the war of liberation, 237.

Catherine, wife of Peter the Great, her early career, 118; her conduct at the Pruth, 131; her reign, 139.
Catherine the Great, her marriage, 153; seizes the throne, 157; her domestic reforms, 162; her foreign policy, 165-70; her territorial acquisitions, 180.
Charles XII. of Sweden invades Russia, 124.
Christianity becomes the national religion, 26.
Constantine, the Grand Duke, refuses the throne, 197.
Cossacks, alliance with the, 100; come under Russian sway, 102; those of the Dnieper maltreated — terrible scenes, 103.
Cracow, republic of, extinguished, 206.

Crimea, the, invaded, 107; invaded a second time, 145; conquered and annexed, 168; visited by Catherine and the Emperor of Austria, 173, war in, by Turkey and her western allies, 208-18.

Dimitry Donskoi defeats the Tartars, 50.
Dimitry, son of Ivan the Terrible, murdered, 75.
Dimitry, the first false, his successes and fate, 80-86.
Dimitries, other false, 88.
Dissent, religious, 247.

Education, national, 250.
Elizabeth, her accession, 148; her cruelties, 149; results of her rule, 153
Empire, the, divided and reunited, 22, 29, 34; extent and population of. 244.

Feodor, the reign of, 104.

Godunoff Boris, his regency, 75; his reign, 78.

Horde, the Golden, 43, 56.

Igor, reign of, 19.
Ivan of the Purse, 49.
Ivan III., 54.
Ivan the Terrible, 57; his good years 59; his resignation and reacceptance of the throne, 62; his terrible cruelties, 65; the murder of the Tsarevitch, 69; his death, 71.
Inkerman, the battle of, 215.

Jassy, the treaty of, 176.

Kainardja, the treaty of, 170.
Kieff, emigration to, 17; becomes the capital, 19; abandoned for Vladimir, 37; destroyed by the Tartars, 42.

Menschikoff, Prince, favourite of Peter the Great, 118, 141; ambassador extraordinary to Turkey, 209.

Michael I., his election and reign, 93, 98.
Moscow, burned by the Tartars, 40; becomes the capital, 48; in possession of the Poles, 89; retaken, 92; burned in resistance to Napoleon, 191.
Munich, Marshal, 144, 149, 154, 158, 160.

Nevsky, Prince Alexander, his opposition to the Tartars, 43.
Nicholas, the Tsar, his accession, 197; conspiracy against him, 198; war with Turkey—the peace of Adrianople, 201; Polish insurrection — seizure of territory, 203; alliance with the Turks, 204; disputes with the Western Powers, 205; Cracow suppressed, 206; the Crimean war, its origin, 208; siege of Sebastopol, 216; death, 219.
Nobility, character of, 250.
Novgorod, traditional history of, 14; seized by Rurik the Varangian, 15; asserts its independence, 37; sacked by Ivan the Terrible, 70; patriotic resistance to the Poles, 91.

Olez, reign of, 18.
Olga, regency of, and conversion to Christianity, 20.

Paul, the Tsar, 183; his foibles, 184; his wars, 185; his murder, 187.
Paris, the treaty of, 218, 230.
Peasantry, character of, 251.
Peter the Great, his education, 108; seizes the throne, 109; creates an army and navy, 112; visits western countries, 114; founds St. Petersburg, 117; marries Catherine, 118; his conflict with Charles XII., 123; the battle of Pultowa, 126; conquests from Sweden, 127; war with Turkey, 129; battle of the Pruth, 131; second visit to the west, 136; his character and achievements, 140.
Peter II., his brief reign, 141.
Peter III., his accession, 151; deposition, 156; murder, 158.

Plevna, the siege of, 238.
Poland, invasion by, repulsed, 92; war with, 98; the first partition of, 165-8; the second partition, 177; opposition suppressed by Suwarroff —the third partition, 179; insurrection of 1830, 203; of 1861, 225.
Population, primitive, 9; amount and distribution of, 245.
Potemkin, Prince, 172, 180.
Pultowa, battle of, 126.

Religion in Russia, 247.
Romanoffs, the, their origin, 95.
Rurik the Varangian, 15; his reign, 18.
Rylieff's, Conrad, conspiracy, 193.

Sebastopol, siege of, 214.
Serfdom, instituted, 77; abolished, 222.
Serai-Batcha, the buried city, 55.
Slavonians, government and manners of, in early times, 11.
Sophia, regency of, 105.
Stefano, San, treaty of, 241.
Suwarroff, Marshal, 175, 179, 185.
Strelitzes, the, 64, 86.
Sviotaslaf, his reign, 21.
Sweden, war with, 97; cessions of territory by, 127, 150, 194.

Tartar, the, domination, 40; its downfall, 55.
Turkey, views of Alexis I. as to, 103; war with, under Peter the Great, 181; under Anne, 165; views of Marshal Munich, 146; war with, under Catherine, 167; views of Alexander I. 189; first war with, under Nicholas, 204; views of Nicholas, 208; the Crimean war, 209-18; war with, under Alexander II., 235.

Vienna, the congress of, 173.
Vladimir I., his reign, 23; conversion to Christianity, 26.
Vladimir II., his reign and character 56.
Vladimir, the city of, 57.

Yaroslaf, the lawgiver, 31.

www.ingramcontent.com/pod-product-compliance
Lightning Source LLC
Chambersburg PA
CBHW021406230426
43666CB00006B/658